AlG

Family, State and Social Policy

Family, State and Social Policy

LORRAINE FOX HARDING

Consultant Editor: Jo Campling

MACMILLAN

First published 1996 by
MACMILLAN PRESS LTD
Houndmills, Basingstoke, Hampshire RG21 2XS
and London
Companies and representatives
throughout the world

ISBN 0–333–57481–8 hardcover
ISBN 0–333–57482–6 paperback

A catalogue record for this book is available
from the British Library.

10   9   8   7   6   5   4   3   2   1
05 04 03 02 01 00 99 98 97 96

Printed in Malaysia

This book is dedicated to my late father, **the Reverend Walter Gill**, who set me off on the academic and writing paths early in life

Contents

Acknowledgements

I would like to acknowledge the help of the following in writing this book: Jo Campling for her unending encouragement and support; Andrew Green and colleagues in the International Division of the Nuffield Institute for Health, Leeds University, for housing me in 'the attic' while I wrote the bulk of this book; Norma Martin Clement of the School of Law, Leeds University, for advice and information on family law, and Jane Pillinger of Northern College for similar help on Europe; Linda Brooke and Carol-Lynn Strickland-Scott for help with references; Julia Wassall for word-processing the bibliography; Terry Wassall for converting the word-processor discs; Mary Lance for the invaluable task of editing and cutting; and, finally, Steve Harrison of the Nuffield Institute for Health for coming up with a brilliant idea every time I passed him in the corridor!

LORRAINE FOX HARDING

Introduction

The key theme of this book is the relationship between family and state in conditions of rapid change. Political and media interest in family change, and the state's response to it (actual, possible or preferred), has intensified recurrently in the 1980s and early 1990s, and did so to a degree in the decades prior to that. In the 1970s, for example, there were debates about family change, especially the needs of the growing group of single-parent families, and about possible 'family impact statements' to highlight the effects of government policies on families of different types. In Britain, both major political parties claimed to be 'the party of the family'. In the 1980s the tone of debate became somewhat more strident, with a backlash against sexual 'permissiveness' and the growth of alternatives to the traditional married family. 'Pro-family' movements, supporting a reversion to traditional forms, appeared on both sides of the Atlantic, and in Britain in 1983 a Cabinet group (called the Family Policy Group) reported on how 'the family' might be strengthened by various government measures. In 1987 an Executive Order from the Reagan Administration spoke of strengthening family stability, the marital commitment and parental responsibility. Later in the 1980s, the British government's expressed concern about the decline of the two-parent family paved the way for the Child Support Act 1991, which aimed to increase absent fathers' maintenance contributions. This was modelled on a scheme for child support set up in Wisconsin. Before this Act was fully operational, further concern about single parents was expressed by government ministers, with suggestions of additional policy change. From time to time the claim has been made that single parenthood occurs by choice, out of a desire to obtain various benefits from the welfare state (and that therefore such benefits should be reduced). In the USA this theme was associated by thinkers such as Murray (1984) with notions of a growing 'underclass', separated by its lifestyle and welfare dependence from mainstream society. During the 1990s pro-family pressure groups and their publications attacked trends such as working mothers, easy divorce, cohabitation, and the apparent weakening of fatherhood and its alleged social consequences (for example, Dennis and Erdos, 1992). They wished to reinstate an earlier family form, perceived as more stable and socially beneficial. At the same time feminist writing and scholarship proliferated and was broadly critical of patriarchal family forms for their adverse effect on women. The debate polarised as family change appeared to accelerate, and was particularly sharp in North America where various types of family change were more advanced than in many west European states.

Dramatic change in families has occurred and continues to occur; this seems undeniable. But there were, and are, deep divisions over the meaning of change, its consequences and its policy implications. It is against this background that this book attempts to tease out the main areas of family change and their significance, what the state does to and for families through law and policy, and how the state's relationship with family life might be understood. The text covers events and legislation up to the time of writing (1994).

Key terms

Some key concepts in this book are 'family', 'state' and 'social policy', the first two of which are particularly problematic. Neither 'family' nor 'state' must be seen as a unitary concept with a single accepted meaning or reference point. Not only are there diverse family forms in modern society (single-parent, cohabiting and step-families, as well as the married, two parent nuclear form), but the notion of 'family' overlaps concepts such as household, kinship, marriage and parenthood; it may also be used metaphorically to describe, for example, a nation, collectivity or group. There are also different values and ideas about what families *should* be like, and what kind of living arrangement acceptably merits the term 'family'. The term '*the* family' is on the whole avoided in this book (see Finch, 1989), as it contains certain values concerning the worth of a particular type of institution – the married, two-parent family form, gen-der-differentiated, stable through time – and assumptions about social stability which accompany the perception of that form. Alternative terms to '*the* family' which perhaps do not carry the same connotations are *family, families,* and *family life.*

Second, 'state' is also a concept incorporating diverse mean-ings. The state, as Frost (1990) argues, is not a unified set of institutions or an internally coherent entity; and this is par-ticularly the case in its relationship with the various family forms. The state is a set of institutions/organisations (such as central and local government departments, courts, the police and quasi-autonomous agencies set up and funded by government) with other institutions – such as the professions – closely linked to it, each body having its own rules, policies and practices which are not necessarily consonant with each other, and do not necessarily reflect one ideology, aim or set of interests. As will be shown in Chapter 6, different practices towards families may be directly in conflict with each other; for example, a particu-lar family form or family role may be rewarded in one part of the system but penalised in another. The 'messages' which the various state agencies give about family life are therefore mixed, often confusing and contradictory. The terms 'state' and 'the state' are used for convenience throughout this book, but it must be borne in mind that this many-armed, many-eyed en-tity does not move in one coordinated direction or speak with a single voice.

Third, policy is understood as the ongoing actions of state organisations which have a degree of stability and which affect many people's lives in significant ways. Policy in Britain includes Acts, statutory instruments, circulars, regulations, codes of prac-tice, directives, reports and reviews, plans, statements of intent as in White Papers, and the thinking and principles which underpin these. *Social* policy specifically is concerned with social purposes and effects, including distribution of life chances, well-being and the quality of life, and also with the social conse-quences of other policies. With regard to families, policy acts *on* them but is also affected *by* how families form and behave. For example, an increase in single parents changes demands on the social security system and on public housing stock. Family members can redefine their own responsibilities in ways which then alter pressure on the state, and this is not entirely controllable by the state. Policies are the object of family behaviour, as families are (sometimes) the object of policies.

Families and the state have a complicated and uneasy relationship, with the effects of action and change working both ways. Many policies, not all of them 'social policies', affect family life (sometimes very significantly), but family functioning may also act on a range of policies. The term 'family policy', as will be shown in Chapter 6, has no clear-cut meaning, but may be a useful device for approaching developments in the actions of the state and their implications for families.

Outline of the book

The essential focus of this book is change in families and the interaction between family and state. It examines specific changes in family patterns such as gender and marriage, policies which impinge on families, and how state–family interaction may be understood. Chapters 1 and 2 focus on various aspects of family change: gender roles, the reproduction of children, ageing and inter-generational relationships, and changes relating to marriage. Chapter 3 addresses the significance of change, as opposed to continuity, in family relationships. Chapter 4 covers the interaction between families, the state and social policy in Britain. The areas examined include family law, incomes policy, housing, community care and child care. The chapter sets out the state of policies affecting families, and explores assumptions underlying policy and policies' influence on families. Policies and their assumptions constrain families but also support them in some ways. Chapter 5 examines seven hypothetical models of the state–family relationship on a continuum of greater and less control. The two extremes are represented by an authoritarian and a *laissez-faire* model, and the intermediate stages by enforcement of responsibilities; manipulation of incentives; working within constraining assumptions; substituting for/supporting families; and responding to needs and demands. Chapter 6 looks at the notion of 'family policy': the meaning of this term; the question of family rhetoric; 'family policy' as smokescreen for other policies; side-effects and the demand for family impact statements; inconsistency in policies;

and briefly whether 'family policy' can be value-free.

Overall, the book will attempt to understand and clarify some aspects of changing family life and the state's role in that life, aspects that are clearly troubling to many people. It does not constitute a full and final interpretation of family change and the family–state relationship, or a prescription for where the family should go or how the state should attempt to get it there.

Chapter 1

Dimensions of Family Change: Gender, Reproduction, Age and Generation

This chapter and Chapter 2 focus on various related aspects of family change: change in gender roles, divisions and relations; reproduction (defined to include the care and socialisation of children as well as physical procreation); ageing and the pattern of relationship between generations; and changes connected with heterosexual couple relationships, including marriage, divorce, single parenthood, remarriage, cohabitation and births outside marriage, which suggest that marriage has been 'transformed'.

Changes in women's position in the labour market, and, more briefly, in other institutions, will be explored, as will the (lack of) change in the domestic division of labour. Ideas about male and female roles, and about the social position of women, will also be discussed, and some consideration will be given to male roles and whether changes here complement changes in female roles. The chapter also looks at the opposite ends of the age spectrum: reproduction and childhood, and old age. With regard to the reproduction of the generations through child bearing and child care, aspects considered include the long-term historical decline in fertility and its ramifications, the more concentrated spacing of births, and the response to childhood and child care. At the other end of the age spectrum, discussion

1

will focus on the general 'ageing' of the population, longevity and the question of generation. Both reproduction and age have a clear gender dimension.

Gender

Women and the labour market

The first aspect of change affecting gender roles concerns changing relations with the labour market. One of the most marked changes in post-Second World War Britain and in many other western societies has been the movement of married women, including mothers, into recorded paid employment, and away from the 'housewife' role where women were supported by husbands to undertake housework, care for children, husbands, the elderly and sick, and also carry out a variety of other roles.

This movement into the labour market may not be all that it seems. Census records were not altogether reliable on female employment in the past. Indeed, to place this development in historical context, it is useful to recall the spread of the idea of the full-time 'housewife' role in the latter part of the nineteenth century and the early part of the twentieth century. This role was something of a historical aberration, certainly as far as the working class was concerned. Prior to industrialisation women had done economically productive work in farms, trades and households; and in the early nineteenth century they had worked in, *inter alia,* factories and mines, though for lower wages (see, for example, Allan, 1985; Gittins, 1985). Industrialisation brought about a separation of home and workplace, and a redefinition of 'work' as only that which took place formally at a place of work, for an employer, for wages. The move to exclude women from the workplace developed from the struggle of working-class men for a 'family wage' that would enable them to support a wife and children, as middle-class men already did; this struggle was in part successful, certainly for the more skilled and affluent working class (see, for example, Allan, 1985; Gittins, 1985).

To some extent the ideology of breadwinner-husband, housewife-wife was accepted by women as improving their lot (Roberts, 1984 and 1988). This was not surprising given the heaviness of domestic duties and the time required for them, and the harshness of much paid work. For men the housewife model removed lower-paid female competitors from the workplace, raised their own wages, and gave them a full-time domestic servicer at home. Earlier in the nineteenth century it had been a financial necessity for working-class wives, and even quite young children, to engage in paid labour, spending much of their time in a workplace. But by the end of the century children aged up to 12 were in school full-time, and married women were at home – at least in the more skilled and organised sectors of the working class, – though often taking in laundry or lodgers, or cleaning, or doing other unrecorded part-time work (for example, Allan, 1985; Roberts, 1988). The presence of the wife in the home, financially maintained by her husband, became part of the notion of working-class identity, respectability and success (Lewis, 1984; Roberts, 1988).

Lewis (1984) comments that the evidence suggests the number of married women working to be markedly lower in the *late* nineteenth and early twentieth centuries than in the *mid*-nineteenth: probably less than half. Walby (1990, p. 25, citing Hakim, 1980) remarks: 'if we go back to the middle of the nineteenth century, we find that the female activity rate . . . was as high in 1861 as it was in 1971, at 43 per cent'. However, there was a growing expectation (certainly in the twentieth century) that single women would support themselves, – and their labour force participation increased (Lewis, 1984; Roberts, 1988).

Around the time of married women's withdrawal from jobs outside the home, housework was becoming less skilled and more reliant on technology, utilities and manufactured goods, so the working-class housewife's life became somewhat easier. Instead of women having more leisure, it seems that standards of housekeeping rose (see, for example, Walby, 1990; Delphy and Leonard, 1992). The family also became more child-centred from the early twentieth century (see, for example, Allan, 1985; Walby, 1990) and therefore child care became more demanding; while in the mid-twentieth century the middle-class household lost servants, creating a heavier domestic role for wives. Middle-class women did not necessarily have less to do, while the lot of working-class housewives did ease in terms of the heaviness of the tasks.

The movement of married women into paid work after the Second World War has to be seen against this longer-term historical background: for the working class, it was a change in terms of recent history only; middle-class women had long undertaken unpaid charitable work, some of which eventually developed into paid professional work, such as health visiting and social work. The idea of a full-time housewife solely supported by a male breadwinner is less long-established than is sometimes believed.

Changes this century are reflected in the statistics for the percentage of married women at work. Married women's employment was first recorded by the census of 1911 in Britain at a level of only 10 per cent, although there was certainly some under-recording of paid activities such as washing and sewing (see Roberts, 1988). Leaving the First World War aside, this proportion did not change radically over the first half of the century until the Second World War: in 1931 it was still around 10 per cent (census data quoted by Lewis, 1984; Joshi, 1989). The First World War had proved an aberration in that women participated in large numbers in occupations connected with the war effort or previously filled by men; but they overwhelmingly returned to domesticity after the war, and it seems there was not much change in attitudes to married women working in the 1920s and 1930s (Lewis, 1984; Roberts, 1988). Between the wars, married women who did undertake paid work tended to leave and not to return after beginning their families (Lewis, 1984). More married women worked in the new light industries (Lewis, 1984; Roberts, 1988).

During the Second World War, women again worked in industry and the armed services; and although many did lose or leave these jobs after the war, their exodus from the workforce in Britain was not as dramatic as after the First World War (Lewis, 1984). Married women's level of labour market participation soon began to rise again. By 1951 the percentage of married women aged 15–59 in the labour force was over a quarter (26 per cent); by 1961 it was up to 35 per cent; and by 1971 nearly a half (49 per cent): a considerable increase from pre-war decades (Allan, 1985; Lewis, 1992). Engagement in paid labour had previously ended for most women on marriage, as marriage brought other duties (and before the Second World War many occupations carried a 'marriage bar' for women: see, for example, Lewis, 1984). In these early post-war decades paid work was construed as ending at the onset of *child bearing* rather than marriage (though possibly with a return to work when children were older). At this time ideology surrounding motherhood – deriving, most notably, from the theories of Bowlby (for example, Bowlby, 1953 and 1969) concerning the adverse effects of deprivation of maternal love – emphasised the importance of the mother's presence in the home full-time when children were young.

During the 1970s married women's employment became a majority pattern; and by 1981 approaching two-thirds, or 62 per cent of married women below retirement age, were in the labour force (that is, in work or looking for work), while 57 per cent were actually in work (Allan, 1985; Lewis, 1992). The rate of married women's employment increased more slowly in the 1980s due to recession and unemployment, but the trend for mothers of young children to join the labour force con-tinued. By the early 1990s the percentages of married women had reached 72 per cent in the labour force and 67 per cent in work (OPCS, *General Household Survey*, 1991). However, much of married women's work was part-time. In 1987 only 30 per cent of married women worked full-time, and rather more, 34 per cent, worked part-time, although 34 per cent were work-ing full-time by 1991 (Central Statistical Office, *Social Trends*, 1990; OPCS, *General Household Survey*, 1991).

The movement of married women into paid work has been experienced by other western industrialised countries. Accord-ing to the OECD (Organisation for Economic Co-operation and Development 1993), the labour force participation of women in all OECD countries has been increasing steadily since the late 1970s. In Canada the participation rate of wives increased steadily until nearly two thirds were working in 1988 (Veevers, 1991). Duffy *et al.* (1989) report that while mid-century only 10 per cent of married women in Canada were in paid work, in the last three decades work has been increasingly dominant in women's lives, and by the late 1980s 66 per cent of women with employed husbands and children under 16 were in paid work. In the USA and Australia nearly two-thirds of married women were in the labour force by the late 1980s/early 1990s (Bittman and Bryson, 1989; OECD, 1993). In other western European countries similar trends have occurred. Pillinger (1992) reports that since the creation of the European Community in 1957 women have increasingly entered the labour market, with the highest female activity rate in 1987 being found in Denmark (at nearly 76 per cent). However, in all member states women earned on average up to a third less than men.

After the Second World War women gave up work when children were young (Lewis, 1992), but gradually this pattern changed. Women returned to work after child bearing, and more rapidly (both after and between births), so that women with younger and younger children were in the labour force, albeit mostly part-time. Kiernan and Wicks (1990, p. 26) comment that: 'each successive group of new mothers returns to the labour market more quickly than the one before' while women's employment patterns have come more to resemble those of men (but not the stereotypical male pattern of life-long employment). Economic activity rates for mothers (those looking for work as well as actually working) were only 24 per cent in 1961, but 39 per cent in 1971 (Lewis, 1992), and 47 per cent in 1973 (OPCS, *General Household Survey*, 1991). Non-working mothers were a minority by the 1970s. By the end of the 1980s, 63 per cent of mothers with dependent children were economically active and 60 per cent were actually working (OPCS, *General Household Survey*, 1990); by 1992, 65 per cent were economically active and 59 per cent in work (OPCS, *General Household Survey*, 1992).

There were more families with children where both parents worked. This was a majority pattern by the end of the 1980s; the Family Policy Studies Centre gives a figure of 58 per cent of married couples with dependent children in 1988 where both partners were working (Family Policy Studies Centre, 1991). More children were accustomed to having both parents out at work, for at least some of the time. However, mothers' paid work was mostly part-time; in 1985–7 only 17 per cent of married women with dependent children worked full-time, while 37 per cent worked part-time (OPCS, *General Household Survey*, 1987; CSO, *Social Trends*, 1990). Nevertheless, even where the youngest child was under two, 11 per cent of mothers worked full-time in 1987 (Kiernan and Wicks, 1990, quoting OPCS, *General Household Survey*, 1987). Where children were 10 and above, a much higher percentage, 30 per cent, worked full-time (Family Policy Studies Centre, 1991).

This pattern reduced the number of married women and mothers totally dependent financially on a partner, but independence was limited by women's tendency to work part-time for low pay. A Gallup Survey in 1990 found a third of all women were completely reliant financially on the man of the house (*Daily Telegraph*, 11–13 June 1990, quoted by Child Poverty Action Group, 1990a). This is a substantial minority; to be completely dependent on a male was still not grossly unusual. Looking at the figures in employment, around 30–40 per cent of wives and mothers below retirement age were *not* working by the beginning of the 1990s.

Mothers in other countries have also moved into the labour force in increasing numbers. An increase in married mothers working is found in other OECD countries (OECD, 1993). In Canada, for example, in 1961 only 17 per cent of wives with children under 15 were in the labour force; by 1971 this proportion had risen to a third, and the trend accelerated in the 1970s and 1980s so that, by 1986, 62 per cent of wives with children under six were working outside the home (Veevers, 1991). Duffy *et al.* (1989) point out that the family form with a working father and mother at home only applied to approximately a quarter of Canadian families by the end of the 1980s (quoting Boyd, 1988), and 'the relatively few women who direct their energies solely to home and family do so for shorter and shorter periods' (p. 11). Goldscheider and Waite (1991) quote an American statistic for 1988 (Bureau of Labour Statistics, 1988) to the effect that over half of mothers of children under one were in the labour force. They comment: 'Since the 1950s, attitudes about whether working women can be successful parents have continuously become more favourable' (p. 10). In Australia, by 1990, 56 per cent of married women with children were in paid work (Gilding, 1991). Pillinger (1992) shows variation among EC countries, however: while in Denmark over 70 per cent of mothers with children under five were employed by the end of the 1980s, the percentages were lower in Belgium and France, and markedly lower in other states, particularly the UK, Ireland and the Netherlands (less than 30 per cent).

The reasons for the move of married women into employment in the post-war period included a labour shortage in the early post-war decades in Britain. The service sector also expanded and provided part-time jobs seen as suitable for, and indeed attractive to, women. The development of domestic technology and services continued to make housework less physically onerous, enabling some women to work outside the home. There was greater capacity to limit, space and control childbearing because of more efficient and more widely available contraception, increasingly from the early 1970s onwards (see Kiernan, 1989).

At the same time, men's wages became less adequate to support a family: the 'family wage' went into decline. F. R. Elliot (1986) and other authors note that in the 1970s families increasingly needed two wage earners to achieve a standard of living which would have been possible with one in the 1950s. Increasing owner-occupation, and relative rises in house prices in the 1970s and 1980s, were also factors in this: two-earner households could bid higher for houses, pushing prices up (see Malpass and Murie, 1987). In other words, there was a move away from the single wage that would support a family, and ideas about acceptable standards of living also changed. The Gallup survey referred to above found that in as many as 72 per cent of working-class households both partners worked because they needed the money, and in only 18 per cent because both wanted careers; the breakdown even for middle-class households was 57 per cent for money and 35 per cent for careers (*Daily Telegraph*, 11–13 June, quoted by Child Poverty Action Group, 1990a). Pahl (1989) also reported a predominance of financial motives for women working, citing studies which found that women's earnings often kept families out of poverty. But women also found paid work socially and personally rewarding (Lewis, 1992).

Women's employment has not brought them anything approaching equality with men; women's position in the labour market remains severely disadvantaged. All that has significantly changed is women's greater participation in (the disadvantaged sectors of) the labour market (see, for example, Walby, 1986 and 1990). The great growth in women's paid employment is mostly in part-time work, so married women are not primary breadwinners in the way that men have been. Joshi (1989) reports that in 1951 only 5 per cent of women were in part-time jobs (no pre-war figures were collected on part-time labour), and in 1961 it was 9 per cent, but by 1971 the figure was 18 per cent and by 1981 it had reached 27 per cent (a three-fold increase since 1961). The percentage of women in *full*-time work remained fairly constant post-war, around 30–32 per cent. Walby (1990) shows that, of all women in employment, nearly 43 per cent were working part-time in 1988, which represents a very substantial minority. Britain has the second highest rate of part-time work among women in the EC (Walby, 1990). Lewis (1992, p. 75) comments: 'All the post-war increase in women's work has been accounted for by an increase of 2.3 million part-time jobs, the number of full-time jobs having fallen by the same number.' Even women *full*-time workers tend to work fewer hours than men full-timers (Equal Opportunities Commission, 1991).

Shorter hours are not the only factor in women's earnings disadvantage. Part-time work itself is often badly paid and disadvantaged, but women's average hourly earnings have always been less than men's and continue to be so, though the gap has narrowed somewhat. Historically women in Britain received about 50 per cent of men's pay in weekly terms (Chiplin and Sloane, 1974, quoted by Reid and Stratta, 1989), 60 per cent in hourly terms (Joshi, 1989); but there was an improvement in relative pay in the mid-1970s with the implementation in 1975 of the Equal Pay Act 1970 (Joshi, 1989). Walby (1990), quoting the New Earnings Survey, reports that in 1986 women earned 74 per cent of men's hourly rate, 66 per cent of their weekly earnings. By 1990, full-time women workers earned on average 77 per cent of the hourly earnings of males; for most of the 1980s there had been little change in the differential, although it did narrow after 1987 (Equal Opportunities Commission, 1991). Part-time women workers received lower hourly earnings still. In general, as Lonsdale (1987, p. 109) says: 'The evidence that is available suggests conclusively that average earnings for women are well below those of men in virtually all industries and occupations and have been so for some time.'

Commenting on the Canadian situation, Veevers (1991, p. 23) says that the disparity between male and female earnings is in part 'accounted for by the fact that women are more likely than men to work part-time. However, even when comparisons are restricted only to persons who work full-time for a full year, the discrepancy is large and consistent.' In all member states of the EC women earned, on average, up to a third less than men (Pillinger, 1992).

Women's occupations are not only less well paid but also tend to carry weaker pension rights than men's, and may carry none where work is part-time. Women have less protection as workers: if working less than 16 hours per week in Britain they have, until the mid-1990s, had significantly fewer employment rights, including maternity rights. Women are also predominant among homeworkers, who are frequently exploited (Joshi, 1989). Clearly equality, however defined, has not been achieved at work. Lewis (1984, p. 220) comments: 'The trend towards part-time, service sector jobs is predicted to continue, and such work tends to be low paid, poorly unionised, lacking in security and other employment benefits, and is labelled women's work.'

Women, then, do not benefit materially from their labour anything like as much as men do, even allowing for their fewer hours of work. Women and men, on the whole, do different kinds of jobs, and 'women's jobs' are less well remunerated. This was also the case historically (see, for example, Roberts, 1988), with women concentrated in textile factories and domestic service; from the late nineteenth and early twentieth centuries junior clerical and retailing positions increasingly became open to them, but their wages and their prospects for advancement were restricted relative to men's (Roberts, 1988). Teaching and nursing opened increasingly to women, but neither occupation was particularly privileged or well paid, and equal pay in teaching was not achieved until after the Second World War. Jobs in the Civil Service also became more available to women, but mostly at the lower ranks, with equal pay again not achieved until after the Second World War (Lewis, 1984). Since that war women have increasingly been employed in the expanding service sectors, both public (most obviously in education, health and social services) and private (such as catering and retailing) (see, for example, Lewis, 1992).

Women are thus employed in different employment sectors from men, overwhelmingly in service rather than industrial sectors, and in different industries within the industrial sector. The Equal Opportunities Commission (1991, p. 13) comments: 'Most occupations remain heavily segregated. In the four occupations in which women were over-represented in 1989, their share of the workforce was 60 per cent or more. In ten of the twelve occupations where women were under-represented, they made up less than 29 per cent of the workforce.' In other words, occupations tend to be polarised between those numerically dominated by women and those numerically dominated by men. Women's work has been overwhelmingly unskilled; or, perhaps more importantly, defined as unskilled. Women's jobs are also less likely to be unionised. Furthermore, the sorts of job characteristically done by women are mostly at the lower levels of a hierarchy. In 1989, about 68 per cent of women's employment was non-manual, whereas men are evenly divided between manual and non-manual work (Equal Opportunities Commission, 1991), but women are concentrated at the *lower* levels of non-manual work. Women are limited in the types of jobs they can take by their domestic commitments, tasks in which they are (as will be shown below) relatively unsupported by husbands, extended family, or public provisions or subsidies. This may lead to them taking work at unsocial hours, or working from home.

Women mostly perform secondary or peripheral and specifically female work, carrying low status, low pay, poor conditions and which is casual and insecure, 'flexible' from the employers' point of view. Sexual segregation is both horizontal and vertical: horizontal in that women occupy different categories of work, and vertical in that in all fields men tend to occupy the higher levels of employment which carry more pay, power and other rewards, even if women are in the majority in that field. There was, however, over the decade 1971–81, a slight decline in vertical segregation for women, though not overall in their horizontal segregation (Walby, 1990).

While the receipt of an income from work does potentially reduce women's economic dependence on men, the married woman's income is usually less than her partner's, often considerably. Joshi (1989) reports that on average wives earn 30 per cent of joint earnings, and therefore husbands earned 70 per cent; Bryson (1992, pp. 195–6) comments on the OECD countries that: 'A rough summary for all nine countries suggests that for women in paid employment, less than 10 per cent earn the equivalent of their husbands and on average they contribute one-third less to the family income, leaving a large dependency-gap.'

What is done with a woman's earnings is crucial to how far paid work enhances her autonomy and well-being (see Brannen and Wilson, 1987; Pahl, 1989). In the early nineteenth century in Britain married women's wages were legally the property of their husbands. Married women could only formally own their earnings after the Married Women's Property Acts of 1870 and 1882. Even so, women may not benefit from their paid work as men do; their earnings may go to buy domestic labour, and women are more likely than men to spend extra income on the home and children (see Brannen and Wilson, 1987; Pahl, 1989). Delphy and Leonard (1992) argue that one aspect of the continuing male expropriation of female labour is this practice of women's earnings being used to benefit the family, or other family members, rather than themselves. They comment: 'wives do not have the same rights to control the money they earn as their husbands or boyfriends have to the money they earn' (p. 118), and: 'in practice in most marriages almost all the wife's income goes into the communal budget over which the husband has overall control, whereas the husband has personal spending money' (p. 131), referring to their empirical work reported in Chapters 7 and 9 of their book. G. Wilson (1987) notes women's greater tendency to use any surplus money they controlled or their 'savings' for collective household consumption, and the trend for men to have more personal spending money and greater financial power and control. Pahl (1989, p. 129) concludes from her research: 'The great majority of women made their wages available for household consumption' rather than using them as personal spending money, and notes that her findings are similar to those of other research.

The implication of all this is that there are limits to how far the entry of women into the labour market can be regarded as a challenge to patriarchy and male power, or as a means of establishing women's independence and equality either within or outside the family (see Walby, 1990). This is reinforced by the primary responsibility for domestic work remaining with women even when they have paid work.

Women's participation in other institutions

A few words may be said about women's entry into education beyond the school-leaving age, and into other social and political institutions. Women have had improved educational attainment since the 1960s. Lewis (1992) gives figures for the number of women first-year university students, which more than doubled from 1965–6 to 1981–2. Nevertheless, full equality in higher education has not been achieved, particularly in science and engineering subjects, and the effects of enhanced educational opportunities are not what might be thought. Lewis (1984, p. 220), for example, comments that it is 'notable that increasing numbers of women have pursued further education and training irrespective of expectations regarding marriage and motherhood, and yet the percentage of women in "top jobs" other than medicine is not much greater than [in] 1911.'

As for other institutions, despite more than 70 years of having been able to sit in Parliament, the percentage of women Members of Parliament has remained extremely low; having fluctuated between 3 and just over 4 per cent in the post-war period, it rose in the 1980s, but only to 6 per cent in 1987, and by 1993 was still less than 10 per cent (Close, 1989; Joshi, 1989; *Guardian*, 7 September 1993). The immediate post-Thatcher Cabinet of 1991 was notorious for containing no women (later, two women were included); under the Thatcher governments for most of the time there had been only one woman in the Cabinet, and that was Thatcher herself. Women remain underrepresented in local government, other public bodies and the media; they have achieved advances in some areas of the professions such as medicine, the law and banking (Hakim, 1979; Lewis, 1984), but still remain largely excluded from powerful positions within these. The judiciary, for example, is overwhelmingly male. Close (1989) gives figures which demonstrate the preponderance of men among judges and lawyers, national government administrators, doctors, economists, accountants, teachers in higher education and others. Lewis (1984, p. 222) comments on the continuance of inequality that 'there has been no steady line of uninterrupted, unequivocal progress for women', and 'Women in the late twentieth century find themselves in the paradoxical position of having more freedom and opportunity than ever before and yet facing inequalities that seem as deeply entrenched as ever.' In all, women remain highly unequal in the public sphere.

The division of labour within the household

The division of household tasks within the family has been slow to change (see, for example, Henwood *et al.*, 1987; Delphy and Leonard, 1992; other aspects of change in marriage will be discussed in later sections). Paid work has not freed women from household responsibilities any more than it has freed them from economic dependency. Most domestic and child-care work is still done by women, even when they also do paid work. In the 1960s and early 1970s, Willmott and Young (1973) claimed the family had become more 'symmetrical', with women doing more work outside the home and men more work within it; these authors have been taken to task for this view which misrepresents the situation. For example, Walby (1990) comments that Willmott and Young purported to show more participation by husbands in housework, but were criticised by Oakley (1974), who notes, 'the argument was based upon husbands "helping" their wives with tasks at least, but not necessarily more than, once a week. That is, the amount of domestic labour which Wilmott and Young found might have been negligible, and is insufficient empirically to ground their argument' (Walby, 1990, pp. 80–1).

Families in which both parties have jobs do not necessarily share domestic work, and neither is equal importance allocated to wives' and husband's work, partly because (as shown) wives tend to earn less. These families may be regarded mostly as 'dual worker' rather than 'dual career' (see Allan, 1985, pp. 26–7), and are not necessarily egalitarian with a fair sharing-out of household work. Detailed information on the division of work within the household was lacking until the 1980s, but the British Social Attitudes Survey of 1988 (cited by Kiernan and Wicks, 1990) undertook an analysis of who in couples was said to be responsible for various household tasks according to different female employment statuses. It was found, for example, that even when the wife was in full-time employment, household cleaning was done mainly by her in 60 per cent of cases, washing and ironing in 80 per cent and preparing the evening meal in just over 60 per cent of cases; she was responsible for caring for a sick child in over 50 per cent of cases. Household shopping was most likely to be shared, being done by both equally in nearly 50 per cent of cases (but still by the woman mainly in over 40 per cent of cases). There was less sharing still where the woman was in part-time work or out of the labour force, although again shopping stood out as the task most likely to be shared. Only to a minuscule degree were the various tasks undertaken mainly by the man.

Allan (1985, p. 51) comments: 'All studies show that the wife continues to bear the brunt of domestic responsibilities irrespective of her employment during the week', and Lewis (1992, p. 88) writes: 'the extent to which unpaid work in the family has remained women's work is seemingly one of the most *unchanging* aspects of post-war life' (italics added). Close (1989, p. 15), having reviewed a number of studies, concludes: 'women, as wives and mothers, participate far more than men in domestic labour (housework, child care)' and this pattern holds 'despite variations between couples with respect to (1) the wife's "employment status" ... (2) the husband's employment status (3) the couple's social class'. In Canada, Boyd (1988) comments that: 'A number of studies indicate that the acquisition of labour force positions by women has not meant equal assumption by men of domestic responsibilities' (p. 93); for example, one study (Meissner *et al.*, 1975) found that when a wife began work the husband increased his share of housework by only six minutes weekly where there was no child under 10, although by 60 minutes where there *was* a child under this age. Again in the Canadian context, Duffy *et al.* (1989, p. 102) observe: 'Family ideology continues to prescribe that a certain core of domestic labour is women's work, regardless of whether a woman engages in wage labour.' Goldscheider and Waite (1991, p. 10), in an American context, refer to: 'substantial disparities between the sexes in time spent on household tasks', noting that, until recently, studies did not document much difference in hours spent in housework between husbands with employed wives and those with homemaker wives, or any increase in time spent by husbands on housework as wives began working in increasing numbers. On Australia, Gilding (1991, p. 126) comments: 'As married women worked more outside the home, surveys consistently indicated that men did little more in the home.' And in Europe, according to Pillinger (1992, p. 22): 'The European Network on Childcare found that the time spent by men and fathers on child care and housework has not increased as more women have entered the labour market.'

The result of women undertaking the double role of paid work and most domestic work has been found to be over-load, conflicts and stress (see, for example, Rapoport and Rapoport, 1976). The type of paid work in which women are able to participate is also limited by this over-load. However, Morris (1990) shows that there was a doubling of male involvement in routine household work in the decade from the mid-1970s to the mid-1980s, although starting from a very low base. It may well be then that patterns of behaviour within the household are changing, but disproportionately slowly in relation to other systems. Goldscheider and Waite (1991, p. 11) give some grounds for optimism, saying: 'there is now some evidence that by the mid-1980s, after a generation of employed women worked a second shift in the home, men are actually *increasing* the number of hours they spend on household work... not only in the United States but also in Canada, the United Kingdom, and Norway' (quoting Gershuny and Robinson, 1988; italics in the original).

Male unemployment does not necessarily lead to men taking on more domestic tasks or to role reversal even where the woman is employed. For example, Morris (1984) showed that, even when men were unemployed and their wives employed, there was not a significant increase in housework by the men (see also Morris, 1985a and 1985b). Morris (1990, p. 100) found: 'little evidence of male unemployment leading to major responsibility for domestic work, nor even to their taking an equal share'.

It may be considered to what extent, and why, the more

private world of the family has lagged behind other changes in the 'public' realm. A similar pattern was observable in the inter-war years, when women had won the vote and other types of formal rights in the public sphere, but on marrying were mostly expected to give up other work and devote themselves full-time to the wife and mother role. Marriage had changed to a degree (see, for example, Lewis, 1984), but not as might have been expected (for the sexualisation of marriage at this time see Jeffreys, 1985). In the later post-Second World War period it became more accepted that married women, even mothers, might assume paid work, but only at the cost of a huge workload as they maintained most of their traditional domestic role as well. Despite changes in the law relating to marriage and divorce, and other external changes, the internal workings of labour in marriage have lagged behind other areas. Notable authors who put forward a view of marriage as essentially unchanged are Delphy and Leonard (1992), who see marriage as continuing in a highly traditional form, with wives' considerable input of labour and loss of autonomy in marriage.

The anomalous nature of traditional marriage and the gender-based division of labour within households, particularly where women work outside the home, is a likely source of women's dissatisfaction and of the increased instability of male–female partnerships. (Ermisch, 1989, for example, found that women with more work experience were more likely to divorce, although other factors may apply here, such as the opportunity to meet new partners.) The continuing high domestic workload of women affects their availability to undertake long hours of paid work. Nevertheless, more women work, and have an independent income which makes it more feasible to break free from marriages in which they are unhappy. These areas will be explored further later.

Changing ideas and attitudes

Despite the limits of objective change, there have been changing *ideas* about women and their roles, although caveats have to be entered about how we interpret different signs of ideological change, and about the representativeness of feminism as a movement and set of ideas. For women firmly committed to traditional roles, feminist ideas may be deeply threatening. There is also a conscious 'backlash' or counter-assault in some quarters against feminism and changes in women's position (for example, Faludi, 1991 argues that backlashes against feminism and women's advances have occurred cyclically).

Looking at the twentieth century as a whole, a 'first wave' and a 'second wave' of feminism in North America and Europe are commonly identified. The first wave occurred at the end of the nineteenth/early twentieth century, with the struggle for the franchise, and the overcoming of other legal and institutional barriers to women's participation in the public sphere, so that women were (formally) enabled to enter higher education and the professions, and to have more equal property, divorce and custody rights in marriage. Delphy and Leonard (1992) identify the first wave with the period 1850–1920, and report that some challenges to the existing form of the family came from feminists during this phase. The focus for change was on laws relating to property and divorce, on achieving a higher valuation of women's work at home, on improving the situation of women outside marriage and of women victims of violence, and of women in the public sphere, especially in education and employment. Other areas of concern were the treatment of prostitutes, the age of sexual consent, and men's sexual behaviour generally. A few 'argued for domestic reform and set up actual reformed communities providing houses for many families living together, with communal facilities' (p. 7). But there was less discussion of the gender division of domestic labour, partly because of the widespread employment of servants; differing roles for husbands and wives were accepted; and 'the ideal of (married or single) women combining employment and family responsibilities was only rarely represented' (p. 8). Marriage and family were presumed, even by feminists, to be a central sphere for women.

The second wave came after a dormant period in the mid-twentieth century when it was thought that the major battles had been won. There was some pressure for reform mid-century, largely focused on women as wives and mothers (see, for example, Williams, 1989). The second wave developed from the late 1960s onwards. The measures of the early twentieth century had made it appear that the essential female equality objectives had been achieved, and that women would gradually reach positions of power and economic advantage on an equal basis with men. But by the 1960s it was strikingly obvious that, despite decades of formal legal equality for women in some respects, nothing like this had occurred. Some institutional barriers to equality remained firm after first wave feminism: different rates of pay for men and women in the same work, conscious occupational segregation, the 'marriage bar' in some occupations up to the Second World War, the legality of discrimination against women in employment, education, hire purchase and mortgage provision, and continuing control of women in the sphere of reproduction through restrictions on contraception and abortion. Delphy and Leonard (1992) identify the second wave with the period 1968–90, and associate it with women's dissatisfaction with marriage as an unequal partnership, especially among women who were educated and who had enjoyed a period of employment and independence before marriage. This dissatisfaction 'produced an explosion of anger which launched the second wave of feminism' (p. 12).

The second wave concerned recognition of women's continuing inequality and pressure for further legal and institutional change: rights to easier abortion and contraception, to more state child care, to maternity rights and equal pay at work, and against discrimination in general. There was also pressure for changes in the relations between men and women within the family and elsewhere, for protection against men's violence, and a more diffuse change in consciousness and practice regarding gender roles and the treatment of women. Delphy and Leonard stress that much of the feminist critique in the early 1970s focused on the private sphere and inter-personal relationships, as well as on the public sphere. The focus on the private – the division of domestic labour, sexual relations, the construction of femininity – and the conscious labelling of this as a political area marked a break with the earlier feminism. Women were seen to be oppressed and exploited, the victims of violence and sexual abuse, and to be engaged in a political struggle with the system of male domination. As Delphy and Leonard say (p. 13): 'From the start of the second wave of feminism there was a clear recognition that marriage and heterosexual couple relations generally were an important element within this sytem.' Marriage and family were seen as essentially unequal, with domestic work falling invariably to women, and 'in the late 1960s and 1970s at least, family and sexual relationships were always stressed as key sites of oppression and in need of radical change' (p. 14).

Attitudes to the acceptability of married women working were changing by the late 1960s, and work was perceived favourably by many women, particularly the educated middle class, who were bored by isolated domesticity; this discontent was a prominent theme early in the second wave of feminism (for example, Friedan, 1963; Gavron, 1966). Women had entered work increasingly during the 1950s and 1960s; but various problems confronted them, notably explicit discrimination at work and the reluctance of men at home to share in domestic work and child care, resulting in the burden of the 'double shift'. Little formal child care was available, (except on a private, paid basis) to free women for paid work and other activities. Resentment of these factors fired second-wave feminism, the 'women's liberation' movement of the late 1960s and early 1970s (largely a movement of young, white, middle-class women at this stage- see Lewis, 1984 and 1992; Delphy and Leonard, 1992). The 'sexual revolution' of the late 1960s had apparently had some adverse effects for women, although the realisation of this was perhaps only gradual (Delphy and Leonard, 1992); while from the early 1970s there were revelations of the extent and severity of the violence experienced by women from their male partners (see Pizzey, 1973).

Women's treatment by the various agencies of the state, and the underpinning assumptions of state welfare that women were mostly the economic dependants of men, also came under fire (E. Wilson, 1977); this feminist critique of the welfare state was to develop further. Significiant measures which attempted to improve women's position in Britain were the Equal Pay Act 1970 (implemented 1975), and the Sex Discrimination Act 1975. The effects of these were mixed and not as helpful as had been hoped; nevertheless, women's relative pay improved slightly in the mid-1970s (Lewis, 1984), and formal protection against discrimination in employment, services and education was introduced. These changes both reflected and reinforced changing attitudes to women's equality.

In the 1980s the term 'feminism' rather than women's liberation was employed, and a body of feminist literature developed, which highlighted and challenged women's inequality and traditional gender roles. Minor objective changes were wrought at work and in social security provision, but other 1980s developments, such as in divorce (see, for example, Lewis, 1984) and controls on public spending, worked against women's interests. The ideology of this time fluctuated: there was talk of 'post-feminism' in the mid-1980s, suggesting that women were already 'equal' enough, and feminism was no longer necessary, or was even disadvantageous. (See Segal, 1987, for comment on how the concerns of feminism itself were changing.) Neo-conservative and 'neo-traditionalist' thinking on 'the family' experienced a resurgence in a conscious counter-reaction against feminism and female equality aims, and in favour of traditional roles. Delphy and Leonard (1992) refer to a 'decline' in the women's movement in the 1980s (p. 262); and Faludi (1991) discusses a 'backlash' against feminism and women's advances in the USA which was evident among opinion leaders and in the media, in fashion, the film industry, politics and popular psychology. This reaction was ostensibly concerned with the supposed adverse effects of feminism for women, but was often based on unreliable or inaccurate evidence, and was at root a struggle to re-assert male power. In the early 1990s there was continuing evidence of a counter-reaction in the 'family values' and 'back to basics' debates, in some extreme anti-abortion movements in the USA, and in the appearance of a literature re-asserting men's needs and rights (see Farrell, 1988 and 1994; Bly, 1991; Lyndon, 1992; Thomas, 1993).

However, the 'backlash' seems to have represented a minority viewpoint; for example, the Gallup survey reported by the Daily Telegraph in 1990 found that 63 per cent of people thought the trend away from the 'traditional' family of breadwinner husband and homemaker-wife to be a good thing (Child Poverty Action Group, 1990a). As for Canadian evidence, Veevers (1991) cites a Gallup poll which found that in 1960 only 5 per cent of respondents said married women should take a job if they had young children, but as many as 47 per cent did so in 1987 – a striking shift. Attitude change is not necessarily consistent or uniform; Goldscheider and Waite (1991) comment that according to American evidence: 'More people approve of women working in the labour force . . . than they do of men sharing in the responsibilities of the home' (p. 11).

The changed consciousness about women and their roles over the 1970s, 1980s and beyond constituted a serious challenge to the ideology of patriarchy, female inequality and traditional gender roles. However, while women's own consciousness changed, this was not necessarily matched by a corresponding change in male ideology about gender, although it would also be incorrect to argue that there was no change in men's views (for changing masculinities see, for example, Segal, 1990). Women changed at a faster rate than men, and some men actively reacted against feminism.

Changes affecting men

The foregoing has concentrated primarily on changes affecting women: their increased labour force participation, the division of labour within the family/household, and changing ideas about their role. However, both men and women within the family have changed their behaviour patterns less than might be expected from the external shifts. What else has happened to *men* in relation to work and family over time?

First, in the later post-war period men's work activity rate declined as women's rate increased. This was due partly to increased participation in higher education taking men out of the workforce for a time (Webb, 1989), but also to recession and rising levels of unemployment. In fact, the 1980s saw *full*-time jobs for both women and men fall sharply, while the *part*-time employment of women rose (Webb, 1989). And *Social Trends* (1991) shows that over the 1970s and 1980s male and female unemployment rates followed a similar pattern, but the male rate was consistently higher. However, methods of measuring levels of unemployment in Britain tend to exclude many women who want a job by not counting those disentitled to social security benefits (many women cannot claim benefits when unemployed, for a mixture of reasons). Walby (1990) gives some figures (from the Labour Force Survey) *not* just for those claiming benefit for 1984–86, where male and female unemployment rates were much the same, at 11 per cent/10 per cent. However, the overall economic activity rate is higher for men than for women (see, for example, Lonsdale, 1987).

Men are more likely to be in work or to be officially counted as unemployed than women, but men are also much more likely to be unemployed than in the earlier post-war decades. 'Full' employment as a goal in the immediate post-war period meant full *male* employment, and this was achieved in part at the expense of women losing their war-time jobs. The height of male *employment* was reached in the mid-1960s, with unemployment then increasing in the 1970s and 1980s, reaching a peak of 13 per cent of the male labour force in 1986 (CSO, *Social Trends*, 1991). The rate then declined, only to rise again in the 1990s, to 13.2 per cent for males (Keegan, 1994).

To some extent there was an (indirect) displacement of men by part-time women workers, with men and women occupying different segments of the labour market; that accommodating part-time women expanded, and that accommodating men shrank. So as men lost one type of employment, women gained another; more marriages contained two earners instead of one, but more also contained *no* earners with both partners unemployed. An article in the *Guardian* by Keegan (1994) underlines the nature of the change, noting that soon the number of women with jobs would exceed the number of men with jobs. Citing the Confederation of British Industry, Keegan states that in the last 25 years the number of men in employment in Europe had fallen by a million, while the number of women in employment had increased by over 13 million. New jobs were mostly those for part-time women workers, while most jobs lost were full-time male posts in manufacturing (3 million since 1979). Some companies employed part-timers to replace full-time staff. The problem for men was that: 'They can't take the full-time "men's" jobs in industry because there simply aren't enough of them and they are culturally – and financially – unprepared to apply for part-time "women's" jobs' (Keegan, 1994).

Change in the male role *within* the household has been slow, with women earners retaining much of their domestic responsibility. Men have taken on more domestic work and child care, and there is evidence of men as carers of adult dependants (Green, 1988), but the shift is not commensurate with the expansion of women's work roles. So as men as a group lost their work role, they did not compensate by moving into a domestic one; again, marriage and marriage-like partnerships are slower to change than other arenas of society. Walby (1990, p. 82) comments: 'Any marginal increase in symmetricality in the family is due to women moving towards a male pattern of engagement with paid work and less housework, not, to any significant extent, to men moving towards a female one and doing housework.'

Some of men's power within marriage has been undermined by both women's employment and their own weakened breadwinning role and unemployment. Evidence for this might be that the divorce rate is higher for unskilled and semi-skilled men (who have lower wages and are more likely to experience unemployment) than for professional men; it is higher still for unemployed men (Haskey, 1984; B. J. Elliott, 1991); and, as mentioned, women with a work history are more likely to divorce (Ermisch, 1989). The balance of *advantage* for women in marriage has worsened (because they are expected to do more work but are less totally supported financially), while the balance of *power* has shifted in their favour (their possibility of independence is greater). If women were being expected to give more while men gave less, while women also had greater ability to manage without a partner (or to search for another one), then more conflict between partners and more separations would be a not surprising outcome. This is Walby's (1990) argument; she says, 'we should expect that, as women gain increasing access to paid employment, they will be less likely to live in marriage relations' (p. 85); and, 'The major causes of change in the household and reproduction are the increasing proportion of women in paid work, and the extension of welfare benefits to independent women' (p. 86). Both give women an income of their own, albeit not a generous one.

This section has considered women's changed position within the labour market: the fact that more wives and mothers are in paid work, but nevertheless disadvantaged paid work, and therefore women have not been freed altogether from economic dependence on men; the marginally changed position of women in relation to other social institutions; the (relatively unchanging) division of tasks in the household; changing ideas about women's roles; and the changing roles of men. The general trend is for important although partial change, with more changes in women's public role than their private one, and asymmetrical change in men's and women's lives and behaviour.

' A useful summary is provided by Armstrong and Armstrong (1988), writing in the Canadian context but in terms also relevant elsewhere; they comment: 'The massive and relatively permanent movement of married women into the formal economy has increased women's strength and choices in and out of the market' (p. 163). They point to women's changed position within the labour market, women's power within households, and their increased ability to leave unbearable marriages. New ideas about women's work and women's place have accompanied the changes; nevertheless they have not all improved things, and the authors point to women's low pay, occupational segregation and part-time work. In fact the changes have polarised women, with differences especially found 'between those career women married to men with good jobs and those women without paid work or employed husbands' (p. 166).

Reproduction

Reproduction means here both the bearing of children and their upbringing, maintenance and care. The term is thus more restricted in its use than when Marxists and others use it to indicate *all* the activities associated with caring for the workforce so that individuals are 'serviced' and enabled to undertake paid work.

A first striking area of change is a significant decline in fertility in Britain, beginning around 1870. Lewis (1984, p. 5) comments: 'Within marriage the most important change experienced by women was the steady decline in the fertility rate until after World War II . . . while in the 1870s there were over 295 legitimate live births per 1000 married women aged 15–44, this figure had dropped to 222 by the first decade of the twentieth century and to only 111 by the 1930s'. The drop occurred first in the middle class. There have been fluctuations in the long-term fertility decline, but the *general* trend in child bearing has been to produce fewer children (although more of those born survive); this has had a dramatic effect on gender roles, changing the pattern of most women's lives substantially.

Titmuss in 1963 noted that the typical mother at that time had had two or three pregnancies, while the typical working-class mother of the 1890s had had 10! A Victorian mother spent on average 15 years in pregnancy and/or with a child in the first year of its life, and was in her mid-50s (at a time when life expectancy was shorter) when her youngest child left school. A mid-twentieth-century mother spent four years in pregnancy and infant care, and her children had left school by the time she was 40, leaving her with another 36 years of expected life. Lewis (1984, p. 6) comments: 'The decline in the general fertility rate was matched by a reduction in family size. In the first decade of this century 55 per cent of women had three or more children and 25 per cent more than five, but by the 1940s these figures were 30 per cent and 9 per cent respectively.' There were class differences, however; working-class families had more children until a later period, and the class differential remained wide until the inter-war years. But, by the end of the inter-war period, the two-child family was the norm across classes. In fact, there was concern about this decline in fertility by the outbreak of the Second World War.

Since Titmuss wrote in 1963, the number of births per woman has declined further, with child bearing starting later and more births being to older women (Kiernan and Wicks, 1990; B. J. Elliott, 1991). Nevertheless the main contours of Titmuss's comparison remain valid: women are freed from continuous child bearing, and the number of years occupied by bearing children and caring for them is dramatically diminished, especially in relation to total lifespan.

The broad pattern of fertility change over the twentieth century has been as follows. A historically high rate of births (accompanied by high levels of infant mortality) fell in the late nineteenth century, and remained low throughout the early twentieth century, with a small blip after the First World War. During the Depression family size was low and childlessness perhaps more acceptable; family planning clinics certainly developed in this period. The Second World War also served to keep child bearing low, with family founding for many couples deferred till after the war. After a peak in births just after the war (1947), fertility remained fairly constant in the early 1950s, but then rose to another peak in 1964 (B. J. Elliott, 1991). This is the period known as the early 1960s 'baby boom'; it occurred because younger age groups were starting child bearing earlier, while older age groups also continued, or started, to have babies.

Since 1964 the general trend in fertility has been downwards, with rates declining gradually till 1971 and then more sharply (B. J. Elliott, 1991); the low point for the birth rate was 1977, after which there was a recovery in the late 1970s (Ermisch, 1990), and then small fluctuations with age variations in the 1980s (B. J. Elliott, 1991). In the latter part of the 1960s and 1970s reliable contraception and abortion became more widely available (Kiernan, 1989), and in the UK contraception became free under the National Health Service in 1973; a relatively liberal 1967 Abortion Act was implemented in 1968. These factors were in part responsible for the fertility decline from the late 1960s. In 1971, however, the fertility rate was still over two children per woman (CSO, *Social Trends*, 1991). (The measure of fertility used refers to the number of children a woman would have if she followed the average trend in each year of her life.) By 1974 the rate had fallen below the replacement level (Ermisch, 1990) for the first time since civil registrations started in Britain (B. J. Elliott, 1991). As Elliott notes, from the early 1950s till around 1970 there was a shift towards earlier child bearing (with more fertility under 25, and teenage fertility peaking in 1971); *since* 1970, however, there has been a tendency for women to postpone having children. Fertility for the youngest groups fell most sharply; conversely, since 1975, fertility for the early 30s age group has risen considerably.

By 1981 the fertility rate was again (slightly) over two, but it was down to 1.8 by 1989, and 1.84 by 1990 (CSO, *Social Trends*, 1991, 1992). Ermisch (1990, p. 6) reports: 'the decline in fertility observed in the 1970s has not been reversed significantly during the 1980s'. It may be noted also that the likelihood of childlessness seems to have increased with successive post-war generations; for example, only 10 per cent of women born in 1945 did not have a child, whereas an estimated 17 per cent of women born in 1955 will not have had one, and 21 per cent of those born in 1965 (CSO, *Social Trends*, 1990; OPCS, *Population Trends* 61, reported in the *Guardian*, 20 September 1990). Family size is usually one or two children; to have more is unusual. Childlessness is more accepted and more people may remain childless in the future. This remains an area for debate, however.

A striking aspect of change in reproduction, then, has been the smaller number of births per woman. The drop in the rate of births has not been continuous, but has included some fluctuations or 'baby booms' at specific periods. Nevertheless, the overall trend has been a reduction in family size, as reflected in the fertility rate. The recent situation is somewhat confused by a rise in the actual *numbers* of births from the later 1980s, caused by the cohort born in the 'baby boom' years of the early 1960s being in their child bearing years; thus there are more births and younger children in the population (Ermisch, 1990).

Alongside the general drop in births per woman and greater probability of remaining childless, there has also been some evidence of a desire for fewer children since the early 1960s (B. J. Elliott, 1991); there seems also to be increased *involuntary* infertility, along with more use of reproductive technologies from the 1980s to remedy this (most notably *in vitro* fertilisation). The 1980s also witnessed an increase in other means of bearing children, such as artificial insemination and surrogate motherhood, raising new questions about the relationship between the biological and the social, the meaning of motherhood and indeed of parenthood, and the relationship between the infertile, the medical profession and the law (see, for example, Stanworth, 1987). Clearly while some childlessness is intentional, some is involuntary and deeply resisted. The traditional 'solution' for infertile couples, adoption, declined after the 1960s as the number of babies available for adoption dropped. This was largely due to more widely obtainable contraception and abortion and a changed attitude to unmarried mothers. (Older children and children with disabilities became *more* available, but such placements led to rather different forms of adoptive family. Adoption of young children without 'problems' became a difficult and competitive business: see, for example, C. R. Smith, 1984.)

There were more births to older women in the 1970s and 1980s; fertility *rates* of women over 30 increased, while those of women in their 20s declined (C. Jones, 1992, quoted by Family Policy Studies Centre, 1992). This was the result of deferring child bearing, and also of remarriage after divorce. Later child bearing was part of a reversal of the previous postwar trend (up to around 1970) to *earlier* first births and more births to those aged under 25 (B. J. Elliott, 1991). As Kiernan and Wicks (1990, p. 11) say: 'Couples marrying since the late 1960s have been delaying starting their families. For example, in 1970 the average age at first birth amongst married women was 24 years, by 1980 the average age of becoming a mother had increased by over a year to 25.2 years and by 1987 had increased still further to 26.5 years.'

In general, in the 1950s and 1960s, births became more concentrated in terms of timing, and so followed a more predictable pattern (B. J. Elliott, 1991). This concentration reduced the total amount of time spent by women in nurturing babies and very young children, while the subsequent trend to later child bearing enabled some women to establish themselves at work before leaving (briefly) for childbirth. Wider birth spacing in the 1970s enabled a return to work between births (see, for example, Brochlain, 1986).

Reproduction, then, has on the whole become more concentrated and limited compared with previous eras. It is worth referring also to infant mortality and its dramatic reduction in the twentieth century, especially in the latter decades. When Rowntree was researching in 1899, the England and Wales rate in deaths per thousand births was 160; by 1961 it was 21.4; by 1992, 6.6 (Tilly and Scott, 1978; OPCS, 1993, reported in the *Guardian*, 10 July 1993). While women were having fewer babies, more of these babies survived beyond infancy and childhood. This meant that women have had to experience fewer births to achieve a given completed family size, and the expectation has been that most children would live to maturity. The once common experience of young child bereavement became exceptional.

The long-term historical decline in fertility is common to most western industrialised countries. For example, in North America, Veevers (1991, p. 25) speaks of a 'Canadian baby-

bust which began in the 1960s', which 'parallels similar declines in the rest of the developed western world'. In 1981 the
fertility level was below the replacement threshold (there was
particular concern about falling fertility in Quebec). Boyd (1988)
notes a fertility rate of 1.6 children by 1985 in Canada,
with increasing rates of childlessness and postponed births.
Goldscheider and Waite (1991) recall a US 'baby boom' from
the late 1940s to the early 1960s, which ended fairly abruptly.
There were then major declines in fertility in the late 1960s
and early 1970s, with no real sign of any increase; the 'current
generation' of women are likely to have an average of 1.8 children, a level below population replacement rate. In Australia
Gilding (1991) shows that in the 1950s there was a 'baby boom',
but in the 1960s more efficient contraception led to more restricted fertility and more widely spaced children. In the 1970s,
child bearing was delayed, the two-child family became the ideal,
and single children and childlessness became more common;
there were also more abortions. Bittman and Bryson (1989)
note that in 1975 in Australia the birth rate fell below replacement level, and by 1986 was at the 90 per cent level. This,
they report, was similar to the England and Wales level but
higher than the level in Italy, Denmark and, especially, West
Germany. As in Britain, successive cohorts of women were more
likely to be childless in Australia.

Similar patterns have occurred in many west European countries. Jensen (1989) records a long period of fertility decline
in Norway, followed by a post-war 'baby boom' which ended in
1964 (as indeed it did in Britain). There was then a downward
trend until 1975. The fertility rate in 1985 was 1.68. Although
there was a fall in family size, there was not a rise in childless
women. Jensen notes that countries such as Denmark and West
Germany have experienced several years of decreasing population, and that fertility rates are well below replacement levels
in several European countries. Pillinger (1992, p. 21) gives figures for declining birth rates for all EC countries between 1960
and 1986, though from a varying base. West Germany had the
lowest birth rate in the world, according to Nave-Herz (1989),
with the rate in 1984 being 1.3 children per woman. There
have been smaller families and more delayed reproduction with
successive cohorts. Even in Roman Catholic southern Europe

fertility rates have dropped, with Italian and Spanish rates well below those in northern Europe (*Guardian*, 25 May 1994, citing World Health Organisation figures). By the 1990s it was Italy which had the lowest fertility rate in the world at 1.3.

There are fewer children, then, but the actual years spent with very young children are not the only indicator of the demands made on women. Another variable is the way that adequate child care – and childhood itself – are construed, and the amount of time and energy that mothers are expected to devote to each child. In the latter nineteenth and twentieth centuries childhood has come to be seen increasingly as a separate stage of dependence and development, in need of special protection, understanding and stimulation, so that family life – and to some extent society – has in principle become more child-centred. Hendrick (1990) sees the developing concept of childhood as moving towards a more universalised concept through various stages in the nineteenth and twentieth centuries. By 1914 a recognisably 'modern' institutionalised childhood was in place (Walvin, 1982). Children had rights which the state would safeguard. They were indeed seen as special (at least by professionals and commentators). Hendrick (1990, p. 55) says: 'For most of this century the widely accepted concept has been refined and elaborated in accordance with the principles of pediatrics, medical hygiene and child psychology, and notably in relation to a politically inspired (but culturally recognized) commitment to "the family".' Relevant here are concepts of motherhood, and the way in which the role of mother, and the ideal of mother–child relationships, are defined. These influence the demands of child bearing and rearing, so that a very small modern family might be as demanding of time and energy as a large Victorian one where, for example, children received less individual attention, and older children were expected to undertake a good deal of the domestic work and look after younger ones.

The period of children's economic dependency has gradually lengthened over this century, as the school-leaving age was progressively raised from 12 to 16, and more young people entered higher and further education (see, for example, CSO, *Social Trends*, 1986). Children were therefore kept out of the full-time labour market for longer periods of time and were

more of an economic liability and less of an asset; the rise in
youth unemployment in the 1980s and 1990s (CSO *Social Trends*,
various years), and the loss or reduction of social security benefits for 16–25 year olds, exacerbated this dependency. While
in the nineteenth and early twentieth centuries young people
generally had a period of some years between leaving school
and leaving the parental home, during which time they were
usually economically active and an asset to parents because of
their financial contribution to the household (see, for example, Humphries, 1981; Walby, 1990), this 'contributing' inter-
val diminished as the age of leaving full-time education rose,
and as (in the early post-war decades) the age of marriage
declined. By the 1960s young people were also leaving the
parental home long before marriage and were therefore contributing less in the early adult stages of life. In the later 1970s
and 1980s this trend to leaving home earlier was reversed in
Britain (Kiernan and Wicks, 1990), due to conditions of economic recession, but higher levels of unemployment also meant
that younger people were contributing less to the family budget
when they were at home. From the late 1980s parental financial obligations to the young also increased further in practice, due to factors such as reduced financial support for those
in higher education (following *greater* suppport in the early
post-war period), and reduced or non-existent social security
benefits for 16–25 year olds (when single and childless).

Goldscheider and Waite (1991), in an American context, note
the rise in non-family living among young adults since the 1950s,
observing that until this time most young people had lived in
their parents' home until marriage. They 'remained at home
for a decade or more after completing schooling to contribute
to the family economy' (p. 17, quoting Kett, 1977). From the
1950s, however, this changed. These authors also comment on
children's reduced regular responsibilities for significant household tasks.

Childhood and youth, and young people's role within the
family, have therefore been construed differently at different
times. As the responsibility for child care within the family has
been mainly the woman's, the change in children's position
has affected mothers more than fathers; however, fathers have
continued to bear the greater part of the economic responsi-

bility, the responsibility for *maintenance*, although decreasingly so with more single parents in the population. It has been suggested that the increased financial onerousness of rearing children to adult independence has resulted in a 'flight from fatherhood' (Walby, 1990, quoting C. Brown, 1981, and Ehrenreich, 1983). That is, when parenthood is financially burdensome, men are more likely to leave parenthood to women. Certainly there is evidence that when day-to-day contact ends, many fathers seem to feel reduced involvement with, and financial responsibility for, their children (see, for example, Wallerstein and Blakeslee, 1989).

Reproduction occupies a smaller part of women's lives in terms of time in the life cycle taken up by babies and very young children; but reproduction seems a more onerous responsibility per child. However, notwithstanding popular ideas in the early post-war period about the importance of full-time mothers at home for young children, mothers with younger and younger children have returned to paid employment. So the part of the life cycle spent in *full*-time child care at home is reduced even further. According to figures given by Kiernan and Wicks, 30 per cent of mothers of children aged 0–2 were in paid work (although only 11 per cent full-time) in 1987 (quoting OPCS, *General Household Survey*, 1987). In terms of the division of labour between partners, however, child care remains a predominantly female task; for example, Piachaud (1984, quoted by Kiernan and Wicks) found that of the 50 hours or so per week involved in looking after children under five, 87 per cent of it was spent by mothers. Children are more 'burdensome' in a sense, but there is a reduction in overall parenting time. There is American evidence of a distinct drop in parental time spent with children from the 1960s to the 1980s (see Family Research Council, 1991; Mattox, 1991) and this is a concern for those who take a 'neo-traditionalist' or 'family values' viewpoint on family life and the consequences of what is construed as a parental retreat from the tasks of child rearing.

The movement of mothers into the labour force clearly gives rise to a need for alternative forms of daytime child care. (Day care will also be discussed in Chapter 4.) State child-care provision of nurseries, playgroups and nursery schools for younger children, and playschemes out of school hours for older children, is restricted in Britain. Not only is provision not universal, but it is mostly limited to children and families deemed to have problems. A contrast is often drawn with the war years when nursery provision was widespread, in order to free women for paid work (see, for example, Lewis, 1992). Mothers now turn to a range of systems for child care while they are working: husbands, relatives and other informal carers; registered (or unregistered) child minders and nannies; private and employer-provided nurseries, and so on. Evidence from the *General Household Survey* (1991) shows that the proportion of mothers of under-fives with jobs was 43 per cent by 1991. The proportion of parents making some form of child care arrangement for their under-fives had reached 64 per cent. Of under-fives' parents, a quarter used, respectively, nursery schools, and unpaid informal care by family or friends; 17 per cent used a private or voluntary day care scheme; 11 per cent a paid childminder or nanny; only 7 per cent a local authority scheme; and only 1 per cent a workplace nursery. So a variety of sources of daytime child care are used, but state *care* (as opposed to education) caters only for a small minority. There is an unknown number of unregistered and therefore illegal child-minders.

The conventional orthodoxy about the need for a continual maternal presence has been challenged at an ideological level, chiefly by feminists aware of the constraints on women which it implies (see, for example, New and David, 1985, who also quote Rutter, 1972). But in the 1980s and 1990s those with a 'neo-traditionalist' view of how families ought to function sounded the alarm on the likely adverse effects on children of working mothers. Such views diverge sharply from the reality of an increasing number of mothers of increasingly younger children (re)joining the labour market; and indeed it is government policy in Britain to encourage *single* mothers to do this (Lord Chancellor *et al.*, 1990). This is even more the case in some American states, where forms of 'workfare' or working for welfare benefits have been instituted for mothers of young children (see, for example, Burghes, 1992). There is controversy about the impact of maternal working on children but, whatever one's position on this, the inadequate, fragmented and partly unregulated nature of substitute child care arrangements can be pointed to with concern. Child rearing increasingly takes place outside the family unit, in a wide variety of other arrangements whose effects are largely unknown. At the same time, children are much less likely to spend all their childhood *living* with both birth parents. A chart presented by Kiernan and Wicks (1990, p. 16) shows that, in 1985, 78 per cent of children were living with both biological parents who were married to each other: certainly a large majority, but not an overwhelming one and a reduction even from the 83 per cent who were in this type of family in 1979. Approximately 10 per cent of children in 1985 were with their mother only; 9 per cent with a mother and step-father; and 2 per cent with cohabiting natural parents. All of these categories had increased since 1979. The cumulative effect of such changes is that children in general are less familiar with those who physically procreated them. On the other hand, the amount of time spent does not necessarily reflect the quality of the relationship; and neither does coresidence necessarily indicate, or lead to, a good close relationship.

An increasing proportion of births outside marriage was a feature of the 1960s, 1970s and particularly the 1980s. This is also found in other western societies. The percentage of births outside marriage in Britain was constant at around 5 per cent in the 1950s; it was 8 per cent by the end of the 1960s (B. J. Elliott, 1991); 11 per cent by the end of the 1970s; and as much as 28 per cent by 1990 (CSO, *Social Trends*, 1992). Thus the percentage more than doubled over the 1980s. Later figures suggest that the rise continued, although not so steeply, into the 1990s (OPCS, *General Household Survey*, 1992). Legal marriage, then, was decreasingly the necessary context for child bearing, while a greater proportion of children were born and raised in cohabitations, in 'reconstituted' families where a partner was present who was not the birth parent of the child, and in single-parent families. The trend was particularly marked among younger groups (CSO, *Social Trends*, 1992). Such changes raise questions about parental roles, and introduce at least a degree of ambiguity into the relationship between children and the adults with whom they live and/or who have physically reproduced them.

This section has covered the general decline in fertility this century, the shortened period of time spent by women in child bearing and rearing, the changes in the dependency of childhood and child care, and the reduced amount of time (apparently) that biological mothers and fathers are with their children. The general pattern is a confusing one because, while ideology this century seems to have become more 'child-centred', while having children can be more burdensome to adults, and smaller families might entail more attention per individual child, the objective evidence would seem to suggest that parents' lives and time are in some ways *less* centred round their (biological) children than they were. This is to neglect the more qualitative aspects of parent–child relationships, however.

Age and generation

The last section looked at the younger groups in the population. This section will consider trends affecting ageing and the gaps between generations in relation to families. It is well known that western societies in general are getting 'older' in that older age groups now form a larger proportion of the population. In Britain, as elsewhere, the pattern of demographic change over the last century has led to a general 'ageing' of the population, a skewing of the population to older age groups, in particular those over retirement age, and, in more recent years, the older groups – over 75, over 85 – *within* the retirement population.

In 1901, for example, only 4.7 per cent of the population was over 65, 1.4 per cent over 75, and a minuscule 0.15 per cent over 85. By 1931 these percentages had risen significantly to 7.4 per cent for the over 65s, 2.1 per cent for the over 75s, and 0.24 per cent for the over 85s. By 1951 the proportions were 10.9 per cent, 3.5 per cent and 0.45 per cent respectively, so that over a tenth of the population was by this time over the retirement age for men, 65. The percentages continued to rise in the post-war decades: 11.8 per cent over 65 by 1961, with 4.2 per cent over 75 and 0.64 per cent over 85; 13.2 per cent over 65 by 1971, with 4.7 per cent over 75 and 0.86 per cent over 85; reaching 15 per cent for the over 65s by 1981, 5.7 per cent for the over 75s, and over 1 per cent for the over 85s (McGlone, 1992, citing census data). More recent figures (1991) are 15.8 per cent for the over 65s (Family Policy Studies Centre, 1991, citing OPCS data), and 7 per cent for those 75 and over (Family Policy Studies Centre, 1992); McGlone (1992) also gives this figure of 15.8 per cent as a 1989-based projection for 1991, with 1.6 per cent for the over 85s.

The figure of 15.8 per cent of the population being over 65 translates into over 8.8 million people; 7 per cent into nearly 4 million; and 1.6 per cent into nearly 900 000 (McGlone, 1992). If we include women aged 60–65 (that is, over their retirement age) as well, we have a figure nearing 20 per cent of the population, or over 10 million people (CSO, *Social Trends*, 1992). The numbers of elderly are projected to increase well into the twenty-first century, but at a slower rate (McGlone, 1992). For example, the 1989-based OPCS projection for 2021 is 18.2 per cent of the population over 65 (10.78 million); 8.1 per cent over 75 (4.8 million); and 2.2 per cent over 85 (1.3 million: see McGlone, 1992).

Two factors are responsible, at one level, for this trend: one is fertility. If the birth rate drops, as it has over the past century, then the population gets relatively 'older' even if other factors remain constant; the *proportions* of people in older age groups will increase as the proportions in younger age groups decrease. The second factor is length of life. The change this century has been dramatic. Life expectancy at the beginning of the century was around 50; in the inter-war years it was around 60; by the early 1950s, around 70 (Ermisch, 1983). (There is always a gender differential, with women living longer.) Ermisch (1990) gives figures of 71.9/77.7 (men/women) for the mid-1980s; and the 1991 figures are 73.2/78.8 (Family Policy Studies Centre, 1992). So at birth the average male can expect to live to over 73, and the average female to nearly 79. On recent changes, Ermisch comments: 'The length of life has increased for both sexes during the 1980s, but more so for men than women' (1990, p. 18).

The proportion of survivors, Jefferys and Thane (1989) point out, especially among the young, has increased at each age, altering the formerly triangular shape of the age structure to something more like a rectangle. Ermisch (1990, p. 19) also comments on the 'rectangularisation of the lifetable', and says, 'deaths are now occurring at much later ages than they did in the past'. While infant mortality has declined, deaths in middle age are also more rare than they were; it has become more common to see one's retirement years. Just over 90 per cent of British women are expected to reach 60 according to present mortality patterns; a century earlier only 46 per cent did. Among men, just over three-quarters are expected to reach their sixty-fifth birthday; a century ago only 40 per cent did so. Looking back to the early twentieth century, Ermisch says: 'When state retirement pensions were introduced, the majority of people did not survive to retirement age, and even those who did were not around much longer' (p. 20). Now survival to retirement age is nearly certain, and there are more years of life after retirement. (So the original introduction of state income for retirement was based on rather different assumptions from those that apply today!) The population over retirement age is also 'older', with a greater proportion being over 75, over 85, and indeed reaching a hundred, with over 7000 centenarians in Britain in the early 1990s (Johnson, 1994, citing OPCS, 1993).

Again, the trend is common to the western and developed world. For example, in Canada the population is ageing as it is in Britain, although the proportion over 65 in 1986 was, at about 10 per cent, lower than in Britain (Veevers, 1991). But here too the proportion of oldest elderly has increased. In Australia, the proportion of 'old age pensioners' increased between 1969 and 1983 from 5.8 per cent to 9 per cent (Bittman and Bryson, 1989). Japan has one of the highest life expectancies in the world, and with it an ageing population (Hendry, 1989).

This major historical shift is commonly regarded as a serious social problem because of the need for care and financial provision for older people and the cost of this, both to the state and families/individuals. Disability and illness show an increased incidence in old age, especially after 70/75. Phillipson and Walker (1986, p. 6) comment: 'As age increases beyond about 50 there is a marked rise in the incidence of disability – particularly at the lower levels of severity – in successively older age groups. Then there is a rapid increase in severe incapacity beyond the age of 70.' The authors estimate that more than an eighth of the population aged 65 and over are severely disabled, and over half of the population of 75 and over are, though they also stress the positive side of this: most elderly people are *not* disabled, not even slightly so. McGlone (1992) notes that the numbers of the disabled, and the severity of the disability, increase steadily with age, especially after the age of 80. Of Britain's 6.2 million disabled people, more than two-thirds are aged 60 or over; this gives a figure of 4 million elderly people who are disabled, with the figure expected to rise rapidly. Moreover, 'From about 75 more people have a disability than do not' (McGlone, 1992, p. 11); while, 'Just under a quarter of people aged 60–69 have a disability, but this rises to nearly 3 in 5 for those aged 80+' (p. 12). Increase in life expectancy has not necessarily shortened the period of disability and dependency before death. Bebbington (1991, p. 28) comments: 'the expectation of life without disability for both men and women is improving far more slowly than is life expectancy, if indeed at all'. Bebbington also points to American findings (Crimmins *et al.*, 1989) which indicate no change in disability-free life expectancy over the 1970s.

There are clearly considerable public expenditure costs to this, as well as demands on families and other sources of help. McGlone (1992, p. 7) reports that those aged 85 and over cost the health and community services, on average, five times as much as those aged 5–64; and 'those aged over 75 and 85 cost the health service more than all other age groups put together'. While elderly people (that is, 65 and over) are only about 16 per cent of the population, they account for over half of all hospital and community health service expenditure, £6.4 billion per annum (1988–89 figures: p. 22); over 45 per cent of the English personal social services budget went on the elderly in 1988–89, namely £1.5 billion (p. 23). McGlone also reports that elderly people consume about half of all spending on social security.

It might appear that increased longevity has brought in its train a huge public burden; however, some have argued for a less pessimistic view of the increased incidence of old age (for example, Jefferys and Thane, 1989; Thane, 1989), and have suggested that older people are also contributors to the economy, family and society (see also Finch, 1989); furthermore, they claim that the nature of old age, and its presumed 'dependency', are socially constructed. Retirement ages, for example, which are set by law and employment practices, are imposed on individuals, and could in principle be changed; if older people are now fitter in their 60s than a generation ago (see, for example, Thane, 1989), then the 'burden' of dependency of old age might not mean what is commonly believed. Also, old people are *givers* of care, both to each other and younger members of the family (for example, to grandchildren). Indeed, 'Research has identified women in their early 60s making the largest contribution to informal caring' (Family Policy Studies Centre, 1992, p. 10). The younger elderly also have a role as voluntary workers (OPCS, *General Household Survey*, 1977; Askham *et al.*, 1992). Most old people's own care needs seem to be met within the family; as McGlone (1992) says: 'The vast majority are cared for in their own homes by husbands or wives or adult children. This shows that family care is alive and well' (p. 42). Although, McGlone reports, more than a half of those aged 85 and over cannot do their own shopping, 'it is important to emphasise that even among very elderly people, large proportions are not dependent on other people for everyday domestic and personal care' (p. 15).

As far as the financial dependency of old age is concerned, however, it must be said that effective retirement ages in Britain have come down, due to economic conditions, rather than risen with greater fitness in old age; a smaller proportion of men aged 60–64 are now in work (55 per cent in 1988, compared with 91 per cent in 1961: Laczko and Phillipson, 1991), and they are not (since 1983) required to register as unemployed. Since the 1970s there has been encouragement of early retirement in order to release jobs for younger workers (for example, the Job Release Scheme, 1977–88). This increases the social security and occupational pension costs of the retired; and it seems unrealistic in conditions of high unemployment to talk about *raising* retirement ages. However, the British government in the early 1990s proposed that this be done for women, in order to align both sexes' retirement ages at 65 and to cut pension costs. How far social security costs will be reduced by this decision remains to be seen, as women aged 60–65 prevented from claiming the National Insurance retirement pension might still need to claim Income Support. They would not necessarily be able to find employment, and many of them would be carers.

A few other characteristics of the elderly population may be noted. There is a gender dimension to ageing, as women on the whole live longer than men. There are more women than men in the older groups, and the older the group the more this imbalance is apparent (Kiernan and Wicks, 1990). Also, over the age of 75 women's rate of disability is higher (McGlone, 1992). McGlone reports that more women aged 75 and over are widowed than men, so older women are more likely to live with children or alone. The tendency for wives to be younger than their husbands makes it more likely still that women rather than men will be widowed. Similar trends are noted in, for example, Canada. Veevers (1991) reports that in 1986, of persons aged over 65, only 13 per cent of men were widowed, compared with 48 per cent of women. This is attributed to women's longer lifespan, their tendency to marry older men, and their reduced likelihood of remarriage once bereaved. Boyd (1988, pp. 99–100) records: 'Fewer than two in five elderly women (aged 65 and older) are currently married, and the percentages decline with increasing age.' So more older Canadian men live with spouses than do older women.

One long-term effect of raised levels of divorce may be an increased number of older women without a current partner. McGlone (1992, p. 21) comments on this: 'A social change that may be important in reducing the future supply of elderly husband and wife carers is divorce.' At present, he notes, the percentage of elderly who are divorced is very low; but it will rise dramatically if current divorce rates continue. In 1989, one out of 31 women and one out of 34 men over 65 were divorced, but the projection for 2019 is one in seven for both (McGlone, 1992, p. 21). This trend would exacerbate the number of *women* alone specifically, as the remarriage rate after divorce for men is higher (CSO, *Social Trends*, 1990). The Family Policy Studies Centre (1991) predicts that the numbers over 65 who are divorced but not remarried will increase four times by 2025, with a higher percentage for women.

Many elderly people, especially women, live alone, and this tendency has been increasing (see, for example, CSO, *Social Trends*, 1986). More than a third of those aged 65 and over in

Britain lived alone in the late 1980s, and over 60 per cent, or approaching two thirds, of women aged 85 and over did so (OPCS, *General Household Survey*, 1989). Nearly half of *all* those aged 75 and over live alone, the percentage being much higher for women than for men (McGlone, 1992). Kiernan and Wicks (1990) show that, of all aged 65 and over in 1987, 36 per cent lived alone, 45 per cent with just their spouse, and relatively small percentages in other arrangements such as with children or other relatives. For women aged 80 and more, however, the position was very different: as many as 61 per cent or nearly two-thirds lived alone; just 11 per cent lived with with their spouse only, but 21 per cent were with children or children-in-law, and 6 per cent with spouse and others or with other relatives (p. 23). Thus both the likelihood of living alone or with other relatives had increased with age, and the likelihood of living just with a husband had sharply decreased.

Living alone, while it imposes certain risks, does not necessarily imply social isolation, and it appears that most elderly people are well supported by family and friends: most old people are in touch with their children and receiving services from them (Wenger, 1986). The Family Policy Studies Centre (1992) quotes work by Wilmott (1986) which showed that most of the population had an extended family network, even if contact was only maintained by telephone, letter or visits; only a small minority, about one in twenty people, belonged to a 'residual' network group where relatives were rarely seen. As McGlone (1992) says, relatives are the main supporters of disabled people, and of the 6 million informal carers, three-quarters of them are looking after someone aged 65 and over. The increase of the numbers in the very elderly groups means that the most obvious carers, the next generation down, are also likely to be elderly, and it may be the grandchild generation who are more fit and able to care; however, ties across two generations may not be as close. The concentration of births this century into the earlier part of the life cycle would tend to exacerbate this situation (that is, very elderly parents with elderly children). However, the increase in births to older women in the 1980s will also mean some relatively 'young' childen around when these women reach old age.

Nevertheless, close family may be lacking for older people;

for example, in 1977, 30 per cent of the over 75s had never had children, and 7.5 per cent had outlived their children (McGlone, 1992). The continuing low birth rate and apparent increase in childlessness will mean fewer children available as carers for elderly parents in the future; the anticipated shrinkage of spouse carers due to divorce is another factor.

Other points about the situation of the elderly concern their poverty and poor housing relative to other groups. Well over half of pensioners live in, or on the margins of, poverty, but there are big inequalities within the pensioner group. An estimated 1.7 million pensioners and their dependents were on Income Support in 1991; and 3 million were on or below the Income Support/Supplementary Benefit level in 1987 (McGlone, 1992). Between 1979 and 1988, the number of pensioners with an income below half the average nearly trebled, increasing from 10 per cent to 17 per cent (McGlone, 1992, quoting Households Below Average Income, annual). There is a growing inequality between pensioners because of the growth in occupational pensions and the fall in the real value (relative to earnings) of state pensions. McGlone see 'two nations' emerging: one group with property and an occupational pension, and another living in rented accommodation and dependent on the state pension. Householders aged 75 and over are also more likely to have homes that are unfit or lack amenities than any other age group. McGlone comments: 'The greater likelihood of very old people living in poor housing is largely explained by the disproportionate number still renting from a private landlord' (p. 35). This may change in future with the general decline in this form of tenure.

What has occurred over the twentieth century, then, is longer life, resulting in more older people in both an absolute and a relative sense, and a reduction in the birth rate, altering the balance between young and old. Successive birth cohorts influence the numbers reaching old age at a later stage, and the lower birth rate between the wars has reduced the growth of the younger elderly by the closing decades of the twentieth century, but the *older* elderly continue to grow, and this is the group most likely to need medical treatment and nursing and social care. In general, the new historical situation of nearly a fifth of the population over retirement age has brought increased

costs in terms of pensions and care, and new demands on
younger members of families.

Finally, the rather separate question of generation also needs
to be addressed. It is clear from the outlined trends in old age
that grandparents and great-grandparents are more likely to
be present in families than in earlier times, although this situation depends not only on length of life but on the spacing of
generations. A useful comment on generations within families
comes from M. Anderson (1983). Pointing out that the concept of a more flourishing 'extended family' in the past in
Britain, with many members living together or nearby, is something of a myth, Anderson nevertheless shows how the pattern
of relations between generations, in terms of the timing of events
in the lifespan, has altered. Shorter life expectancy, higher infant
mortality and a larger number of children per woman combined to give the family of the past a very different shape. In
the early 1770s around 12 per cent of young people were or-
phaned by the age of 25, and the approximately median age
at which one lost one's father was 32, and one's mother 34;
these figures did not change markedly over the next century,
but by the 1921 birth cohort, only 2 per cent lost both parents
by 25, and the median ages for parental death were 41 (for
fathers) and 47 (for mothers). Of those born in 1946, only 1
per cent would lose one parent by age 25, with median age
for father loss being 45, mother loss 53. The twentieth-century
decline in family size and clustering of births in the early years
of marriage have also been significant, with median age at the
marriage of one's last child, and at birth of the last grandchild, declining this century, while age at death rose. So it
became more likely that individuals would live to see all their
children married, and all their grandchildren born. The 1861
birth cohort was the first in Anderson's study where a majority
would know all their grandchildren; the average woman can
now live long enough to see all her grandchildren *marry*.

There are various implications from these estimates, concerning relationships with particular kin, and the time that
women have free between the birth of their last child and of
their first grandchild. Earlier generations of women saw their
lives bound up with caring for their children and then their
grandchildren, with less space in between, and there was more

possibility of reciprocal family care, such as grandparent to grandchild; (grand)child to (grand)parent. Nowadays,

> the trends of the twentieth century have changed all that. Increasingly in the 1960s and 1970s women, free of their own child care responsibilities by their forties, returned to work – and worked right through the period when their grandchildren were born. And now that they themselves are entering old age, with around 20 more years to live, they find that their own children have in turn had their families and returned to work. (M. Anderson, 1983, pp. 8–9)

That is, possibilities of reciprocity of the three-generation sort found in the traditional working-class communities have largely vanished. Anderson may be overly pessimistic; his view should be contrasted with comments from the Family Policy Studies Centre (1992) on mutual help betwen the generations. But Finch (1989) makes the related point that the time when one generation needs help does not necessarily coincide with the time when another generation is free to give it; 'family' time and 'individual' time do not necessarily harmonise. Anderson also notes that, in terms of the ratio of survival years of older people to number of living children, the burden falling on each child has increased. These changes are highly relevant for policy. (See also *New Society's* special supplement, 18 September 1987.) Discussing the Norwegian situation, Jensen (1989, pp. 123–4) comments: 'By the year 2,000, when the economically active mothers of today will be about 50 to 60 years old, they will have built up long careers in the labour force ... [yet] They will face a demand for care from their parents and parents-in-law which far exceeds that presented to the middle-aged women today.' This represents a challenge.

So different generational patterns have changed families, and women's lives, quite drastically; and they have changed the basis for support between kin of different generations, although the empirical evidence for the continued existence of family helping and care for old people should be borne in mind (see also Wenger, 1986; Wright, 1986; Lewis and Meredith, 1988; Qureshi and Walker, 1989).

This section has discussed the general 'ageing' of the population in Britain brought about by reduced fertility and greater longevity, some of the public cost implications of this trend, some characteristics of the elderly population, and the separate but related question of generation. The situation facing Britain and many other western societies seems historically unprecedented and throws into question earlier assumptions about family care of the elderly, although at present family care does still seem to be fairly active.

Conclusion

This chapter has examined change in the areas of gender, reproduction, ageing and generation. The picture is, overall, one of extensive, and interconnected, change. Women have moved into (disadvantaged) paid work; they have changed their public role more than their private one, but are nevertheless to a degree freer of marriage than they were. Fertility has declined and women spend less time than in the past in child bearing and care, although the ageing population is potentially another great demand. Ageing also affects women disproportionately because they live longer than men and are more likely to age alone. Different generational patterns have also changed family life.

Chapter 2

Dimensions of Family Change: Marriage Transformed

Chapter 1 examined various changes in gender roles, fertility, age and generation. This chapter will now examine changes in marriage, which have been significant. Marriage is occurring later and less often; divorce has become more common, as have families with only one resident parent (usually the mother). Second and subsequent marriages after divorce, heterosexual cohabitation without formal marriage, and child bearing and rearing outside formal marriage, sometimes in a cohabitation but sometimes also by a mother alone, have become more common features of society. Particular emphasis is placed on the significance of these changes in terms of a rejection of formal marriage.

Clearly different areas of change feed into one another. Changing gender roles have dramatically affected marriage, patterns of child care, and the ability of families to provide care in old age; while changes in male–female relations in marriage and other heterosexual couplings have affected gender roles in other contexts, and have had an impact on children and on experience in old age. The issue of gender, particularly, needs to be examined in close relation to changes in marriage, and vice versa. Women seem to be more independent of marriage, and to have less to gain from it. Age and generation are also factors which have bearings on marriage: with an increased lifespan marriages potentially last longer (perhaps causing more strain); while the freeing of women from many years of child and grandchild care opens up new opportunities, making them less confined within marriage. Changes in marriage and marriage-like relations themselves have implications for childhood and old age: for example, in rupturing parent–child links, and increasing the number of divorced elderly people in the future.

Connections between the different dimensions of change should be constantly borne in mind. No change occurs in isolation, and straightforward linear causal chains are extremely difficult to trace.

Marriage

In considering the apparent transformation of marriage, and the increasing appearance of alternatives to formalised, legal marriages, it is useful to start with institutionalised marriage itself: a partnership between a man and a woman formalised by either a religious or civil ceremony and having a particular status in law as well as in social custom. In the early post-war decades in Britain marriage became increasingly popular and occurred earlier, compared with the pre-war years; but after about 1970 this trend was reversed.

The increased incidence of marriage in the 1950s and 1960s was partly the result of a more even sex ratio in the population: in earlier decades a 'surplus' of women meant that many (in a society where marriage was monogamous and mostly lifelong) remained unmarried. In Victorian times a higher death rate for males, especially in infancy, and the disproportionate effect of wars and emigration, resulted in an excess of women over men; the Finer Report (Department of Health and Social Security, 1974, quoted by B. J. Elliott, 1991, p. 23) recorded that: 'in mid Victorian England, almost one third of the women aged 20 to 44 had to remain spinsters because differential mortality rates and large scale emigration so depleted the reservoir of men, that there were not enough to go round'. Lewis (1984, p. 4) reports that many women never married, and this was: 'partly due to the imbalance in the sex ratio, which increased steadily from 1871 to 1911, and dramatically as a result of World War I'. By 1921 there were only 894 bachelors for each 1000 spinsters in the age group 15–54 (B. J. Elliott, 1991).

For the first half of this century, then, as well as in the last century, women outnumbered men. Marriage rates were higher for men than for women from the turn of the century till the late 1940s; not until 1961 did men outnumber women in the 16–44 age group, a trend which has intensified. This demographic imbalance in the past, linked with a system of marital monogamy and relatively rare divorce, ensured that a proportion of women faced involuntary spinsterhood. This status was socially stigmatised and often economically insecure, given women's poor position in the labour market and the restricted number of occupations open to them; they also faced particular problems as they aged (Lewis, 1984). The spinster's fate invites an analogy with unemployment: marriage was women's primary role – a 'marriage ethic' – but it was structurally impossible for them all to marry, a situation for which the victims were frequently blamed. Some unmarried women, however, were supported within the family as carers, particularly of elderly parents (Lewis, 1984).

From the 1940s, marrying became a more universal experience, especially for women. Since the early 1950s women's marriage rates have been higher than men's (B. J. Elliott, 1991). Both men and women married earlier, with marriage rates for the under 25s increasing. The marriage rate for men in their early 20s rose rapidly through the 1950s and 1960s, while for women *teenage* marriage increased markedly. The median age at first marriage was 26.8 for men and 24.6 for women in 1951, but by 1971 it had fallen to 24.6 and 22.6 respectively (B. J. Elliott, 1991). Apart from the more even sex ratio, another factor was increasing economic prosperity and full (male) employment, which enabled couples to marry and begin families earlier, with the resources to do so and a reasonable prospect of a secure economic future.

The turning point in this trend came after 1970, which was the peak year for marriage (B. J. Elliott, 1991). After 1972, first marriage rates for both men and women declined quite steeply, so that by 1987 the first marriage rate for women was only half the 1970 peak, and for men the rate had dropped even lower. In the 1970s and 1980s, in other words, marriage became steadily less popular. The drop in the 1980s was somewhat steeper for men than for women, and the overall decrease continued into the 1990s (OPCS, 1991a).

Thus, median age at first marriage has risen since the early 1970s. In 1951 the median age of first marriage was 26.8 for men and 24.6 for women; by 1971 these ages had dropped to 24.6/ 22.6 (B. J. Elliott, 1991). But by 1987 the age had risen again to 25.3 for men and 23.3 for women (Kiernan and Wicks, 1990); by 1991 the median first marriage age was back to that of the early 1950s: that is, well over 26 for men and well over 24 for women (OPCS, 1991a). The fall in first marriage rates post-1970 was largely due to people under 25; the marriage rate declined quite steeply for men aged 20–24 (up to the 1980s), and even more dramatically for women aged 20–24, while teenage marriage rates fell (B. J. Elliott, 1991). The trend has changed the prediction of those ever marrying/never marrying quite drastically; the Family Policy Studies Centre (1991, p. 1) records: 'The majority but a declining proportion of people eventually marry. If present marriage rates continue, then the expected proportions of men and women married by age 50 would be around 77 per cent for men and 78 per cent for women, compared with 93 per cent of women and 96 per cent of men in 1971.'

It is not yet apparent whether all this means that young people are simply marrying later, or whether they are turning away from marriage altogether; as Elliott (1991, p. 89) says: 'What is not yet clear is whether the recent decline in marriage rates in this younger age group is due to young people marrying at progressively older ages, or from an increasing section of the population rejecting marriage altogether.' The relation of cohabitation to this trend will be discussed below. The switch to later marriage/less marriage among the young after 1970 coincided with economic decline and rising unemployment.

There has been a decline in the percentage of marriages solemnised in church and therefore a greater proportion of civil marriages (see Fletcher, 1988b). Elliott (1991) gives a figure of 48 per cent of marriages solemnised by a civil ceremony in England and Wales in 1987, with rather fewer in Scotland and a much smaller percentage (13 per cent) in Northern Ireland. She notes that the proportion of civil ceremonies has increased in all these regions since the Second World War.

Social Trends (1993) gives the proportion of civil marriages in Great Britain in 1990 as 47 per cent, compared with 40 per cent in 1971, with Christian marriage ceremonies declining. This increase in civil marriages is undoubtedly connected with the rise in the number of second and subsequent marriages after divorce, where remarriage in church is often not allowed; but the trend is also consistent with the decline in (mainstream) Christian practice (see CSO, *Social Trends*, 1993), and the general secularisation of society. It may also mark a change in the understanding and meaning of marriage: an ideological shift in which marriage is seen more as a terminable 'contract' rather than as a life-long and religiously sanctioned commitment connected with a system of moral rules and entailing an inescapable set of duties. Various redefinitions or reconstructions of marriage may have deeply affected its social meaning. (See here, for example, Finch and Morgan, 1991, who argue for a more 'realistic' understanding of marriage in the 1980s.)

Similar trends in marriage are found elsewhere, too. For example, Veevers (1991) notes a decline in marriage rates in Canada for both men and women since the 1950s, with the average age at first marriage being 26.7 for men and 24.6 for women by 1985, which is an increase of about two years from the early 1970s and similar to Britain's. There had also been a 'precipitous' (p. 14) decline in teenage marriage. Boyd (1988) notes similar figures, arguing that they reflect more common-law marriages in Canada, and also recession and awareness of women's issues. Goldscheider and Waite (1991, p. 13) comment on the USA: 'Since the 1950s, the American family has retreated from a pattern of early and stable marriages, with extremely high proportions marrying. Not only are young people marrying later but more appear not to be marrying at all.' Between 1960 and 1985 the percentage of single American women in their early 20s rose from 28 per cent to 58 per cent, while the percentage single in their mid–late 20s rose from 10 per cent to 26 per cent. However, Goldscheider and Waite's comment on the historical normality of this is worth quoting; they say: 'The current average marital age and projected proportions marrying are not at all exceptional in contrast to the more distant past; it is the baby boom period that was unusual' (p. 14). They also say that the vast majority still expect and prefer to be married. In Australia we have similar trends: Gilding (1991) notes that in earlier post-war decades couples married at progressively younger ages, but from the early 1970s they progressively delayed marriage.

Divorce

The previous section, showing a reduced tendency to marry since the early 1970s (or certainly a tendency to marry later), raises questions about the 'decline' of formal marriage. However, a more obvious trend, which raises the question of the health of marriage as a social institution, is the increase in divorce. It may be that more frequent divorce in a society does not so much indicate a rejection of marriage *per se* as a rejection of a particular marriage and a desire for a better one (see, for example, Fletcher, 1988b); nevertheless, more divorce does clearly indicate a weakening of the practice and the concept of the *life-long* pattern of marriage.

The point to be considered here is the changing incidence of divorce this century. In the last century divorce was extremely rare, and in practice confined to the very wealthy. Until 1857 in England (and since the sixteenth century) it had required an Act of Parliament, and was therefore a lengthy and expensive – and very public – process. The grounds were very restricted and were different for men and women: a wife could (eventually) be divorced for adultery alone, but in the rare case of a wife suing for divorce, the husband's adultery had to be aggravated in some way (by, for example, incest, cruelty or bestiality). The Matrimonial Causes Act of 1857 changed the process so that a divorce could be obtained by order of a special court, but the narrow and discriminatory grounds remained (until 1923), and there were certain bars such as collusion and condonation. Divorce was still only available to those who had the material resources to undertake lengthy legal proceedings. Marriages still broke down, of course; how frequently, and how far the modern tendency to divorce represents only an increase in *formal* termination of marriage, is an area for debate (see Stone, 1990). Spouses might simply live apart, or regularise their separation by deed or order; but only full divorce enabled a former spouse to marry again.

In the early years of the twentieth century, divorce still occurred at a minuscule rate by comparison with recent decades.
For example, at the start of the First World War there were
less than a thousand divorces per annum in England and Wales
(Goldthorpe, 1987) compared with 153 000 in 1990 (CSO, *Social
Trends*, 1993). The usual measure employed is the number of
divorces in a given year per thousand married couples/mar-
riages. This rate was under one per thousand until the Second
World War, compared with figures of around 12 to 13 in the
1980s (*Social Trends*, various years). Thus it was very low in the
early years of the century and divorce remained unavailable to
most people; as Lewis (1984, p. 4) says, 'Prior to 1914 divorce
was largely confined to the middle and upper classes'; but
'Change in the aid given to poor petitioners in 1914, together
with the effects of World War I, produced an increase in the
divorce rate after 1918' (Lewis, 1984, pp. 4–5). The incidence
of divorce was rising, and the First World War gave a boost to
the rate. This was connected with the general social disruption of war, which to an extent weakened the rather rigid social
controls on sexual behaviour (for middle- and upper-class women
at least) of the Victorian and Edwardian eras: births outside
marriage also rose at this time, and there was a more relaxed
attitude to them. Goldthorpe (1987, p. 41) refers to 'the enforced separations, hastily contracted marriages, and other
abnormal circumstances associated with two world wars', which
led to a steep increase in divorce. The two peaks were in 1919–
20 and 1947 and, although the numbers fell back, it was to a
point higher than the pre-war level. In England and Wales the
rate of petititioning more than doubled from 1913 to 1922;
'an unwillingness to condemn war-time divorces extended into
the 1920s and 1930s' (Goldthorpe, 1987, p. 41).

There were changes in the law at this time; the discriminatory basis of divorce law *vis-à-vis* husbands and wives was removed in 1923; help to poor petitioners was extended in 1926
(Goldthorpe, 1987); and the grounds for divorce were extended
in 1937 to include desertion, cruelty and incurable insanity
(Dewar, 1992). Behind this change was a feeling that the restricted ground of adultery led to artificial situations where an
apparent 'adultery' was manufactured to meet the court's requirements. As Dewar (1992, p. 258) says 'Ingenious means

were devised for manufacturing the evidence necessary [prior
to 1937]' and 'the allocation of "fault" by judicial process was
increasingly seen as an unreal characterisation of the true causes
of divorce'. Nevertheless, in these inter-war years the 'offence'
basis of divorce law was retained. Divorce remained largely
unobtainable by the working class, and 'Prior to World War II
working class couples made use of judicial separation machinery
rather than divorce, but the number of informal separations
was undoubtedly larger than the number that came to court'
(Lewis, 1984, p. 5).

Post-1945, the opportunity to divorce widened further. Divorce had become more common during the war, reaching a
peak in 1947 as some ill-judged wartime marriages were un-
ravelled. After the war the greater availability of legal aid for
divorce from 1949 brought it within reach of a cross-section of
the population for the first time. The divorce rate did reduce
after the immediate post-war peak, but did not come back down
to 1930s levels: 'in 1950 the rate of petitioning was more than
four times as high as it had been in 1937' (Goldthorpe, 1987,
p. 42).

However, during the prosperous and full employment 1950s
the rate was static or declining, at around two divorces per
thousand marriages (Allan, 1985; B. J. Elliott, 1991). Goldthorpe
(1987, p. 42) comments: 'Throughout the western world, divorce rates fell during the 1950s and appeared to stabilize at
levels which though higher than before the war were far below the post-war peak. This contributed in no small part to a
generally optimistic mood about the stability of family life at a
time when there were many other reasons for optimism.' (p.42)
Nevertheless in 1947 wives became more likely to petition for
divorce than husbands (Smart, 1994), probably in part because
of the granting of legal aid. A Royal Commission on marriage
and divorce in the early 1950s saw the emancipation of women
as one factor in divorce, and it favoured retaining the 'fault'
basis of the law, as was indeed done until 1969 (Smart, 1994).
Issues such as maintenance and custody were overshadowed by
the question of who was to blame. There was still considerable
social stigma attaching to divorce at this time (Smart, 1994).

In the 1960s, 'the underlying upward trend reasserted itself'
(Goldthorpe, 1987, p. 42) The rate 'initially increased quite

slowly during the early 1960s so that by 1968 the rate had only climbed to 3.7 per 1,000, a figure exactly comparable with the 1946–1950 post-war rates' (B. J. Elliott, 1991, p. 91). There was preparation for further easing of the legal restrictions, with the 'fault' basis of divorce law coming under increasing criticism. A commission appointed by the Archbishop of Canterbury was critical of the offence-based grounds and wished to see them replaced by the sole ground of irretrievable breakdown of marriage (Dewar, 1992), seeing this as less adversarial and better according with social realities (Archbishop of Canterbury, 1964). The way was now clear for further reform; the subsequent legal change which occurred in 1969 was also a response to greater *demand* for divorce, and the debate about the need to enable dead marriages to be legally terminated more easily. By 1969 the divorce rate was 4.1 per thousand marriages (Allan, 1985), or nearly double what it had been at the beginning of the 1960s.

The Divorce Reform Act of 1969, implemented in 1971, changed the general ground for divorce to the irretrievable breakdown of marriage; however, to demonstrate this it was necessary to show one of five specific grounds. The first three retained the idea of fault: desertion, adultery plus finding it intolerable to live with the adulterous partner, or unreasonable behaviour. The other two may be seen as true 'no fault' grounds: two years' separation with the consent of the other partner, or five years' separation without consent. In 1973 a more streamlined legal procedure for divorce was introduced, which reduced the judicial function to a minimum; divorce became more of an administrative process in most cases (Dewar, 1992). Divorce effectively became much easier; and while the situation was not strictly one of 'divorce on the demand of one partner', it was arguably becoming closer to this in practice (Dewar, 1992).

While the 1960s was the decade of preparation for divorce reform, it was the 1970s which was really the 'divorce decade' in Britain, in the sense that the divorce rate rose even more steeply than before, and divorce became part of many people's experience at first or second hand. It became much less stigmatised, indeed, it became 'normal' to be divorced, both in the sense of being statistically common and being consonant, to some extent, with social norms. Divorce became 'approved of' as part of the search for personal fulfilment and high quality relationships: it became acceptable, indeed legitimate, to abandon one relationship in the search for a better one. Allan (1985) quotes Farber (1973), who sees the change in orientation towards divorce and marriage as part of a shift from a 'natural family' to a 'legal family' model. In the former model, marriage has consequences for others apart from the couple and is governed by quite rigid rules; under the latter: 'the purpose of marriage is not to sustain social order but to satisfy the idiosyncratic, and changing, personal needs of the couple' (Allan, 1985, p. 102). Under this model, the divorce procedure does not allocate blame but, since marriage is more of a private arrangement, the court's role is rather to facilitate the separation so that interests are protected. The Divorce Reform Act of 1969 is a reflection of this changing paradigm of the family and marriage; however, it also 'legitimates and hence reinforces this transition' (Allan, 1985, p. 103), thus perhaps bringing about further change.

In 1971, the year of the implementation of the new Act, the divorce rate was six per thousand marriages (CSO, *Social Trends*, 1991, 1992); by 1972 it was 9.5 (Allan, 1985); by 1976 it was 10 (CSO, *Social Trends*, 1991, 1992); by 1979, 11.6 (Allan, 1985); and by 1981, 11.9 (CSO, *Social Trends*, 1992). That is, rates doubled in the 1970s, as they had done in the 1960s from a lower base. There was a 'blip' in 1972 due to a backlog of effectively finished marriages which could now be terminated (Allan, 1985; B. J. Elliott, 1991), but the rate continued to rise after this; hence the description of the 1970s as the 'divorce decade'.

In the 1980s divorce continued to rise but much less steeply, and there were fluctuations. After 1978 the rate remained fairly stable for some time, although there was a temporary rise following the Matrimonial and Family Proceedings Act of 1984, which enabled petitions to be presented after one year of marriage rather than three. This produced a short-term 'blip' in 1985 (B. J. Elliott, 1991). There was then a falling back and minor fluctuations (CSO, *Social Trends*, 1990, 1991, 1992) with the rise perhaps reappearing in the early 1990s. In 1990 the rate was 12.6 (CSO, *Social Trends*, 1993) – that is, not much more than the level in 1981 – but in England and Wales at least, it rose in 1991 to 13.5 (OPCS, 1991a). In the 1980s, then, divorce rates levelled. However, the 1990s may herald another manifestation of the long-term historical rise.

Other measures besides the number of divorces per thousand marriages also reflect the likelihood of divorce. Estimates based on late 1980s trends show (Haskey, 1989) that 32 per cent – that is, nearly a third – of marriages contracted in 1987 in England and Wales were likely to end in divorce during the first 20 years, and ultimately nearly four out of ten marriages would have ended in divorce before their thirty-third anniversary. Kiernan and Wicks (1990, p. 13) comment:

> The speed of change is most clearly seen when one considers the divorce behaviour of people married in the same year. For example, 10 per cent of couples who married in 1951 had divorced by their 25th wedding anniversary. However, amongst those marrying in 1961, 10 per cent had divorced by their 12th wedding anniversary, whilst amongst those marrying in 1971 and 1981 the analogous durations of marriage were 6 and 4.5 years.

An often quoted figure is that almost a quarter of children are likely to experience their parents' divorce before the age of 16 (Haskey, 1991b). Disruption of family life has become the experience of a substantial minority of adults and children, and the indicators are that it will become more common in the future. This may further reduce the stigma.

With the growth of remarriage – that is, second or subsequent marriage after divorce – *redivorce* has become a more common phenomenon. The Family Policy Studies Centre (1991) reports that from the early 1970s to the late 1980s the percentage of divorces involving a second or subsequent marriage for one of the partners more than doubled, from 7 per cent in 1971 to 16 per cent in 1989.

The trends to increased divorce in Britain are common to most western industrialised countries, although there are variations in level: for example, the UK had the second highest divorce rate among EC countries in 1990 at 12.6 divorces per thousand marriages, just behind Denmark at 12.8 (CSO, *Social*

Trends, 1993). However the USA has always had a higher rate
than any western European country (Goldthorpe, 1987). Earlier
this century the American rate rose slowly but steadily (Besharov,
1989). Some recent figures are given by B. D. Whitehead (1993):
in the 1950s and early 1960s the US divorce rate was less than
10 per thousand married couples. There was then a sharp increase from about 1965, the rate reaching a peak of 23 in 1979,
which is well above the highest British level of 13. The rate
levelled off at about 21 in 1991. Whitehead states that half of
American marriages end in divorce (presumably on current
trends), the corresponding British figure being four in ten.
Goldscheider and Waite (1991, p. 14), however, claim: 'Recent
studies estimate that about 2 out of 3 first marriages will end
in divorce or separation' (quoting Martin and Bumpass, 1989).
A third to a half of all American children born to married
parents will experience parental divorce before 18 (Besharov,
1989, quoting Glick, 1979).

So the USA, like Britain, had a steep rise in divorce in the
late 1960s and 1970s, followed by more of a plateau in the
1980s. Veevers (1991, p. 17) says of Canada: 'In 1961, the divorce rate was 164 per 100 000 married women; by 1985, the
rate was 1004 per 100 000, a sixfold increase,' Canadian divorce law was liberalised in the late 1960s, the grounds now
including divorce on demand after five years' separation. The
divorce rate soared after this, and: 'Recent analyses indicate
that if current divorce trends persist, more than one in three
marriages is likely to end in divorce' (Boyd, 1988, p. 95, quoting Statistics Canada, 1981). Veevers (1991) notes that in 1985
the American rate was more than twice as high as the Canadian rate, but she comments: 'The ubiquity of the divorce experience has meant that divorce has become a "normal"
experience that touches virtually all families directly or indirectly.' (p. 17). It is not necessarily a source of stigma, therefore. The Canadian divorce law was liberalised further in 1986.

Australia experienced an immediate post-war peak in the
divorce rate in 1947, followed by a drop, but with a rise in the
1960s and 1970s (Gilding, 1991). An Act reforming divorce in
1975 introduced a single new ground, irretrievable breakdown
demonstrated by twelve months' separation (Bittman and Bryson,
1989). The rate of divorce steadied in the 1980s (Gilding, 1991).

What is remarkable is the similarity between the English-speaking countries' experience of divorce.

One interesting aspect of change in divorce in Britain is the increased prominence of wives as petitioners. In the past men had more frequently been the ones who divorced their wives; and B. J. Elliott (1991) reports that in 1946–50 less than 45 per cent of petitions were from wives. It was at this point that wives began to overtake husbands as petitioners. By the end of the 1970s the proportion of wife petitioners was over 70 per cent, and it has stayed at around 71–73 per cent ever since. The most common ground used by wives was 'unreasonable behaviour', employed in 52 per cent of cases in 1987, and the next most common was adultery, in 25 per cent of cases; husbands divorcing their wives were most likely to use adultery, with 45 per cent of divorces granted to husbands in 1987 being on this ground (B. J. Elliot, 1991).

The significance of the shift over time to a greater number of wife petitions is not easy to assess; as Elliott says: 'we can make no assumptions about which partner really initiated the dissolution of the marriage or why' (p. 93). It is not clear from the legal fact of wives being more often the petitioner that they were the chief instigator of the ending of the relationship (in so far as this is ever clear-cut). However, the finding may mean that wives' greater economic independence, plus the fact that marriage has become more disadvantageous to them because of asymmetrical change, has made them more prepared to end unsatisfactory marriages. A husband's adultery or violence might once have been endured because ending the marriage seemed difficult or impossible. An easier process of divorce, legal aid, somewhat better treatment of women subject to domestic violence, women's stronger property rights and their improved general social and economic position, may all have acted to shift women's threshold of tolerance for a distressing marriage.

Other patterns in divorce relate to age and social class. Marriages made at a younger age are more likely to end in divorce (see, for example, Ermisch, 1989). However, one can scarcely draw from this (as Fletcher, 1988b, tends to do) the conclusion that delayed marriage will necessarily bring the divorce rate down, since in the 1970s and 1980s marriage occurred at later ages, yet the divorce rate (especially in the 1970s) went up. There is also a time and generational pattern. For example, there is the observation made by Kiernan and Wicks (1990) that 10 per cent of marriages which had taken place in 1951, had ended in divorce 25 years later; of marriages taking place in 1961, 10 per cent had ended within 12 years, half the time. And of marriages taking place in 1971, 10 per cent had ended in divorce by 6 years; while of those taking place in 1981, 10 per cent had ended by 4.5 years. In other words, successive generations of those marrying were divorcing at an earlier stage. The OPCS found in 1991 (OPCS, 1991b) that, of marriages made in 1974, 6 per cent ended within five years, while the incidence of early termination among marriages occurring ten years later, in 1984, was up to *10* per cent. Projecting trends of this kind into the future indicates *more* divorces, not fewer, and at shorter durations of marriage.

While there is not a totally straightforward class gradient (class 3 is anomalous), divorce is less common among social classes 1 and 2, the professional and managerial groups, and more common in classes 4 and 5, the semi- and unskilled; the incidence is higher still where the husband is unemployed. Haskey (1984) showed an age-standardized divorce ratio (constructed to compare rates with the national average) of 47 for husbands in class 1,220 in class 5, and 225 where the husband was unemployed. This suggests a link with affluence/poverty. However, as Elliott (1991) notes, the finding that divorce is also particularly high where the husband is in the armed forces (that is, 270), 'would suggest that economic forces cannot be the sole explanation for the current differentials between divorce rates in different social classes' (p. 93).

In connection with the changed social significance of divorce, it has been suggested that the attitude to divorce has changed, and it has become a less stigmatised process. The change in social status was especially marked for women, whose 'respectability' had been threatened in earlier times by the label divorcee (see, for example, Smart, 1994). This greater acceptability of divorce was both a *consequence* of its becoming more common and, arguably, a driving *factor* in more divorces occurring: there was less of a deterrent in terms of social disapproval and exclusion. In addition, as there are more divorced people, even as a temporary stage between marriages, they might feel less isolated and be treated as less deviant than in the past. Are we, then, even discussing the same social (and legal) institution when we talk about divorce in the 1920s or 1950s or 1980s? The same sort of point may be made about births outside marriage.

Finally, does an increased incidence of divorce indicate a rejection of marriage? Some commentators maintain that it does not: Fletcher (1988b), optimistically in his own terms, sees divorce and indeed most recent changes in family life as certainly *not* suggesting a turning away from marriage and the nuclear family. While a 'traditionalist' in many ways, and strongly disapproving of, for example, cohabitation, Fletcher supports liberal divorce laws as allowing people to find better marriages than the ones they currently have. He claims: '[it is] astonishing that the much emphasized and publicized statistics of marital breakdown should have been allowed to spread so false a picture as that of a decline of the family in Britain' (p. 83). Other earlier commentators in the recent history of family change (for example, the Family Policy Studies Centre's publications in the early 1980s) tended to stress that more frequent divorce did not necessarily signify rejection of marriage. Divorce can be seen as heralding the search for a more fulfilling marriage: indeed, some people divorce in order to remarry a specific new partner. The idea that some divorcing people might be recoiling altogether from the prospect of marriage is seemingly unacceptable to some. However, the rise in divorce has to be seen in conjunction with other changes: the reduced propensity to marry in the first place, or to remarry after divorce, and the increased propensity to cohabit or live alone, and to procreate without marriage. Taken together, the changed behaviour patterns do firmly suggest that the increase in divorce *does* indicate a greater wariness about marriage – whatever marriage itself may now mean.

Consequences of divorce

Single parenthood

One of the most obvious consequences of divorce is an increase in single-parent families. Where there are children, divorce creates, at least for a time a single-parent–child(ren) household, and it is overwhelmingly the case that it is the mother who remains with the children and the father who is absent; this fact has various consequences. In most cases care of the children is not disputed, and in most cases also the mother has care of or coresidence with them (Hoggett, 1987), with fathers having varying degrees of what was called access, but is now under the Children Act 1989 known as contact. The vast majority of single-parent families formed after divorce, then, are mother-headed (see figures below).

Single-parent families include those formed after separation and divorce (still the largest group in the late 1980s: see Haskey, 1991b), those where there has never been a marriage and the single-parent status either occurs after a breakdown of cohabitation or has been in existence since the child's birth, and those resulting from the death of a parent. The group where there was no marriage has been a growing one, particularly in the 1980s and 1990s; the widowed group has shrunk over time in both absolute and relative terms as deaths in mid-life have become less common.

The number and proportion of single-parent families in Britain rose slightly over the 1960s and more markedly over the 1970s, 1980s and 1990s. Haskey (1991b, pp. 21–2) says: 'The number of one-parent families in Great Britain has increased considerably since the early 1970s, from around 600,000 to just over one million – by more than 50 per cent.' Haskey notes that this growth is common to most industrial countries, although the largest increases are found in Britain, Australia and the USA, with most countries showing an increase of 30–50 per cent over the 1970s and 1980s (pp. 22–3). The number of single parents in Britain passed the million mark in the mid-1980s, standing at 1.01 million by 1986 and (provisionally) 1.15 million in 1989 (Haskey, 1991a). More recent figures are 1.25 million in 1990 and 1.3 million in 1991 and 1992 (CSO, *General Household Survey*, 1992; Roll, 1992; CSO, *Social*

Trends, 1994)). Numbers of children involved also reflect the rise: in 1971 there were a million children in single-parent families, but by 1986 there were 1.6 million and, by 1989, provisionally 1.9 million (Haskey, 1991a): that is, almost double the 1971 figure. More recent estimates show 2.1 or 2.2 million in 1991 and 1992 (Roll, 1992; CSO, *Social Trends*, 1994).

Looking at percentages rather than absolute numbers, in 1961 only 6 per cent of all families with dependent children were single parent; by 1971 the proportion had risen slightly to 8 per cent, but by 1981 to 12 per cent, and by 1987 to 14 per cent (Kiernan and Wicks, 1990; CSO, *Social Trends*, 1993). More recent figures from the *General Household Survey* show a level of 17 per cent (1989), 20 per cent (1990), and a slight falling back to 19 per cent (1991), followed by a rise to 21 per cent (1992). The percentage of *children* in Britain in single-parent families was just over 13 per cent in 1986–88 (Haskey, 1991b), and will be well above this now.

Both the absolute numbers and percentage figures only give the picture at one moment in time; families continuously move in and out of the single-parent category, so that the proportion of adults and children experiencing this status *at some stage* of their life course would be much greater. That is, single parenthood is a more common experience in society, and statistically more probable for individuals, than 'snapshot' figures would suggest. Hardey and Crow (1991) say that the numbers passing through the single-parent stage may be one in four. Length of lone parenthood is also a factor not reflected in one-moment-in-time statistics. For example, the trend in the 1970s appears to have been to *shorter* spells as a lone parent than previously. Ermisch (1989, pp. 53–4) says: 'the expected duration of lone parenthood may have fallen off by as much as 4 years after the Divorce Reform Act took effect in 1971'; and 'lone parenthood lasted longer when it was less common'. There is also a marked regional variation (and by social class and ethnic group) so that the experience would feel more common and less deviant for certain social groups and in certain areas.

Consideration of a longer timescale, stretching back to the early years of this century and the centuries before, shows that the single adult plus children unit is not as historically aberrant as a comparison with the recent past might suggest. There was a high incidence of widowed families in earlier generations, due to more deaths in mid-life. Millar (1989, pp. 14–15) notes: 'the proportion of women potentially lone mothers through either widowhood or marital breakdown was very similar in 1861 (8.1 per cent) and 1981 (8.9 per cent)'; and B. J. Elliott (1991, p. 92) writes 'Going back to the 1890s, approximately 30 per cent of the cohort of couples married in 1896 experienced marital break-up before their twentieth wedding anniversary due to the death of their spouse. Assuming current divorce rates the extent of marital break-up is remarkably similar for couples in the 1980 marriage cohort.' This interpretation does blur the differences of meaning and experience which arise from the *causes* of single parenthood: how accurate is it to refer to widow(er)hood as marital breakdown, for example? However, poverty-stricken widowed families, and their deprived and neglected children, were a recognisable and not uncommon group up to First World War times (Lewis, 1984). They were among the earliest groups for whom social security benefits were made available, with widows' benefits being introduced in 1925. Because of widow(er)hood, remarriage and step-families were also relatively common in the past. The newness of single parenthood as a 'problem' has to be seen in this context.

The sharpest increase in single parenthood came in the 1970s rather than the 1980s; for example, while the increase between 1971 and 1981 was over 70 per cent (CSO, *Social Trends*, 1989), from November 1979 to February 1986 the number grew by 20 per cent (National Audit Office, 1990). It was single-parent families arising from marital breakdown/divorce which rose substantially during the 1970s; and just as the 1970s was the 'divorce decade' – much more so than the 1980s – it may also be regarded as the 'single-parent (divorced) family decade'.

The growth in single-parents is common to most industrialised countries, with the largest increases in Britain, Australia and the USA (Haskey, 1991b). While there are variations in different countries, there has been a rise in lone parents in most OECD countries, with the majority – 80–90 per cent – headed by mothers (OECD, 1993). Bryson (1992, p. 193) states: 'The proportion of single parent households has virtually doubled in the USA, Sweden, Australia, France and West Germany . . .

over the last two decades.' In the USA the percentage is higher than Britain's at 25 per cent (Kiernan and Wicks, 1990), although this figure masks racial variations; for example, Bryson (1992) reports that for the white population the percentage of single parents is 14 per cent, and for the black population 65 per cent. Besharov (1989) reports that of children born in America in 1980, on existing trends 60 per cent would spend part of their childhood in a family headed by a mother who was divorced, separated, unmarried or widowed. In Canada, the 1986 proportion of single-parent families was 13 per cent (Veevers, 1991, quoting Moore, 1989), similar to the British percentage at that time. For Australia, Bittman and Bryson (1989) give a percentage of over 14 per cent in 1985, a proportion which doubled between 1969 and 1985. The highest rate for the 'advanced' societies is given by Bittman and Bryson as Sweden's, at around 30 per cent. Britain stands high in the European league table of nations in terms of incidence, having the largest proportion of single parents in the EC; Spain, Greece, Ireland and Italy, for example, had only 5–9 per cent of families who were single parent in 1989 (Roll, 1992). Germany, the Netherlands, France, Belgium and Portugal occupied an intermediate position with 10–12 per cent (Haskey, 1991b; figures for 1989).

The trends over time have been different for different types of single-parent family. As Haskey shows (1991b), the largest percentage increase over the decade 1976–86 was found for both the never-married mothers (up 77 per cent) and divorced mothers (up 78 per cent), while separated lone mothers increased only marginally and the number of widowed lone mothers fell by 30 per cent. Slightly after this time, never-married or single mothers became a more prominent group; between 1986 and 1989, Haskey (1991a) shows, these mothers had an average annual increase of 19 per cent, while divorced mothers actually showed an annual *decrease* of 2 per cent. According to the *General Household Survey*, in 1990 unmarried mothers represented 6 per cent of all families with children; in 1971 they had been only 1 per cent. Ermisch (1990) shows that while never-married mothers were only 16 per cent of all *single* parents in 1971, they constituted 23 per cent in 1986. Thus divorce, while still significant in producing single-parent

familyhood, has been gradually giving place to *unmarried* motherhood. Being widowed is of declining significance in single-parent
familyhood. The decline of widowed parenthood and the rise
in divorced and unmarried motherhood are common to a
number of countries (see, for example, Roll, 1992; OECD, 1993,
p. 5). The OECD (1993) comments: 'While the most common
route into lone motherhood is through the breakdown of a
marriage or marriage-like relationship with the father of the
child, there is also an increase in the numbers of unmarried
women with children.'

While a small percentage of single-parent *fathers* is found in
many countries, it is sometimes higher than Britain's percentage of less than 10 per cent. Veevers (1991) gives a figure of
17.8 per cent in Canada in 1986 (quoting Wargon, 1987); the
OECD (1993) gives approximately 80–90 per cent of single-
parent families headed by mothers, thus 10–20 per cent by
fathers. The percentage of father-headed families actually decreased in Britain in the 1980s to 9 per cent (Haskey, 1991b)
and then to 8 per cent in the early 1990s (Garnham and Knights,
1994). As a group, they present a different profile from the
mother-headed families; a higher proportion are widowed (about
a quarter, as opposed to around 7–8 per cent of lone mothers);
and a much smaller proportion are single (5 per cent, compared with 28 per cent of the lone mothers); the proportions
of divorced and separated are about the same. Lone fathers
differ from lone mothers in age, employment and income. *Mother*-
headed single-parent families tend to experience poverty, at
least for some of the time that they are single parents; while
father-headed families are better placed, although they still tend
to be worse off than two-parent families. Among the mothers,
the single or never-married seem to be the most disdavantaged,
and are the least likely to receive maintenance, although they
are also single parents for shorter periods of time (Ermisch,
1989). Single mothers and their children are usually younger,
while widowed families are older, with the separated and divorced somewhere in the middle (Family Policy Studies Centre, 1991). Single or never-married mothers are more likely to
live with their parents or other relatives, although they are now
more likely to live by themselves. Beginning in the early 1970s,
the shift to single-household living for single mothers was

particularly pronounced in the mid-1980s (Haskey, 1991a and 1991b). Widowed, separated and divorced lone mothers are overwhelmingly likely to head their own households.

The OECD reports that in OECD countries as a whole, the most disadvantaged lone mothers are those who have a child while not living with the father; this group is younger, and less likely to have support from the father, or to have previous employment or education. By contrast, widows are much better off (OECD, 1993). Boyd (1988), in the Canadian context, notes the poverty of female-headed single-parent families, and reports that they are more likely to rent accommodation; they have low wages and inadequate child support payments; also their relative economic deprivation is increasing over time. Besharov (1989) claims that the poverty rate of female-headed families with children in America was almost three times higher than that of other families with children, and quotes Garfinkel and McLanahan (1986), who said: 'Families headed by single women with children are the poorest of all major demographic groups regardless of how poverty is measured' (p. 148). Bryson (1992) comments that in Australia about 43 per cent of single parents were below the official poverty line (quoting Raymond, 1987), with some improvements since 1987.

The ethnic minorities as a whole are over-represented among single-parent families. In Britain 11 per cent of households among ethnic minorities were single parent in 1986–88, while the figure was 4 per cent for households headed by a white person (Haskey, 1991b). However, this statement conceals great variations *between* different ethnic groups. Almost one in four households headed by a West Indian [*sic*] contained a single-parent family living alone in 1986–88; Africans were the second highest at one in 9; but single parenthood was relatively uncommon within one-family households headed by persons from the Chinese, Indian, Pakistani and Bangladeshi groups at around one in 20 (Haskey, 1991b). Haskey (1991a, p. 39) also comments:

One-parent families occurred in relatively large numbers amongst families headed by those of West Indian, mixed, and African ethnic groups; about every other West Indian family was a one-parent family, as was approximately every third African and mixed ethnic origin family. However, the prevalence of one-parent families amongst Indian, Pakistani, and Bangladeshi ethnic minority families was well below that amongst White families.

The percentage of lone mothers who are economically active declines with the number of children, has been at a lower level (49 per cent) than the economic activity rate of *married* mothers (around 62 per cent using 1987–89 figures: see Haskey, 1991b), and declined during the 1980s. The *General Household Survey* of 1990 showed 42 per cent of lone mothers actually working, as opposed to 63 per cent of married or cohabiting mothers. For lone fathers the economic activity rate (at 76 per cent) was much higher, but still appreciably lower than for married fathers (96 per cent) (Haskey, 1991a). The OECD (1993) notes that while in some OECD countries labour market participation rates for lone and married mothers have increased together, in others (Canada and the USA) the *increase* in married mothers' participation rate over the last ten years has co-existed with relatively *stable* participation by lone mothers, and in yet others (the UK) an increase in married mothers' participation has actually been accompanied by a *decline* in lone mothers' participation. Bittman and Bryson (1989) comment that Australia is like New Zealand and the UK in having *lower* labour force participation rates among lone mothers than among married mothers. Low labour market participation is clearly linked with to poverty.

There are geographical differences within Britain. Haskey (1991b, p. 42) comments: 'Almost invariably, it is the metropolitan counties which show the highest relative concentrations of one parent families.' The highest relative concentrations are in the London boroughs and the largest cities. Lambeth is top of the list, then Hackney, then Hammersmith (1981 figures, p. 43). Kiernan and Wicks (1990) give a percentage of single parents for inner London, in 1981, of over 26 per cent. Areas of greater deprivation, therefore, are also areas where single parents are more commonly found. This complicates the connection between single parenthood *per se*, poverty, social class, and other factors such as poor educational performance.

The immediate factors behind the rise in single parents are

clearly divorce and family founding outside marriage. One deeper aspect concerns stigma and social attitudes surrounding single parenthood. As with divorce, greater acceptance has both reflected and fed into change. An aspect of the reduced stigma surrounding *unmarried* motherhood in particular has been a blurring of distinctions *between* types of single-parent family, and indeed the adoption of the very term 'single-parent family'. The National Council for the Unmarried Mother and her Child became the National Council for One Parent Families in 1973, committed to campaigning for similar provisions for all types of lone parents (Hardey and Crow, 1991). Widowed mothers had in the past enjoyed a higher social status and more 'respectability' than separated/divorced mothers, with specific provision being made for them through insurance benefits from 1925 (Lewis, 1984). Unmarried mothers were probably the most disadvantaged, facing difficulties in obtaining maintenance from the child's father and assistance from the state, and often under pressure to give their children up for adoption (see, for example, McIntyre, 1977; Hartmann, 1987; Howe *et al.*, 1992). The collapsing of distinctions between one-parent families was intended to reflect an acceptance of *all* types of single parent as disadvantaged, and a preparedness to advocate on behalf of them all.

Another aspect of this new acceptability was the phenomenon of 'single parenthood by choice', but it appears that although this became more prevalent in the 1980s (see, for example, Renvoize, 1985), it remained a minority pattern. Hardey and Crow (1991, p. 8) say: 'Despite the growth in their numbers over recent years ... single mothers by choice remain a minority among lone parents as a whole (Cashmore, 1985; Close, 1985).' It remains problematic to define what 'by choice' might mean. Women might not set out consciously to become single parents, but might prefer this as an option, on balance, once in that situation. Hardey and Crow (1991) quote several authors who have found single-parent women aware of distinct advantages – notably autonomy – in single parenthood as opposed to conventional marriage; and Bradshaw and Millar (1991) found that their respondents most commonly mentioned independence and freedom as the best features (loneliness and financial difficulties as the worst). The positive aspects of single parent-

hood usually co-exist with financial hardship and social pressure to reform a two-parent unit. It might be thought that the
difficulties would pressure single mothers into partnership with
a male, yet a declining rate of remarriage has also increased
single-parent families; that is, not only has the flow of families
into this category increased, but the flow *out of* it has decreased
(Haskey, 1991b).

All of this probably relates back to changes affecting gender
roles as discussed in an earlier section. Women more often
prefer to live outside full-time, permanent and institutionalised relationships with men. One is returned to the essentially
patriarchal nature of established forms, and the asymmetrical
change in the roles and consciousness of men and women which
have rendered institutionalised marriage less appealing to women
while *enabling* them to reject it more easily. Men in partnerships have, perhaps, with varying degrees of success, tried to
operate the system as before, to follow outmoded scripts and
cling to structures that are crumbling before their eyes. Men
may therefore *also* experience disillusionment with marriage
and marriage-like relationships.

Remarriage

Another possible consequence of divorce is a second or subsequent marriage. A legal divorce declares the parties free to
remarry; this is one of its purposes, and one argument for more
liberal divorce is the need to be free to remarry. Some seek
divorce specifically to remarry with a new partner who has already been found; some seek the general freedom to remarry
should a new partner *be* found. Fletcher (1988b) is one author
who, though writing in the late 1980s, belongs to a slightly
older 'school' on this point (and on others) and, while taking
a traditional view of marriage in many ways, he argues for relatively easy divorce as a means to better marriage. He also puts
the view strongly that divorce and remarriage figures indicate
a strong continuing attachment to marriage as an institution.

This is in keeping with commentators who argue that a greater
propensity to divorce does *not* indicate a turning away from
marriage as an institution, but only a search for a better quality marriage with another partner. Owens (1988, p. 46) says

that the figures on early breakdown of marriage 'cannot be taken simply to imply disillusionment with marriage itself. Remarriage is common.' Owens quotes a study by Leete and Anthony (1979, p. 46), which 'showed that in three quarters of those divorcing in 1973, one or other partner remarried by the end of 1977, with both partners remarrying in over one-third of the cases. Remarriages also tended to be quick.' However, while remarriage is more common in an absolute sense, the *propensity* to remarry has in fact been declining since the early 1970s.

B. J. Elliott (1991) indicates that about a third of marriages each year in Britain are second marriages for at least one of the partners, usually after a divorce rather than widow(er)hood. (*Social Trends*, 1991, shows a percentage which is steady at around 35–36 per cent in the latter half of the 1980s.) Looking back to 1950, Elliott states that: 'the increase in the proportion of remarriages as a percentage of all new marriages from 20 per cent to 36 per cent is wholly due to the increase in divorced persons remarrying' (pp. 94–5). The remarriage and divorce trends ran almost parallel until 1980, with the peak in divorces after the war mirrored by a peak in remarriages, and the second peak in 1971/2 after the Divorce Reform Act similarly reflected in remarriage rates. A table presented by Elliott (p. 95) using OPCS data shows, however, a *decline* in remarriage *rates* after the 1971 peak, which is particularly noticeable for men. A similar diagram presented by Kiernan and Wicks (1990, p. 9) shows a decline in the remarriage rate per thousand divorced people between 1971 and 1987, especially for younger age groups and for men. And Ermisch (1990, p. 15) shows the trend more dramatically, with remarriages of divorcees falling for both men and women (the rate always being lower for women) from 1972 to the mid-late 1980s. He notes that the remarriage rate of divorced women has also declined in the USA. While there are more remarriages in an absolute sense, then, there are *fewer* as a ratio of those eligible to remarry.

Elliott (1991), like Owens (1988), quotes Leete and Anthony (1979), and notes their finding that, of their sample of those divorced in 1973, 56 per cent of men and 48 per cent of women remarried over a $4\frac{1}{2}$-year period; much remarriage was rapid so that within a year 60 per cent *of those who were to remarry in this time* (that is, $4\frac{1}{2}$ years) had already done so. If people were going to remarry, then, they tended to do it quickly. But Elliott refers to a further study by Haskey (1987) of those who divorced in 1979; as the remarriage rate had declined slightly during the 1970s, a *decrease* in the proportions remarrying was found. Class was shown to be a variable, with middle class men *more* likely to remarry, but middle class women *less* likely to do so.

There are also important gender and age differences in the proneness of divorcees to remarry, with men more likely to do so than women (Kiernan and Wicks, 1990; CSO, *Social Trends*, 1990) and younger divorcees more likely than older ones. Ermisch (1989, p. 51) states clearly: 'Older women are less likely to remarry, and this probably reflects the poorer marriage market for older women because of the steep decline with age in the ratio of unmarried men to women.' The population of older divorced women feeds into the large number of women pensioners who are without a current partner. While widowhood is a more significant factor at present, divorce as a factor (with the reduced likelihood of remarriage, both in general and for older women in particular) is becoming more important, and is likely to become more important still (McGlone, 1992). However, compared with the past, fewer older women are likely to be in the never-married category (aged spinsters were formerly a significant group).

Other factors influence remarriage: for example, Ermisch (1989) found that women with work experience in their first marriage and higher educational attainment were more likely to remarry quickly. He speculates that work experience improves the prospects for finding a new partner. Interestingly, the prospects of remarriage were better after 1971; Ermisch thinks the implementation of the new divorce act produced a better marriage market for women.

What is the significance of the remarriage trends? The 1970s and 1980s fall in the remarriage rate increased the number of single-parent families, as the flow of families out of this category slowed (Haskey, 1991b). Remarriage – or cohabitation – is an important route out of poverty for single-parent women, although it is repartnering with a *working* partner which makes the difference (Ermisch, 1989; Millar, 1989). A declining rate of remarriage is thus increasing family poverty. As Ermisch (1989, p. 45) says: 'it is very important to take account of remarriage in assessing the economic consequences of divorce in Britain'. However, his analysis also suggests that the average duration of lone parenthood was *shorter* after 1971 (his finding that re-marriage was more likely after 1971 has been referred to already). Remarriage prospects were better from this time because there were more potential partners; yet there was a declining rate of remarriage overall. Trends are somewhat contradictory, therefore; and Ermisch himself comments elsewhere (1990, p. 16): 'By *increasing* the duration of single parenthood, the *decline* in the remarriage rates of divorced persons has been working to increase the number of one-parent families' (p. 16, Italics added). The enhanced opportunity to remarry has not prevented a decline in the remarriage rate, and this suggests a definite turning away from (formal, legal) marriage as an institution. Connected with this is the growing popularity of cohabitation between marriages.

A word must be said about *re*divorce and subsequent remarriage. A logical outcome of easier divorce is that some will remarry not just once, but several times, giving rise to a pattern sometimes described as 'serial monogamy'. Veevers (1991, p. 20) uses the phrase in discussing the Canadian situation, stating: 'The increase in divorce rates does not indicate a movement away from marriage, or an evolution of new marriage forms. Rather, it seems indicative of a trend toward serial monogamy.' Veevers notes a move to a 'permanent availability' for marriage of individuals, whether currently married or not. It has been found that remarriages are at greater risk of break-up than first marriages (for example, Kiernan and Wicks, 1990), but this would seem to be linked to the presence of step-children. Kiernan and Wicks (1990, p. 16) comment that material from the USA shows that 'couples in which only one of the parties has been previously married and where there are no step-children have the lowest risk, whilst those marriages where both husband and wife are remarrying and both have children from previous marriages have the highest risk'.

It may be argued that such serial partnerships have fundamentally changed the widely understood concept of marriage in the last few decades. Marriage (or any particular marriage) is not axiomatically a life-time commitment, but may be seen more realistically as a *stage* in the life course.

In general, the number and proportion of remarriages have increased in English-speaking countries. In Canada, for example, by 1985, more than a quarter of marriages involved at least one divorced person, according to Veevers (1991) (remarriages were a *third* of all marriages according to Boyd, 1988). Gilding (1991) notes that in Australia remarriage became more common in the 1970s and 1980s, with 33 per cent being a remarriage by 1986. He also notes that men and younger people were more likely to repartner, and that second marriages were more likely to end in divorce. Veevers (1991) shows that in Canada the remarriage prospects of older women are poor relative to those of older men, due to an imbalance of the sexes in the second half of life, and the norm that husbands should be older than their wives; she states that for women in their 50s 'there are only 50 potential grooms per 100 unmarried women' (p. 152).

Remarriage tends to produce 'step' or 'reconstituted' or 'blended' families and more complex family forms; these have become more common since the 'divorce decade'. With an existing couple there may be, as well as the children of their current union, the children of either or both of them from previous partnerships, while children from previous partnerships may also be living in other households, with varying degrees of contact with their 'absent' parent. Partners, ex-partners, biological children and step-children may all be linked in complex chains of households which could be seen as a new form of 'extended' family, which is certainly different from the conventional nuclear family with two biological parents and their children. According to Stepfamily (1993), there are no formal statistics on step-families, but we know there is an increasing number because of divorce and remarriage. In fact, the *General Household Survey* of 1991 claims that 8 per cent of families with children contain one or more step-children. Step-families show very varied patterns, and the picture is complicated by child bearing in cohabitations which subsequently break up, and where the parents then form new relationships. Step-parents have no legal or financial obligations unless they adopt (a declining pattern), or unless they achieve parental responsibility through a residence order (Section 8 of the Children Act).

Such elaborate patterns of family living present new challenges, and the step-parent/step-child relationship seems to bring particular difficulties. Stepfamily notes reports of the pressures of step-family life for both adults and children, and that step-families are different in many ways from other families. According to the Family Policy Studies Centre (1991), reporting on other research (see also Kiernan, 1992), step-children are at greater risk in various ways than children in single-parent families. Wallerstein's work in an American context (Wallerstein and Kelly, 1980; Wallerstein and Blakeslee, 1989) is not reassuring on the effects on children of remarriage after divorce; and B. D. Whitehead (1993), also in an American context, quotes work by Zill and others which is pessimistic in its assessment of the benefits of step-families for children. Again, step-children appeared to be more disadvantaged than single-parent family children. (Note also the comment above about the greater likelihood of redivorce when step-children are present.)

One of the problems for reconstituted families seems to be the absence of ready-made scripts and models for step-relationships to follow although, viewed in a longer historical timescale, such relationships are not new, owing to the greater incidence of widow(er)hood in former times. Step-families will not be discussed further here, but the research done in this area should be noted; it seems that such families need to be a focus for further study, given the ongoing complexity and shifting nature of family forms.

Alternatives to marriage

Cohabitation

The decline of formal marriage has been accompanied by a marked rise in both the acceptability and incidence of cohabitation of couples in a heterosexual relationship, and – in the 1980s and 1990s particularly – in an increase in family founding in such informal unions. This shift is connected with wider changes in attitudes to sexuality, with greater tolerance of sexual relationships of many kinds outside the confines of marriage.

The dominant morality in Britain and many other western countries in the last century and the early part of this one forbade sexual activity outside marriage and, while this prohibition was not universally observed, it was supported by social sanctions which drove pre- or extra-marital sexual relationships 'underground'. Cohabiting couples (perhaps unable to marry because one partner was unable to divorce) might present themselves socially as married; or an illegitimate birth might be concealed.

Cohabitation is now often quite open, with different surnames used by the two partners, and no pretence of marriage or of children being born into a marriage. It is salutary to recall how dramatic a change this is compared with the first half of the century, or even the 1950s. The change mostly came about *after* the big rise in the incidence of divorce in the 1960s and 1970s; while one argument for easier divorce rests on the importance of the freedom to remarry, in a sense such freedom has become less necessary as partners often cohabit after divorce instead. Indeed, the two groups most likely to cohabit are young never-marrieds (who may subsequently marry each other) and the divorced.

As B. J. Elliott (1991, p. 89) comments: 'From the early 1970s onwards, a growing number of couples have chosen to live together as husband and wife without formalising their union with a marriage ceremony.' Elliott also thinks, however, that 'there is evidence of stable, non-marital, relationships including childrearing in earlier periods' (p. 90, citing A. Brown and Kiernan, 1981). The incidence of 'informal marriage' (before, after or as an alternative to, formal marriage) in various historical periods should be borne in mind if attempting to view cohabitation as 'new' or 'deviant'. The evidence from the past is not reliable and makes it difficult to form a balanced picture but, among the poorest groups in the last century, in certain areas at least, informal marriage seems to have been common (see, for example, Mearns, 1883). This raises fundamental questions as to what marriage is understood to be in any society.

It was calculated in 1991 that 1.2 million out of a total of 13.9 million couples (one in 12) were living together in Britain in 1989; the pattern was more common where the man was in his twenties (Haskey and Kelly, 1991). The *General House-*

hold Survey has collected data on cohabitation for women only since 1979, and for men since 1986; this has shown that, in 1979, 9 per cent of single, never-married women aged 18–29 were cohabiting (A. Brown and Kiernan, 1981). The 1979 *General Household Survey* also found evidence of a marked increase in the incidence of *pre*-marital cohabitation during the 1970s; of first marriages in 1971–73, only 7 per cent were reported as having been preceded by cohabitation, compared to 19 per cent by 1977–79. By the early 1980s, the figure had risen further to around 26 per cent. 'Pre-marital' cohabitation was much more common for second marrriages: 60 per cent of couples, where at least one had been married before, who married in 1979, reported cohabitation beforehand (B. J. Elliott, 1991).

Looking at the 1980s, Kiernan and Wicks (1990) report that the proportions of single women cohabiting increased from 8 per cent in 1981 to 17 per cent in 1987; however, the median duration of cohabitation for this group changed little (18–19 months). Ermisch (1990) gives a figure for the percentage of never-married British women aged 18–49 who were cohabiting; this was 20 per cent by 1988. Kiernan and Wicks, and Ermisch, all conclude that cohabitation provides a partial explanation for the decline in marriage rates: 'Nowadays, it is virtually a majority practice to cohabit before marrying' (Kiernan and Wicks, 1990, p. 8). The authors quote a 1987 figure from Haskey and Kiernan: 48 per cent of never-married women had cohabited prior to marriage (p. 8). The Family Policy Studies Centre (1992) also points out that about a half of brides marrying for the first time had already cohabited with the man they married. This contrasts with the figures of 7 per cent for 1971 and 26 per cent for the early 1980s, given above. *General Household Survey* data suggest that the length of cohabitation before first marriage increased during the 1970s and 1980s (Kiernan, 1989). Among couples marrying for the first time, the median duration of cohabitation was 10 months in the 1970s, but 13–15 months in the 1980s. This is a factor in delayed or declining marriage among younger groups. Elliott (1991) comments: 'cohabitation was probably an important part of the reason for fewer young people getting married in the 1970s' (p. 90), although this can be only a *part* of the explanation for this trend. Cohabitation has perhaps replaced the formal 'engagement' as the precursor to marriage, although couples may both cohabit and be engaged.

Seven out of ten *second* marriages, Kiernan and Wicks (1990) say, were preceded by a period of cohabitation in 1987. The figure was 60 per cent in 1979, and only a quarter back in the 1960s (Family Policy Studies Centre, 1991). The length of time that divorced women cohabited increased: for example, from 28 months in 1979 to 34 months in 1987 (Kiernan and Wicks, 1990). Cohabitation between marriages is part of the explanation for the decline in remarriage rates in the 1980s; divorced people have been cohabiting, and for longer periods.

So cohabitation has become much more common, is seemingly practised as an *alternative* to marriage in some cases, and appears to be becoming almost institutionalised as a preliminary to (re)marriage.

The move to cohabitation or informal marriage is found elsewhere: Scandanavia has traditionally been 'ahead' of Britain on this score. Veevers (1991) gives Canadian figures which show an increase in cohabiting: in both 1961 and 1971, fewer than 3 per cent of households involved a common law union (citing Hobart, 1983). Such unions were counted by the census from 1981, and the figures then showed an increase from 6.4 per cent of heterosexual couples cohabiting in 1981 to 8.3 per cent in 1986, mostly among the younger age groups. In 1984, as many as 29 per cent of women aged 18–49 had been in a common law relationship at some time. In Australia, Gilding (1991) notes more couples cohabiting in the 1970s and 1980s, with legal reforms in the 1980s putting *de facto* unions on almost the same footing as marriage.

One important aspect of the question, Do cohabitations resemble marriages?', concerns their stability over time. Marriage is a less stable institution than it was, being more likely to end in divorce, and more quickly. But cohabitation may be even more likely to break down. Cohabitations, although getting longer, tend to be short-lived, lasting for up to a few years, after which they either break up or are transformed into marriages. Kiernan (1989) suggests that cohabitation is not a permanent alternative to marriage – 'the likely explanation for what has taken place is a shift in the timing of marriage' (p. 33) – but she admits that we do not altogether know. Are cohabitations somehow more unstable or does the choice to cohabit say something about the way the partners view relationships in general? Haskey (1992) found that divorce is more probable if the couple cohabited first. The data, taken from the 1989 *General Household Survey*, showed that married couples who had cohabited were about 60 per cent more likely to have divorced or separated within 15 years than with those who had not cohabited. In other words, pre-marital cohabitation was associated with a raised risk of divorce. Possible explanations included that having cohabited indicated a weaker commitment to marriage, and that cohabitation was practised by the less conventional, who were also therefore readier to divorce. These two explanations would appear to be conceptually linked: the 'less conventional' may be construed as both having a weaker commitment to marriage and being more prepared to divorce. Haskey (1992) also quotes a study in France by Leridon (1990), which found that consensual unions break down slightly more frequently than marriages.

As with so much else in the field of family change, the meaning of the change is an area for debate. Fletcher (1988b), for example, clearly regards the increase in cohabitation as only a superficial change – it is, 'on the face of it . . . an abandonment of marriage on the part of *some*' (italics in original, p. 70) – but he is also severely critical of cohabitation (see, for example, p. 85). Why be so critical if the differences between marriage and cohabitation are so insignificant? Those who wish to defend a 'continuity' position may point out that men and women are living as couples and having children in a framework which may be indistinguishable from marriage apart from the legal sense. This raises fundamental questions about how cohabitation is seen, what it means to the participants, how partners behave in cohabitations and are treated by others, and why the choice to cohabit is made. Here empirical findings become important, but are often absent. Owens (1988, p. 47), for example, says of cohabitation: 'For many it is a prelude, while many others view their cohabitation as a relationship which while not formal, has the same rights, expectations and obligations of marriage proper', but presents no evidence to support this view. It is not objectively and *legally* the case that cohabitation carries the same rights and obligations as marriage: in

Britain there is not quite the same liability to maintain, for example, while certain social security and tax privileges are lacking, and the legal procedures for ending marriage do not apply. However, the courts have extended some property rights to female cohabitees, and the status of children born out of marriage and their fathers has moved closer to that of the children of the married and *their* fathers (for example, under the Family Law Reform Act 1987 and the Child Support Act 1991). Cohabitees *are* obliged to maintain each other under social security legislation, were liable for each others' community charge (1990–93), and lost a tax advantage which they had had in relation to mortgage interest relief in 1988 (this bringing them into line with the married).

Cohabitation and marriage may be converging; even so, the precise social meaning of the incidence of cohabitation is difficult to determine. It appears that many more people are cohabiting, or are prepared to admit to cohabitation; but in what sense this is because of an explicit rejection of marriage, or to what degree cohabitation should be regarded as simply a form of marriage, is unclear.

Births and child rearing outside marriage (in cohabitations, intermediate relationships and single-parent families)

The change to be discussed here connects with the rising incidence of both single parenthood and cohabitation, but is also a change worth commenting on in its own right. It is the rise in the proportion of all births occurring outside legal marriage (what was called the 'illegitimacy' rate before the Family Law Reform Act of 1987 ended the use of the term 'illegitimate' in legal documents). The changed legal and social status of people born outside marriage, and attempts to end the discrimination and stigma they had long suffered, constitute a striking area of social change. Traditionally common law had regarded the child born out of marriage as *filius nullius*, the child of no one, and a considerable number of disadvantages attached to this status; until the last few decades of the twentieth century 'illegitimate' birth was regarded as shameful and was often disguised through means of adoption or secrecy about the circumstances of birth. Unmarried mothers were particularly badly treated by the Poor Law (they were unlikely to get outdoor relief, and could be detained under mental health legislation if deemed mentally handicapped), and by society at large. Up to the 1960s, much pressure was applied for them to give up their child for adoption (see, for example, Howe *et al.*, 1992). In the latter decades of the twentieth century, however, both the legal disadvantages and the social stigma surrounding 'illegitmate' birth and unmarried motherhood have diminished dramatically. Particularly noteworthy is the 1987 Act which made the position of children born out of marriage and their fathers very close to, although not identical with, that of children born within marriage and their fathers.

As should be clear from the last section, an increasing number of births, while 'outside marriage', have occurred in cohabitations. Births occurring in cohabitations are not counted as single-parent births while the cohabitation lasts, and therefore a rise in births to cohabiting couples does not directly feed into the single-parent figures (Haskey, 1991b). Cohabitations may break up, however, and there are indications that they are somewhat less stable than marriages; there has also been an increase in extra-marital births occurring to a mother living alone, who may or may not have an ongoing relationship with a non-coresident father. 'Intermediate' relationships may be identified where the couple are involved with each other and the child(ren), but do not actually live together. The patterns are difficult to categorise in any clear-cut way.

In the first half of the twentieth century, the percentage of English and Welsh live births which were out of marriage was only 4–5 per cent, with a blip in the First World War (*Social Trends*, 1992) due to the relaxing of social controls over sexual behaviour at that time. After a Second World War peak of 10 per cent, the proportion of extra-marital births dropped back again to 5 per cent and stayed fairly constant in the 1950s (B. J. Elliott, 1991) at a level only slightly higher than the early years of the century, so there was a re-instatement of the Edwardian pattern. It was in the 1960s that the rate of births outside marriage began to rise, with the sharpest increase two decades later. From 1960, levels rose steadily, to 8.4 per cent in 1968; there was then a flattening due to the new abortion law which, in making it easier for unmarried pregnant women to terminate their pregnancy, reduced the number of actual births to this group. Notwithstanding this, the rate then rose steeply from 1976 (B. J. Elliott, 1991). By 1979 it was 11 per cent (*Social Trends*, 1992), and by 1981 nearly 13 per cent (Haskey, 1991a). More dramatic change was to come: by 1986 the proportion of births outside marriage was a fifth, and by 1988 a quarter (*Social Trends*, 1990; Haskey, 1991a). The figure hit 28 per cent in 1990, 30 per cent in 1991 (*Social Trends*, 1992), and nearly 32 per cent in 1992 (*Social Trends*, 1994). The figure was still rising, therefore, but the period of sharpest increase was the early to mid-1980s (see also Cooper, 1991).

The 1960s, often identified as the origin of 'permissive' sexuality and liberalising legislation (Weeks, 1985), marked the beginning of this important social change. There was an increase in *pre-marital* pregnancy rates for young women in the 1960s, with a fifth of brides being pregnant at marriage (the proportion was only one-eighth later, in the mid-1970s to mid-1980s: see Kiernan, 1989). The proportion of first births *outside* marriage went from 7 to 14 per cent in the 1960s; where marriage did not take place, young women were still encouraged to place the children for adoption. This changed later. While, at the beginning of the 1970s, young pregnant single women were most likely to opt for marriage, and much less likely to opt for having an illegitimate child or an abortion, by the end of the 1970s they were most likely to opt for an abortion, next for having the child outside marriage, and only then, the least popular alternative, for marriage (Kiernan, 1989). In the 1980s they were more likely to have the child out of marriage.

Reproduction outside marriage is more common in the younger groups. For those under 20 births outside marriage were already the majority by 1982 in Britain (Moss and Lau, 1985); and by 1992 such births accounted for as many as 84 per cent of all those to women under 20 (*Social Trends*, 1994). However, the rise in extra-marital births is also linked with the rise in births to somewhat older women. The Family Policy Studies Centre (1992) comments that births outside marriage to the over 30s trebled in the 1980s, and were closely linked to cohabitation.

Most European countries and the USA also showed an increase in the extra-marital birth rate between 1960 and 1990,

although most European countries have a smaller percentage
than Britain (Ermisch, 1990). Nevertheless in Sweden, just over
a half of births were outside marriage in 1989 (Ermisch, 1990;
Social Trends, 1992: see also Kiernan and Wicks, 1990). Child
bearing within cohabiting unions is a more long-standing pattern in Sweden and Denmark (Family Policy Studies Centre,
1990). In Sweden, for example, while in the early 1960s most
women started their family life by marrying directly, by the
late 1960s they cohabited but married prior to the birth of a
child; in the 1970s cohabitation stretched for a longer period,
and there was then a growth in the numbers having a child
while cohabiting. This was a majority pattern by the late 1970s.
This leads Kiernan (1990) to ask whether Britain is likely to
follow the same path as Sweden, since the same changes have
occurred in Britain at a slightly later period. As Kiernan points
out, it was during the 1970s that we saw child-free, short-lived,
pre-marital unions appearing in Britain. During the 1980s there
may have been the critical transition to child bearing within
cohabiting unions.

Roll (1992) shows the increase in extra-marital births in all
EC countries since 1970. Denmark has the highest EC proportion at 45 per cent, with France and the UK next, and the
lowest rates in Greece and Spain. According to the OECD (1993),
never-married mothers have increased in all OECD countries.
Veevers (1991) notes the increase in parenthood without marriage in Canada, and the increasing tolerance of 'illegitimacy'.
The rate of births out of marriage increased from less than 5
per cent before the 1960s to 19 per cent in 1986; as in Britain
there was a reduced tendency to have these children adopted.
Veevers notes that the child born out of wedlock may be born
to cohabiting parents, or is not necessarily without a known
father. 'Illegitimacy' had in fact been abolished in four prov-
inces by 1988. Besharov (1989) observes a startling rise in extra-marital births in the USA, with the incidence being the highest
ever observed since national statistics were first collected in
1940. Between 1950 and 1984, the number of births to unwed
mothers more than quintupled; and the percentage of children born out of wedlock was 4 per cent in 1950, but 20 per
cent by 1984 (citing US Bureau of the Census, 1981 and 1985).
Never-married mothers were a relatively young group, with 70

per cent of all out-of-wedlock births being to mothers aged 15–24. Besharov also notes that never-married mothers are poorer than divorced mothers (this is also broadly the case in Britain). They are also less educated, less likely to be in paid employment, less likely to receive child support, and are on welfare for longer. In Australia, Gilding (1991) notes more teenage *pregnancies* out of marriage from the 1940s to 1960s, but with more women entering *motherhood* without marriage in the 1970s and 1980s, with the percentage of extra-nuptial births being 10 per cent in 1976 and 19 per cent by 1988 (a very similar picture to that in Britain and Canada).

Another important change in extra-marital births concerns the proportions of these births registered by both parents, rather than the mother alone, and the proportions registered by couples apparently cohabiting. Both types of registration (that is, joint registrations, and joint registrations from the same address) have grown in Britain, absolutely and in relation to all extra-marital births. In 1961 only 38 per cent of the (much smaller number of) extra-marital births were jointly registered, and the proportion was still a minority – 49 per cent) – in 1975 (*Social Trends*, 1990). By 1989, the percentage of births outside marriage which was jointly registered was over 70 per cent; and of these joint registrations, in over 70 per cent the two parents gave the same address; 75 per cent of out-of-wedlock births were jointly registered in 1992, and 75 per cent of joint registrations were by couples at the same address in 1990 (*Social Trends*, 1990 and 1994; Haskey, 1991a). This suggests, then, that over half of the births were to cohabiting parents. So it is more common than it was for fathers of extra-marital children to acknowledge them, and for the father to be living with the mother. On the other hand, there are more of these births in the first place. Children, then, are more commonly reared in cohabitations; there were by 1986/7 estimated to be more than 400 000 dependent children living in cohabiting couple families, about 4 per cent of all dependent children (Haskey and Kiernan, 1989). Other out-of-wedlock children know their fathers, but not as a coresiding figure.

There is some evidence that families founded on cohabitation rather than legal marriage are less stable over time. Millar (1989, p. 20) suggests that 'de facto two-parent families may be more likely to separate than married two-parent families'. Millar is here quoting A. Brown (1986), who looked at evidence from the OPCS Longitudinal Study, based on the 1981 Census, concerning legitimate and illegitimate children born in the decade 1971–81. It was found that at all ages the legitimate-born children were *less* likely to be in a single-parent family than the illegitimate; the latter were *more* likely to be in such a family, whether registered by both parents or not. Brown claims that only about 60 per cent of jointly registered illegitimate children aged under 10 were living with both their natural parents, as compared with about 90 per cent of the legitimate children. However, joint registration of a birth is not identical with cohabitation; in about three-quarters of cases of joint registrations, parents give the same address, which means that in a quarter they do *not*. In other words, as some of these jointly registered illegitimate children were never living with both parents in the first place, one has to be cautious about conclusions on the stability of 'cohabiting families' from this data.

While cohabiting families are growing more common, something should be said about births *not* in cohabitations: that is, child bearing in single-parent units from the start, and what have been called here intermediate relationships (including single parenthood by design). Clearly not all the increase in extra-marital child bearing is accounted for by cohabitation births (about half of British extra marital births are *not* to cohabitees); some of the increase is due to women alone having children. Single parenthood by choice seems to be a minority pattern, but is clearly a more feasible and common option than it was. Whether or not it was chosen from the start, single parenthood for the young unmarried woman is a great deal more common than in the past. These families are known to be mostly poor and on benefits, and are more likely than others to be sharing accommodation with another household, but their situations are also more fluid than those of other single parents and they more rapidly cease to be single parents.

A feature of the late 1980s, and again of the early 1990s – in both Britain and the USA – was the political criticism that young women were having babies outside marriage (or cohabitation) deliberately, in order to obtain public sector housing or other presumed material advantages; or because it was a

route to adulthood or an 'independent' life on welfare benefits; or out of an almost perverse rejection of marriage (see,
for example, *Guardian*, 7 October 1993, 12 October 1993, 21
June 1994; Marchant, 1993; Sutton, 1993, for attacks on single
mothers by British politicians such as Lilley, Howard and Red-
wood). A relevant factor here, however, is the rising incidence
of male unemployment, plus the depression of wages for some
men. Where male income is low, or consists only of social security benefits, a live-in partnership may not be advantageous to a
woman; poverty with autonomy can seem preferable to poverty
without autonomy. The choice of single parenthood may be a
rational one, therefore, given the restricted range of options
which face some women at some stages of their lives. Pregnancy may also not be intentional; for example, an article on
pregnant care-leavers (Rickford, 1992, p. 10) comments: 'Several recent studies of teenage mothers have found that the
great majority of girls become pregnant accidentally, from a
combination of naivety and ignorance, not, as some politicians
have claimed, in a bid to get a council home.'

Adoption is declining in significance, particularly the 'traditional' (that is, earlier twentieth century) type, where a baby
was legally adopted by a (married) couple and all contact with
the genetic parent(s) was severed, with some secrecy observed
and the identity of the parties usually remaining unknown to
each other. The child became legally (after the Adoption of
Children Act 1926) and socially the child of the adopting
couple. The child was thus 'lost' forever to the original parents
(usually a lone unmarried mother). This pattern was well established in the middle decades of the century, and was considered the optimal 'solution' for the unmarried pregnant woman
(although not necessarily by the woman herself: see, for example, Howe *et al.*, 1992). Adoption, avoiding as it did the stigma
and difficulty which surrounded child rearing alone, neatly
'solved' another problem, that of the involuntarily childless
married couple.

By the late 1970s and 1980s this pattern was much less common, and the number of adoptions (particularly of this type)
had declined markedly (see, for example, C. R. Smith, 1984).
As mentioned, the preferred options for unmarried pregnant
women were by this time abortion or single parenthood, and

less frequently adoption or marriage. The result was more single mothers/fewer adoptions/more childless couples unable to adopt. What might be called 'non-traditional' adoptions increased from the 1970s: that is, adoptions of older, disabled, black and mixed race children; step-parent adoptions (until discouraged by the Children Act 1975); and adoptions where some contact with the original family continued (favoured by government reviews of adoption in the 1990s: see Department of Health, 1992 and 1993). Through the 1975 Children Act and later developments, some adult adoptees were able to locate their original parent(s), and so were not altogether 'lost'.

Finally, the meaning of all this, as of so many other family changes, needs considering. As B. J. Elliott (1991) says, it may be argued that from the late 1970s the nature of illegitimacy (*sic*) changes. As many couples (and women on their own) have been having children out of wedlock intentionally, without fear of discrimination or social rejection, the meaning of the term 'births outside marriage' is no longer what it was in, say, the 1950s or 1920s; so this is not so much a growth of a deviant behaviour pattern as a change in what is perceived as deviant. Family founding can acceptably occur in informal unions – or in no union – and does so increasingly. The trend is not without its opponents, however, and one strand in the resistance comes from governments, which have found the shift to child rearing outside marriage causing an increased demand on the social security budget.

Other alternatives to marriage

Cohabitation and child bearing/rearing outside marriage have been considered as, in a sense, 'alternatives' to marriage. Single parenthood and step-parenthood could also be viewed as alternatives to the conventional nuclear family form of once-only married parents and their biological children. Not discussed here, but also relevant to the transformation of marriage, are homosexual partnerships and lifestyles, collective or communal households, experimental forms of marriage such as open marriage and 'swinging', and diverse variants of the non-celibate 'singles' lifestyle (for sources on some alternatives see, for example, Rigby, 1974; Abrams and McCulloch, 1976; Chester and Peel, 1977; Anderson, 1980; Rapoport and Rapoport, 1982; Macklin and Rubin, 1983; Leonard and Hood-Williams, 1988; Bunk and van Driel, 1989; Weeks, 1991). All of these patterns are in some sense 'alternative' to the traditional Christian view of how sexuality and procreation should be expressed; all are more widely accepted and practised than they once were.

Conclusions

Changes in the areas of marriage and related patterns have been examined in this chapter. Formal marriage is becoming a less common pattern in society, while divorce, single parenthood, cohabitation without marriage and reproduction outside marriage have all increased in incidence. Women are much more likely than men to be living on their own with children. Men are more likely than women to remarry, although their tendency to do so has declined. Heterosexual relationships are less stable than they were, and less likely to involve coresidence. A general theme of disengagement may be identified. The social meanings of states such as marriage, divorce, cohabitation and 'illegitimacy' have all dramatically changed. The changes influence, and are influenced by, those affecting gender, reproduction and ageing outlined in Chapter 1.

Chapter 3 will now go on to consider the central question of *how much* change may be identified, as opposed to the degree of *continuity* in family patterns.

Chapter 3

Continuity and Change

This chapter will focus on the question of continuity versus change in family life. So far the emphasis has been mainly on the various changes. This chapter will attempt to stand back a little further to try and assess the meaning of change. How much has *really* changed in family life? Are the changes merely superficial? Are the continuities more important? Are the changes which have occurred simply changes in form (for example, fewer legal marriages), while the social institutions, in a deeper sense, remain essentially the same? Different reactions to change are also based not only on whether change is seen to be significant/'real' but on the onlooker's own values, ideology and ideas about families, gender, parenthood and so on, and how these institutions *ought* to function.

Two broad camps may be distinguished, advocating on the one hand essential continuity and on the other fundamental change. It may be helpful first to look back briefly over a longer historical period than that which is the focus of this book – that is, to previous centuries – and to consider a few authors who have taken this historical view and arrived at differing conclusions about family change in Britain and Europe.

Historical continuity

The name most obviously associated with a continuitarian position on marriage, houesholds and the nuclear versus the extended family in Britain is Laslett who, in a number of works (for example, Laslett, 1971, 1972 and 1980), has emphasised that, despite some changes in family life, western European family forms have shown remarkable continuity over several centuries, and that the most common family household type today (the two-generation nuclear family as a separate household) antedates industrialisation and urbanisation by many years, rather than (as was popularly believed) being *produced by* these changes. The western European family has had certain characteristics since the Middle Ages, being based on the simple nuclear household; the absence of child or arranged marriages; marriage not being universal; and lax kinship bonding or flows of support beyond the nuclear unit (see Laslett, 1980). Other authors who have broadly taken a similar view of the longstanding nature of nuclear units in this country include W. Goode (1964) and McFarlane (1978). M. Anderson (1980) is another writer who has looked at the development of family patterns over time, occupying a broadly continuitarian position, and being sceptical about the incidence of flourishing extended families in the past.

Another author who is not an altogether academic source but who has used Laslett's work to argue for continuity in pair bonds, marriage and parental affection is Mount (1982). Mount is a right-wing political philospher who was an adviser to the first Thatcher government, and his work conveniently emphasised the theme of independence from the state. A writer who has argued for continuity in the specific field of parent–child relationships is Pollock (1983), opposing authors who have emphasised change in the nature of childhood and weak parent–child bonds in the past (see below). Pollock argues, in contradiction to these change-oriented authors, that contemporary sources show that parents of the past were emotionally involved with their children and concerned for their welfare; that brutality was on the whole rare, and there has been considerable continuity in methods of child discipline over time; while frequent child deaths did not mean that parents became accustomed to such loss or emotionally distanced from their children. Contrary to the view of, in particular, Aries (1962, see below), Pollock maintains that there *was* a concept of childhood as a separate stage of life in previous centuries. In general she sees a good deal of continuity in the parent–child bond through time, while also perceiving diversity within any one particular time.

Historical change

What of those authors who are more conscious of *change* in family structures over time, and who tend to see a succession of different phases over a long historical period? One author who occupies this position is Shorter (1975). Shorter sees the family as having, over the centuries, withdrawn from the wider community and from kinship ties, and as having entered a more private world. He suggests that a 'surge of sentiment' in three areas helped to bring about this shift, these three areas being courtship, the mother–child relationship and the boundary between the family and the surrounding community, with the boundary becoming less permeable and the family becoming more of an emotional unit. The modern, domestic, nuclear family was born, a unit which was more affectionate and less instrumental than the family of earlier times. This change, in Shorter's view, became established in the nineteenth century.

Another writer who outlines a pattern of historical change is Stone (1977), who looked at family and sexual patterns over three centuries. Stone traces the development of the modern family through the sixteenth, seventeenth and eighteenth centuries in England, seeing major structural changes by stages. But the critical change is from distance, deference and patriarchy to what Stone calls 'affective individualism', in which there is a focus on freely chosen emotional bonds. In the sixteenth century and before that, there was what Stone calls an 'open lineage family', with permeable boundaries and loyalty to ancestors and kin. This was gradually replaced by the 'restricted patriarchal nuclear family', which was more closed off from external influences. Then there was the 'closed domesticated nuclear family', the product of the rise of affective individualism. This was organised around the principle of personal autonomy and bound together by strong affective ties; husbands and wives chose each other, and there was more time, energy and love invested in the children. Stone sees this family type as beginning to appear as early as the late seventeenth century.

With regard to the position of childhood, in particular, an often-quoted author is Aries (1962), mentioned above, who sees the modern concept of childhood – and the modern private family – as having appeared from the sixteenth century onwards in Europe (at different times in different places and social classes), and childhood in the modern period as being fundamentally different from the mediaeval concept. Children in the Middle Ages, according to Aries, did not occupy a separate world or a separate set of roles once they had left infancy; there was no period of transition before maturity; and in a sense children above about seven were 'little adults'. They were also treated with indifference and sent away from their families at an early age. The emergence of the idea of childhood, Aries claims, occurred with profound changes in European civilisation associated with the Renaissance and Reformation, and contained ideas both of childish innocence which was in need of protection, *and* the need of children for discipline and control due to their association with evil qualities, which served to emphasise the need for education and to separate children from adults. Treatment became harsher, and parent–child relationships grew more authoritarian and remote. The child was removed from adult society. In time also, the family (at first the middle-class family) separated itself from society into a private unit; the modern concept of childhood also appeared first in this class rather than the family of either the aristocracy or the labouring class. Pollock (1983), as noted above, has taken issue with Aries's interpretation, arguing with his use of contemporary evidence, and drawing on other sources to argue for a concept of childhood as a separate state well *before* the time that Aries identifies.

It can be noted that Aries, Shorter and Stone all see the development of the family from an emotionally distant and permeable arrangement to a much closer and more private unit, although their perception of the precise timing of the shifts differs. Relationships within the family became more intensive over time, it seems, and there was more investment in child socialisation. The contrast is with authors such as Pollock and Mount, who regard this emotional quality of nuclear family relationships as having been in existence for longer.

Various qualifications need to be made about the problems of tracing the development of the family unit over time: for example, *variations* within any one historical period (a point stressed by Pollock: these variations would be expected according to class, region, and other dimensions); rapid fluctuations within periods according to changing circumstances and conditions; and the extremely difficult problem of sources and evidence, how representative the available data is, and what the evidence does in fact tell us. Knowing about the composition of the household, for example, does not necessarily enable inferences to be made about the emotional quality of relationships. As M. Anderson (1980, pp. 57–81) says: 'the family and marriage, even if in structural terms they look very similar today to the pattern of two hundred years ago, are changed in many important ways'.

Clearly over time there has been significant change in the conditions *surrounding* the family, such as industrialisation, urbanisation, vast technological change, change in government, the labour market, the law and other social structures. It could hardly be argued that the family has been unaffected by all this, as the conditions in which families are formed and maintained, the work which individuals must do to sustain the resources coming into families, other social institutions and so on, are all factors which fundamentally affect how families function and the constraints upon them (see here, for example, Donzelot, 1980). But has the *internal* nature of marriage and family life fundamentally changed over several centuries? Here the obvious answer must surely be that it has, although precisely in what way is a matter for debate. The changed general social relationships between men and women and their relative social, economic and political positions would produce some internal family change; and a similar statement could be made for parent–child relationships and the general position of children, who now have a quite different relation to the state, for example, compared with previous centuries. Yet have people in western societies, at a deeper level, long continued to seek (at least for a time) exclusive sexual pair bonds and to raise children who are identifiably 'theirs' within this context, and to be emotionally involved in this unit?

What views may be taken of what has occurred in the twentieth century, and specifically the latter half of it, in terms of continuity and change? Two broad positions will be examined, one emphasising an essential continuity in family patterns, and the other emphasising striking, and possibly fundamental, change.

Recent continuity

One notable author who has taken a continuitarian position
in relation to more recent change is Fletcher (1988a and 1988b),
whose writing has already been referred to. Fletcher (1988b),
while chronicling much that has changed, insists that some
essential 'the family' is what most people in Britain want and
have. 'The family remains intact' is his overall conclusion
(p. 123). He also sees 'the family' as a virtual universal in human
societies. Having quoted from Anderson, Fletcher takes from
his work the idea that 'the casting aside of historical myths
and faulty perspectives can give us an altogether different and
more positive appraisal of the nature of marriage and the family today' (pp. 127–8): that is, more positive than superficial
change might suggest), although he admits that there are some
problems; the situation with the family is not trouble-free. For
example, Fletcher is fairly scathing about the shift to cohabitation, seeing this as a very negative development. While broadly
within the functionalist school of sociology, Fletcher is in a
sense part of the 'neo-traditionalist' or 'family values' lobby in
that, apart from supporting liberal divorce laws, he is committed to a conventional family form and is sceptical about
alternatives, and about many developments in lifestyles stem-
ming from the 1960s. But his insistence is on continuity at a
deeper level, in conjugal and parental sentiments, for example,
although he also thinks that sentiment has declined. One is
tempted to suspect an element of wishful thinking on his part:
Fletcher desperately *wants* to believe that the conventional two-
parent married family is alive and well in Britain, while his
attacks on feminism, single parenthood by choice, homosexuality and cohabitation suggest strongly that he is aware that it
is not.

Another author who perceives essential continuity in the midst
of change, is Chester (1985), who speaks of the 'neo-conventional family'. Here developments such as divorce, cohabitation and married women being in paid work are not seen as
introducing major discontinuities in family life. Writing in the
mid-1980s, Chester stressed continuity rather than change, commenting: 'Of course, some changes have occurred in marriage
and family patterns. Their importance cannot be ignored. But

they must be seen in the context of major continuities in family life' (p. 185). He pointed out that six out of ten people were at that time in parent–children households, and a further 20 per cent were married couples who mostly had had, or would have, children. He usefully shows the need to look at people's situation in the context of their life cycle, rather than merely at 'snapshot' figures. Having children is a normal developmental phase; while there *is* change (for example, mothers in employment) there is no drastic re-ordering, he argues. Chester does not see a flight from marriage, only a delaying of it, while cohabitation is not perceived by him as a permanent alternative to marriage. His overall conclusion is that 'there is a very strong framework of continuity' (p. 188).

These continuity authors wish to defend earlier patterns, but a quite different type of 'continuity' position may be taken by some feminist writers who see continuity negatively. They see patriarchy as continuing; indeed, radical feminist writers would tend to see patriarchy as ahistoric and universal in human societies. Walby (1990, p. 173) comments: 'Radical feminists have generally concluded that for every victory won by women there has been a patriarchal backlash in another area.' One view is thus that while patriarchy has perhaps changed its form and become less blatant in the late twentieth century, marriage and marriage-like heterosexual relationships continue to oppress, control and disadvantage women, and women continue to be very unequal both within families and (partly because of their family roles) outside them. Change in the family is not all that it seems, and is not necessarily helpful to women. Greater sexual freedom, for one, has been regarded by some feminist writers as not necessarily advantageous for women (see, for example, Jeffreys, 1985). Cohabitation in some ways leaves women more vulnerable than does patriarchal marriage, lacking some of marriage's legal protection. Single parenthood frequently spells poverty. Divorce and the absence of remarriage have brought poverty for older women.

An example of a feminist continuitarian view would be work by Delphy and Leonard (1992), radical feminist authors who present a highly traditional version of marriage, with husbands in control and wives servicing them in a variety of ways (see, in particular, their Chapter 9, 'The variety of work done by

wives'). The authors see such a form of marriage as continuing, despite two waves of feminism and some changes. Women
are depicted as having to accommodate their lives to their
husbands, and as having fewer resources and less power within
marriage than men. Husbands are assumed and asserted to be
'heads of households' because they are males, and various arguments about their degree of power then follow from that.
The authors' thesis is essentially that women's labour continues
to be expropriated by men in marriage; marriage thus operates in men's interests in a variety of ways and is a key part of
women's oppression. While men may have to struggle to maintain their dominant position within the family, 'that is not to
say that a patriarchal hierarchy does not exist and is not being
continued' (p. 100). Men and women are seen as opposed class
factions, and 'The head of a family enterprise . . . has in common with the head of a firm that he owns property and the
products produced by his subordinates, and that he is conse-
quently the one able to exchange them' (p. 158). The model
of marriage which Delphy and Leonard deploy at times sounds
oddly Victorian, implying a degree of male control which, it
might be argued, is being somewhat over-stated in terms of
late twentieth-century conditions. For example, they say 'wives . . .
are not free to sell their labour to a third party without their
household head authorizing it' (p. 118). Delphy and Leonard
no doubt intend, and would defend, this approach, since it is
their purpose to show that women's labour is *still* expropriated by men through marriage, that women continue to service male partners in a whole range of ways, and that therefore
marriage even now operates over-poweringly in men's, not
women's, interests. It needs to be considered how accurate,
representative and up-to-date their picture of marriage is. Interestingly, they do tend to write about *marriage* rather than cohabitation; although they are clearly aware of cohabitation, they
note that it does not necessarily make things better for women.
Their work is supported by reference to two empirical studies
of factory-workers' families in Britain and farm families in France.
These writers stress continuity, then, but a continuity which is
highly disadvantageous for women.

A more 'middle ground' continuity position is occupied by
Walby (1990), who broadly sees a shift from private to public

patriarchy, with women less trapped than they were by individual men in marriage, freer to take part in the public world, but still subordinated in the world outside the family such as at work. Walby sees only slight qualitative change in women's position in employment, for example (women are no longer excluded from the labour market but remain segregated within it). She comments (p. 174): 'British feminists have won significant reforms which ameliorate a number of the features of patriarchy, but some have resulted in a different form of patriarchy . . . Private patriarchy has given way to public patriarchy.' Private patriarchy is based on the household and involves the control of women by individual patriarchs; public patriarchy is based on other structures or institutions conventionally regarded as part of the public domain. However, patriarchy *has* declined in degree as well. Both continuity and change are acknowledged here: patriarchy continues but is weakened; its *form* has changed. 'Women have entered the public sphere, yet are subordinated there' (p. 180). This weak public position of women would rebound on their power position in marriage and the family (see also Walby, 1986).

A moderately continuitarian position on recent family change was also taken by the publications of the Family Policy Studies Centre (formerly the Study Commission on the Family) for a number of years. While change was documented, a broad emphasis on continuity was maintained. It was pointed out that most young people continued to marry, most became parents, most children were born within wedlock and so on (see, for example, Study Commission on the Family, 1982 and 1983). However by the turn of the decade 1980s–1990s, a shift of emphasis was noticeable (see below).

Also on continuity writing, Finch and Morgan (1991), in a review of marriage in the 1980s, quote a number of studies which support a 'continuity' position; they say that 'a number of quite disparate sociological studies published in the 1980s do contain evidence which points to continuities with the past, rather than to dramatic changes' (pp. 56–7). They cite Burgoyne (1987), and five studies which reflect on marriage: Askham (1984), Mansfield and Collard (1988), Brannen and Collard (1982), Burgoyne and Clark (1984) and Lawson (1983). One theme from the 1980s is that: 'most people continued to hold in high regard the concept of a "successful marriage"... The way in which people apparently were thinking about successful marriages does indeed come through as rather conventional' (p. 57). And Finch and Morgan go on to show how little un-equal gender relations and the division of labour within the family had changed in reality. They also comment on the cover of the Family Policy Studies Centre's 1987 publication *Inside the Family* (Henwood *et al.*, 1987). While this showed, appar-ently, a type of 'new man' holding a baby, the content of the publication 'exploring the actual divisions of labour between women and men in parenting and in the home, suggests much more continuity in terms of the "traditional" model than is suggested on the cover' (p. 77).

Finally, as an aside, a 1994 American survey on teenagers' expectations may be mentioned. It apparently found that 'Many boys still believe in a traditional fifties-style marriage, in which the wife stays home, raises the children, cleans the house and does the cooking, while the husband is responsible for making money and mowing the lawn'! But only 7 per cent of the girls said they expected to stay home when married. A marked dis-sonance was noticeable between the responses of the girls and the boys. 'While girls expect their husbands to share in man-aging the home, many boys seem committed to avoiding it' (*Guardian*, 14 July 1994, from *New York Times*). We have here an asymmetrical pattern of continuity/change in the attitudes of the genders.

Recent change

To turn to other writers and commentators who have focused on change and discontinuity rather than continuity in recent decades, one group who do see family change in the latter decades of the twentieth century as real and significant may be summarised by the 'neo-traditionalist' or 'family values' or 'moral lobby' label (see, for example, Berger and Berger, 1983; Durham, 1991). The reaction of this group to perceived fam-ily change is on the whole negative. Recent change is mostly seen as adverse, and there is a wish to reverse it. Divorce, freer sexual morality and single parenthood are in particular deplored; there is a wish to restore 'traditional' gender roles and establish more time for parenting, with a general stress on familial obligation and duty. So married women should not be in paid work but in the home and available to care for children, grand-children, the elderly and any other family members needing care; sexuality, heterosexual couple relationships and parenting should only occur within the context of legal marriage, which should be monogamous and for life (so presumably divorce should be made difficult or impossible, and any children born out of marriage should all be placed for adoption with married couples); having children *would* occur, almost universally, within marriage, however. Families, therefore, would virtually all be two-parent plus children, and the shifting and ambiguous patterns of various sexual and parental relationships, sequential partnerships, single-parent and cohabiting families (and so on) would stop. All married women and children would be supported by a male breadwinner (or male claimant if he was unemployed or sick/disabled). This appears to be the logical end point to which the preferences and ideals of this group of commentators would tend, but the point here is that change *is* acknowledged, albeit perhaps even over-stated?

Examples of such writing are the publications of the National Campaign for the Family/National Family Trust, D. Anderson and Dawson's work, *Family Portraits* (1986), and publications from the Institute of Economic Affairs such as Dennis and Erdos's *Families without Fatherhood* (1992) and Davies's *The Family: Is it just Another Lifestyle Choice?* (1993). In the USA writing by right-wing commentators such as Murray (1984), by pro-family bodies such as the Family Research Council (for example, Mattox, 1991), and others associated with the New Right, moralists, and the 'family values' and anti-abortion lobbies has both recognised extensive family change and deplored it (on American 'pro-family' movements, see, for example, Faludi, 1991). The role of the religious, fundamentalist right wing in this critique of family change may be mentioned, this being a more strident influence in the USA than in Britain, say.

The neo-traditionalist movement and the 'moral lobby', then, embody a number of strands, but constitute a general counter-reaction against what is seen as the permissive and liberal ethos of the 1960s. They are also associated with an anti-gay 'backlash' and a moral panic about AIDS. While the appearance of various moralistic and pro-family groups has been more high profile in the USA, these groups have made their presence felt in Britain, and have presented something of a problem for Conservative governments in the 1980s and 1990s. In terms of rhetoric and presentation of their policies, the Thatcherite Conservatives of the 1980s might have seemed to embrace a similar ideology to the moral pressure groups, but the government was subject to other pressures, and was caught between authoritarian and libertarian strands in Conservatism itself when faced with the demands of these groups for the reversal of change, proposals tantamount to much greater social and state control over various areas of people's personal lives (see Durham, 1991; Abbott and Wallace, 1992). Politicians must have been uncomfortably aware that many of the changes of which the moral/traditionalist lobby were critical were being actively practised and endorsed by the majority population.

It is also possible to construct an 'optimistic' view of the reality of family change: for example, to argue that substantial change *has* occurred, and that this has involved a very real increase in women's rights, opportunities and autonomy, which has made a substantial difference to women's oppression, although perhaps still bringing women nothing like equality. Here it may be argued that gender roles and relations are fundamentally changed in the late twentieth century, even compared with the early and middle decades. Some social policy, left-wing and feminist writing would support what are seen to be women's increased freedoms and the shift away from private dependency on male partners. Single-parent familyhood can be construed as 'liberation' for women, and the freedom of women to choose to procreate without a male partner may be celebrated similarly (see, for example, Fox Harding, 1993). It can be argued that there has indeed been a shift in power relations between men and women, and that women are now significantly freer to avoid oppressive relationships, either by existing outside male–female partnerships altogether or by negotiating a more egalitarian arrangement within them. The point here is that change is acknowledged, and is seen positively. Walby (1990, p. 173) identifies such a positive view of the extent of change affecting women with *liberal* feminism: 'Liberal feminists have usually painted a picture of progress composed of the winning of the vote, entry into education, growth in the number of women in top jobs and the increase in the number of women in public life ... Such advances accumulate and provide the basis of the next reform.'

Finally, the writing of the Family Policy Studies Centre has already been mentioned as having stressed continuity until the end of the 1980s, and then having somewhat shifted ground. For example, writing in a publication from the Centre, Kiernan and Wicks (1990, p. 31) acknowledged:

> We have argued that both continuities and changes are central to any balanced understanding of family life. Often in the past we have stressed continuity, not least to balance a debate in Britain that has been over-obsessed with change. We now feel, however, that the 1980s may have been a watershed in which some traditional features of family life were challenged. Both cohabitation, coupled with child-bearing, and divorce have changed fundamentally our understanding of the family in Britain.

This comment is of considerable interest, coming as it does from a body noteworthy both for its detailed collection of empirical material and its broadly continuitarian position in the past.

Continuity or change?

The present will now be examined briefly in relation to what does and does not appear to the author to have changed in the last few decades. The contours of change have been outlined in Chapters 1 and 2. The most striking areas of change are the increased wariness about formal marriage and the readiness to seek openly other alternative kinds of context for sexual and parental relationships; the decline of fertility and the ageing of the population; and the slight but significant shift in the power and (in)dependence of women. Individuals may be turning away from relationships that look as though they are too binding. At this point a major change will be suggested, which is a significant shift in the *patriarchal* nature of marriage, a shift which has – in the short term at least – made the institution more fragile. To a far greater extent than in the past, women have rejected (or, more precisely, been *able* to reject) the patriarchal basis of traditional marriage and have sought (and been *able* to seek) something different. The result is an attempt to change individual marriages in a more egalitarian direction, which may then cause them to fail, or a turning away from patriarchal marriage/marriage as an institution altogether, in favour of other types of relationship which may look 'freer'.

This is on the women's side. On the men's, it can be argued that there is an attempt to defend patriarchal marriage (at least up to a point) as this is the type of institution which is most in line with men's interests. (The enhanced legal and social freedom to end a marriage, of course, not only frees wives to reject husbands, but husbands to reject wives.) Men may turn away from particular marriages which become intolerable because they are not patriarchal enough, and seek either alternative marriages (an interesting and extreme example is to seek a wife from another culture with more patriarchal practices), or different forms of relationship which are less committed and binding, and which therefore may make less demands and be more easily jettisoned if they are not entirely satisfactory. Both trends, those affecting women and those affecting men, would lead to greater instability in relationships.

In both cases the basic view of marriage is that it is primarily intended for both male and (to a lesser extent) female individual need satisfaction, that, indeed, Stone's (1977) 'affective individualism' has been carried very far, and marriage is not primarily, for example, seen as a set of duties, a means of procreation, or simply as an unavoidable social pattern. The view of marriage is characterised by both individualism and a form of contractualism. Dennis and Erdos (1992), and Halsey, in his introduction to their work (see also Halsey, 1993), argue that marriage has become *merely* a contract, with no special status, which is terminable like any other contract. But is marriage now *less of* a contract than it was, more easily broken, terminated with greater impunity than other forms of contract, or not seen as a contract at all? Child rearing is also perhaps increasingly seen as to do with (adult) need satisfaction, rather than as a set of duties or something which almost inevitably follows from having a sex life (as it did until relatively recent times). A crucial point here is that the changes can only occur in a context which *does* make the search for alternatives and the exercise of choice possible. The opening-up of choices, due to a variety of technological, economic and legal changes, is one of the significant ways in which marriage and family life in the late twentieth century are very different from before. The ability to choose was relatively absent in the past. The opening-up of choices, and a less contractual view of relationships, has made them less binding; and there are much greater possibilities of disengagement from what would once have seemed inescapable. At the same time reduced fertility in principle frees adults, particularly women, from family caring work, in that the burden of child rearing is (on the face of it) reduced. The need for care has shifted to the older end of the age spectrum. But care of elderly relatives is perhaps less of an imperative than care of one's young and may be more easily avoided.

What, however, has *not* changed? It is suggested here that many men and women still have positive ideals about ongoing sexual partnerships and relationships with children, and seek to make them a reality. The pursuit of these ideals in the face of institutionalised relationships which are clearly problematic is the impetus behind the flowering of many different relationship forms, including homosexual ones. Most people, it is argued, still seek companionship, affection, intimacy, support, security, reliability (a partner's fidelity but not necessarily their own?), to play a parental role, to have children to carry their identity into the future, and to appear as a public family unit. Individualism has not (yet) been carried to its ultimate conclusion. These social and psychological needs seem to be most readily met in a pair bond and parent–child nucleus of some kind. Interestingly, the British Social Attitudes Survey of 1993 (reported in the *Guardian*, 1 December 1993) found that only 12 per cent of respondents rated personal freedom above the companionship of marriage. And a study conducted by the European Values Group found that most Europeans' overwhelming moral commitment was to the family, although there was a growing reluctance to tolerate unsatisfactory marital relationships; people believed in the pursuit of personal happiness (Bakewell, 1993). Also, enough of the traditional patriarchal structures remain for women still to be drawn to men as a source of economic maintenance, and men to be drawn to women's servicing and giving of their unpaid labour (although to say this does imply that women and men having different and complementary roles rather than similar and parallel ones, and the *interdependence* of these roles are indeed part of the reason people seek out and stay with heterosexual partners). But it is suggested that the needs are expressed in, as it were, not just one 'attempt' at a relationship but many. There are perhaps many more partial and ambiguous relationships, and more fluid ones; there are more people who do not share their actual household with anyone else, but the basic search for relationship of some form continues.

The author's position on family change is on the whole discontinuitarian. Fundamental change *did* occur in the 1970s and 1980s (although the nature of change was somewhat different in these two decades), and relationships are now more tenuous than in the past. Yet individuals mostly appear to continue to seek some sort of close relationship, and a modified patriarchal framework is still in place. It would also be oversimplistic to assume that any change or trend is irreversible, or can be straightforwardly projected into the future. Divorce has not risen in a linear way over the decades, for example; it could in principle decline in the future. The same could occur with births outside marriage and cohabitations, the two most notable changes of the 1980s. Such reversals would, over time, reduce the number of single-parent families. Discontinuities have occurred, therefore, but they need not be permanent. On the other hand, new family forms altogether may appear.

On the significance of change, a quotation from B. J. Elliott (1991, P. 106) is useful:

> The identity of a family is now more diffuse as it is increasingly likely to undergo a series of transitions; metamorphoses involving both fission and fusion. This makes it more difficult to identify and follow the life cycle of a single family and necessitates focusing on the life histories of individuals instead, as they join and leave these more transitory family units.

That is, families as groups or units have a less continuous and defined identity; it is *individuals* we must track as they move from one relationship context to another. But perhaps the individuals have a less fixed identity as well?

This section has reviewed the issue of continuity and change in marriage and the family, and different viewpoints which may be taken; also, what (in the author's view) has and has not changed. A continuity and a change position have been outlined in relation to both the more distant and the more recent past. Positive or negative viewpoints may thus be taken of both continuity and change. Different positions on family change may be demonstrated by Figure 3.1.

Figure 3.1 Positions on family change

	Continuity	**Change**
Positive reaction	(1) Continuity recognised and welcomed (some neo-traditionalists)	(2) Change recognised and welcomed (some feminists; supporters of 'sexual revolution'?)
Negative reaction	(3) Continuity recognised and deplored (some feminists)	(4) Change recognised and deplored (most neo-traditionalists)

Broadly, neo-traditionalist writing tends either to welcome family continuity or, more usually, to recognise family change and deplore it. Feminist work, conversely, tends either to welcome some change in patriarchal structures, or to acknowledge and lament continuity.

The author's position is that in recent decades there *has* been fundamental family change, but that the importance of close relationships continues in a modified patriarchal framework. The weakening of patriarchy has made these relationships more fragile.

Chapter 4

Areas of Interaction between Family and State

Chapters 1 and 2 focused on family change, and Chapter 3 on continuity versus change. This chapter will consider the general area of interaction in Britain between families in their different forms, and the machinery of the state, concentrating on what is generally known as the 'welfare state': that is, mechanisms which act to offset some of the adverse effects of the market, and which attempt to provide citizens with employment, reasonable standards of living, minimum incomes and other minimum standards, and a range of services such as health, education and social care. The laws which the state makes to regulate family life will also be included. As most individuals live in a family *of some kind* (defining family broadly) at some stage of their lives, much of this state activity – even if directed at individuals – does in practice impinge on families; while some of it is specifically designed with families of various kinds in mind. The discussion will focus first on the state–family interaction in general, and then the different areas of interaction in the British context, including family law, incomes policy, housing policy, community care of adults, and child care. It will attempt to give an overview of the 'state of play' in recent policies affecting families. Key themes will be the assumptions about families which seem to be implicit in policy, and the influence which the law and the state have on families. The discussion will form a backdrop to the consideration of more generalised models of the family–state relationship in Chapter 5. Some specific questions relating to the notion of 'family policy' will then be addressed in Chapter 6.

State–family interaction: control and support

The early history of welfare measures in Britain shows an explicit interlinking with social control measures. The Poor Law of the nineteenth and early twentieth centuries not only attempted to avert civil disorder and enforce the work ethic, but it assumed a large number of genetic relatives would maintain each other, thus reducing the cost to the poor rates. Relief was administered in a deliberately deterrent fashion: for example, by requiring individuals (sometimes some members of a family but not all) to enter the workhouse. Early twentieth-century welfare improved the lot of specific groups and began to replace the Poor Law with other, less deterrent, systems; and the framework which developed after the Second World War and the Beveridge Report of 1942 was administered on rather easier terms and more generously. Until the repeal of the Poor Law in 1948 a large number of extended family members – third generations and collaterals such as brothers and sisters – were deemed responsible for maintaining each other. In the postwar period, the range of relatives liable to maintain a person who would otherwise be dependent on the state has been much narrower: spouses, cohabitees and parents of dependent children.

While the long-term trend until the 1980s was to shrink the range of family members financially responsible for each other, since then the range has *de facto* expanded, because of reductions and inadequacies in social security benefits. Most notable here is the reduction of benefits to those under 25, which puts pressure on their parents to help support them although not legally liable to do so, and the payment, through social security, of fees for independent sector residential and nursing homes which often did not meet the full amount charged. This latter policy in the 1980s and early 1990s put pressure on family members to top up payments even in the absence of a legal liability to do so. The scope of family responsibility also expanded under the *law*, through the Social Security Act 1990 and the Child Support Act 1991, which extended the liability of 'absent parents' to maintain both their children and the other parent. In contradiction to general twentieth-century trends in state welfare, then, these measures *broadened* the range of liable relatives deemed responsible for maintenance, extending the scope of *private* dependency and restricting dependency on state benefits.

State welfare systems, in the need to protect themselves from uncontrollable demand, embody rules which make assumptions about how people should behave in maintaining others for whom they are deemed responsible. The state, directly or indirectly, attempts to enforce this behaviour. Where society itself commonly recognises assumptions about family obligations, and about these coming into play *before* state obligations, then there are legal rules to ensure that this is the order of priorities. Problems arise where the assumptions that the state makes are not, or are no longer, in line with general societal perceptions of family relationships and obligations.

State–family interaction is never likely to be free of an element of coercion where state welfare is provided, because of the contested – and shifting – boundary between state and family responsibility, and the state's incentive to get the family to do more. There is an ideological divide between left and right here, with the right much more insistent then the left on the responsibility of family members for dependency. This area of ambiguity applies to cash income from the state versus maintenance by a relative, and to other kinds of care and help, and indeed to some extent to education and socialisation. Examples of contested and shifting boundaries, where both state and family are recognised as having some (but an unclear) degree of responsibility, would be the social care of the elderly, the care of children outside school (whether on a full-time or part-time basis), child socialisation and sex education.

Where family responsibilities are not 'properly' met, a number of state responses may come into play. These range from deploying direct punitive sanctions against family members (including the use of the criminal law, for example, to punish parents for their children's offences, or prosecutions for non-maintenance of dependants), through removal of dependent individuals from the family (notably children, but also perhaps older people), through deductions for maintenance from wages or benefits, to abandoning state responsibility on the assumption that family members will meet *their* 'responsibilities' (which sometimes means leaving dependent persons vulnerable to neglect, destitution, homelessness and so on).

Another mechanism by which the state defines family responsibility is by passing laws which regulate the membership of families and what family membership means. Most obviously this is done by the laws governing marriage and parenthood. It can also be argued that where the state bases policies on certain *assumptions* about how families operate, then these assumptions will be reinforced, whether or not they were correct in the first place, and whether or not they are deemed legitimate by the groups affected. For example, feminist writers on the welfare state have argued that assumptions about women's economic dependency on men in the tax and benefits systems have made it more difficult for women to escape that dependency, and assumptions about child care have made it difficult for women to reduce their amount of care. In other words, the assumptions are self-fulfilling prophecies. A more positive approach from the state is to offer a variety of forms of help and support to family members so that they are enabled to carry out their responsibilities (but without families feeling that they are no longer responsible at all).

The power of the state, then, can be deployed against families and family members, in an attempt to get them to behave in particular ways. The appearance of a 'welfare state' complicates, and perhaps makes more subtle, this relationship of power, but does not remove the underlying coercive base of the state–family interaction. However, much of the welfare state's activities may also be seen as actively assisting families and rendering family roles less burdensome than they were in earlier times. While the power to give and therefore withhold aid can indeed be used as a sanction, the value of this aid when given should not be overlooked. Obvious examples include state-provided free health care, assistance with the financial cost of rearing children, financial support for elderly and disabled family members, and free education (all of which were more the responsibility of charity, the private sector and the family in the past).

The roles and experience of women within families have been transformed by various health and welfare measures: childbirth is much less hazardous than it was and can be controlled; there are provisions for child health; children are at school for a large part of each day; the needs of elderly parents are provided for to some degree; and various divorce, income maintenance and housing provisions make it infinitely more possible than it was for women to escape or avoid marriage, or to live outside any confining family structure at all. There is a debate within feminism, however, about the ambiguity of state welfare measures for women; the state, while doing much that is helpful to women, remains largely male-controlled and can also oppress.

The experience of children is also markedly different in the late twentieth century from the past, due to the interventions of the welfare state. Children have more extensive, though certainly not foolproof, state protection against abuse and neglect; they experience free education at least up to 16 and possibly beyond; some income from the state is provided for them, although admittedly not paid directly to them. However, the state, as well as the family, also controls; there are rules about what children may or may not do at particular ages; up to a certain age they *must* attend school (or otherwise receive an appropriate education) and their labour market participation is restricted; and special systems come into play when they offend against these rules or against the general criminal law.

As far as men are concerned, the state has done much to undermine what may be described as 'private patriarchy' (see Walby, 1990): their control over 'their' women and children in the family. At the same time though, feminists rightly argue that much patriarchal power is *upheld*, intentionally or not, directly or not, by the various systems of the welfare state: for example, in the assumptions made about how family members should support each other. Men, of course, also benefit from welfare systems such as income maintenance, housing, health and social care; but they are less reliant on *state* systems because they have greater access to (often more favourable) alternative systems, such as occupational benefits and the private sectors of health and care (see, for example, Rose, 1981; Mann, 1992).

The state's attempts to both control and help, and the assumptions which it makes in so doing, influence families by putting constraints on them, by making certain courses of action easier and others more difficult, and by influencing the way family relationships are construed. However, the effect of state actions is never straightforwardly predictable, will not affect all families in the same way, and may actually be the opposite of what is intended. For example, policies designed to strengthen family links may in fact weaken them. Two contrasting ways in which this can happen are as follows: that by providing a certain amount of support and care to dependent individuals, the state may cause family members to withdraw; or, conversely, by attempting to *enforce* burdensome and unacceptable responsibilities on family members the state may cause individuals to evade them. The influence of policies on families is therefore not straightforward.

The area of family law will first be considered as an important means by which the state regulates families, in laying down ground rules for family formation and dissolution and for the rights and responsibilities which are incurred by various family roles. The main areas of welfare provision which affect families will then be considered from the point of view of family–state interaction, including incomes policy, housing policy, community care, child care and, more briefly, health and education services.

Family law

Dewar (1992, p. 1) comments on the definition of family law, saying that the term 'family' has no legal significance in itself, and the subject of family law 'usually comprises a mixed bag of legal rules and concepts, such as those concerned with marriage, divorce, parents and children and property, each possessing a different historical origin and pattern of development'. They all in some way concern the family, but Dewar is sceptical about the idea of family law as a coherent area of study because taking the family as a starting point, and looking at *all* areas of law relevant to it, would lead us to include a much wider area of law than 'family law' as interpreted. In addition, the family is itself, at least in part, a legal construct, and this also makes it difficult to arrive at a fixed definition of family law. Indeed the law itself is not a discrete social system, and just focusing on the law/legal system may be too narrow. In other words, there is a degree of arbitrariness in deciding what the field of family law should encompass. Similar problems of what to include/exclude arise with the delineation of the field of 'family policy'.

What will be considered briefly here, with particular emphasis on recent change, are the areas of law concerning marriage; divorce; cohabitation, in so far as the law has anything
to say about this; what was in the past termed child custody,
and related matters such as maintenance and access (the legal
terms for custody and access now being residence and contact); what was known as 'illegitimacy' (that is, births outside
marriage); adoption; equal opportunities legislation; and, more
briefly, homosexuality, abortion and reproductive technology.
In these areas the law regulates behaviour and status, using
various sanctions; equal opportunities law is included here for
its relevance for gender. Child care and child protection, involving local authority powers to remove and care for children
(public child care law), will be considered under a later section on child care.

Marriage

Although, as Dewar (1992) says, the legal distinction between
formal marriage and informal marriage or cohabitation is becoming blurred, and therefore marriage is losing its significance as a determinant of status, it is still surrounded by certain
formal rules, and has certain discernible legal effects. Formal
procedures are required before a marriage can be deemed to
have taken place; it can only be celebrated in certain places;
and it must be public and recorded. It is legally defined and
has to have certain required elements to be valid: it is 'a heterosexual and monogamous union to which the parties have
freely consented and in which they are able to enjoy at least a
minimum of a sexual relationship, between individuals who are
not related to each other in a certain number of ways, who
are of requisite capacity and who have complied with the necessary formalities' (Dewer, 1992, p. 38). It can be made void if
the required elements are not present; there are rules about
who may marry (at all) and who may marry whom. Being married makes a legal difference to the parties: it confers certain
rights and remedies (that is, a status). Marriage has consequences:
for example, for the right to maintenance/obligation to maintain, for property (particularly significant on divorce), inheritance (especially in intestacy cases), and children.

Of particular interest, since it is an area of change in the early 1990s, and has considerable significance for the implied nature of marriage, is the question of rape within marriage. Until the 1990s, while a husband could be liable to a charge of assault against his wife in certain circumstances, he was usually exempt from a charge of rape, this exemption deriving from the common law view that the wife in marrying was deemed to consent to sexual relations in a general sense: to 'all sexual demands made of her by her husband by virtue of the fact of marriage itself' (Dewar, 1992, p. 56) That is, a clear function of marriage was to provide men with sexual servicing. The scope of the rape exemption was, however, narrowed by court decisions in the 1980s which found that the husband could be charged with rape in certain circumstances (where there was a *decree nisi*, judicial separation, or non-molestation order, for example). But in 1990 the Law Commission recommended the removal of the exemption altogether, with the traditional view that the wife was deemed to give a *general* consent to intercourse now being seen as inconsistent with modern notions of marriage as a partnership of equals. And in 1991 the House of Lords held that the marital rape exemption was no longer part of the common law; again, modern marriage was seen as a partnership of equals, and the notion of consent to sex under all circumstances was seen as unacceptable. Dewar (1992) considers, however, that a change in statute law may also be necessary to give effect to this ruling.

Of interest also is the legal response to other forms of violence within marriage. While in previous centuries the use of physical force (within limits) by a husband against his wife was accepted as a legitimate extension of his authority (the 'rule of thumb', for example, reflected an eighteenth-century judge's opinion that to beat a wife with a stick no thicker than a thumb's width was allowable: see Pahl, 1985), the twentieth century has found physical violence between family members (not only of men against women, but of parents against children) increasingly unacceptable. Safeguards against assault by one's spouse have improved and proliferated in the later post-war period, with the possibility of injunctions to prevent an abusive spouse molesting their partner, and/or to force them to leave the matrimonial home. These may be accompanied by a power of arrest. Relevant legislation here includes the Domestic Violence and Matrimonial Proceedings Act 1976 and the Domestic Proceedings and Magistrates Court Act 1978. Criminal charges were also increasingly used, and police practice has improved in terms of readiness to regard domestic violence as indeed a criminal (and not just a private) matter. Refuges for women victims of domestic violence have developed within the voluntary sector since the 1970s.

Marriage, then, remains a specific legal status with rights and obligations, but has also changed, in a legal sense, over time. The most significant area of change is the greater protection for women as victims of rape or physical abuse, and the corresponding diminution of the rights of husbands to have sex with their wives without consent or to use physical force against them.

Divorce

The divorce law in Britain has been progressively 'liberalised' by means of a widening of the grounds, the lower standards of proof required for these grounds when the divorce is not defended, the extension of legal aid, and the loosening of the divorce process so that, as Dewar (1992) says, it is now an administrative rather than a judicial process, and comes close to divorce on demand of one of the parties. Divorce:

> refers not only to the formal legal termination of the relationship of marriage, but also to the process by which all aspects of the parties' relationship, such as money, property and children, are 'adjusted'. The overwhelming concern in modern divorce is with these matters, rather than with the formal legal issue of the fulfilment of the statutory grounds of divorce. (Dewar, 1992, p. 259)

So the law's concern is with *how* matters should be settled at divorce, not so much with whether divorce shall be granted at all. In reviewing current divorce law, the Law Commission (1988a, 1990) preferred divorce by 'process over time' after twelve months; this time would be used to resolve differences relating to property, finance and children, emphasising also mediation or conciliation. Such an approach was intended to eliminate the 'fault' basis of divorce. However, the proposals were not accepted by government, perhaps because they were seen as making divorce even 'easier'. Such an interpretation is questionable; Dewar (1992, p. 265) thinks that in some ways the process would have been made harder, although he admits that the proposed scheme 'marks the final withdrawal óf any normative or evaluative content from the divorce law', with a focus on managerial goals. Similar proposals were introduced by the Lord Chancellor in a Green Paper in 1993 (Lord Chancellor, 1993); but the position at the end of 1994 remains that 'irretrievable breakdown' must be demonstrated by either separation or one of three 'fault' grounds (desertion, adultery, unreasonable behaviour).

Most divorce petitions are not defended (that is, they are not legally fought by the respondent), and the procedure is straightforward. Legal aid is not available for undefended divorce; it *is* available in principle for defended cases (although in practice it may be difficult to obtain), and for ancillary matters. Where divorce is not appropriate a procedure for judicial separation exists, with the same specific grounds as for divorce, which also enables the settlement of ancillary matters such as children and property. The crucial difference is that it does not free the parties to remarry. This separation procedure is now little used.

In both divorce and separation, courts may make orders concerning the allocation of income and property. The present legal framework is embodied in the Matrimonial Causes Act 1973; prior to 1970 (and the Matrimonial Property and Proceedings Act), property entitlement in divorce was determined according to the ordinary principles of property law, and maintenance decisions were often influenced by parties' conduct and moral considerations. From 1970 the objective was to place the parties in the position in which they would have been had the marriage not broken down. This was later recognised as unrealistic where the assets sustaining one household were to be split between two, and the defensibility of continuing maintenance obligations after divorce was questioned (Dewar, 1992). The (English) Law Commission (1981) suggested greater self-sufficiency after divorce, and their proposals were embodied in the Matrimonial and Family Proceedings Act (MFPA) 1984, which restricted maintenance after divorce. Dewar (1992, p. 299) comments: 'since the introduction of the MFPA 1984, it has been statutory policy to discourage the use of spousal mainte-nance, although . . . the courts have sought to restrict the impact of this legislation'. There was an *increased* emphasis on support for children, and a *decreased* emphasis on support for the ex-wife in her own right (as opposed to as carer of the children).

As well as maintenance, lump sums or property can be allo-cated to one spouse, and the court can also order property to be sold. A number of orders are possible in dealing with the division of the owner-occupied matrimonial home; here: 'The objective is to ensure that . . . the parties are adequately re-housed' (Dewar, 1992, p. 330). The courts also have the power to transfer publicly or privately rented tenancies.

Divorce, then, like marriage, is regulated; but it has become increasingly easy to obtain, while the courts have focused more on the division of resources and the care of children post-divorce. Women have achieved greater equality in property mat-ters and (looking at a longer timescale) in the grounds for divorce, although their maintenance rights have diminished with corresponding effects on their income rights in retirement.

Cohabitation

Cohabitation under the law differs in certain important ways from marriage, although it is not completely unregulated by law. Dewar (1992, p. 62) comments: 'The attitude of English law has been to leave the parties to their rights and remedies as individuals rather than as bearers of a special status.' That is, cohabitees have not shared the special status of the mar-ried. Cohabitees are not obliged to maintain each other under private family law (but they *are* expected to do so under social security law, although this obligation cannot be formally en-forced). They *are* liable to maintain their children, under the Children Act 1989, and now the Child Support Act 1991. The procedures available to married couples to resolve disputes about money and property are not available to cohabitees; they must rely on the general law of property. But cohabitees, unlike married couples, *can* make enforceable contracts governing property and finance, and may also use conveyances and declarations of trust 'to achieve a finality as to their property ownership which is not available to married couples, since a divorce court has complete discretion to review the divorcing couple's needs and resources and distribute property and income accordingly' (Dewar, 1992, p. 61). So in a sense the cohabiting couples have greater control over their arrangements. The unmarried mother, but not the unmarried father, even if cohabiting, has automatic parental responsibility for a child, although the father may obtain it by a court order or agreement with the mother. Cohabitees do not have the same pension rights, inheritance rights or occupation rights in relation to the family home, that married people have.

However, there are some rights which have been extended to cohabitees, such as succession to tenancies and inheritance in certain circumstances, and the right to have orders made to restrain violence. Otherwise they must fall back on the general law of tort, general intestacy rules and the law of property and contract. Not all the legislation relating to domestic violence applies to them as it does to married couples. Cohabitees thus are less regulated by the law overall. Homosexual cohabitation is not specifically regulated at all and parties must fall back on the general law (Dewar, 1992).

There is a debate as to whether the legal regulation associated with marriage should be extended to cohabitation, or whether change should go the other way, 'deregulating' marriage. As Dewar notes, however, *parenthood* is becoming the increasingly important determinant of rights and responsibilities in the 'new' family law, which is more concerned with economic reality than legal status.

So the legal situation on cohabitation remains somewhat ambiguous, although the law has made some strides in catching up with social change. It is not necessarily the case that women's interests are more safeguarded in cohabitation than in marriage, and indeed they may be less so.

Children in private family law

Under the Children Act 1989 married parents (and unmarried mothers) automatically have 'parental responsibility' in relation to their children, with the emphasis on responsibility rather than on rights. This responsibility cannot be voluntarily surrendered or transferred (that is, without a court order), and it continues after divorce; parenthood, with its various obligations, is increasingly seen as 'for life'. Unmarried fathers can acquire parental responsibility through a court order or formal agreement (Section 4 of the Children Act 1989). Under the Child Support Act 1991 they have a liability to maintain whether they have parental responsibility or not (which may seem anomalous). Parental responsibility can also be shared between a number of parties. As Dewar (1992) stresses, it is parenthood rather than marriage that is now likely to have a significant effect on the rights and responsibilities of family members. Dewar (1992, p. 109) comments: 'The concept of parental responsibility . . . reflects, in part, a change in thinking about the legal relationship between parents and children that became prominent during the 1970s and 1980s. Instead of conferring rights, parenthood was increasingly seen as a status which facilitated the protection of children's interests . . . The idea was well-captured by the notion of a trust.' So rights were to be exercised in children's, not parents', interests. 'Children's rights' have become increasingly dominant as a concept, and this may signal a transformation in the distribution of power between children and parents. This could well be the trend for the future (see Harding, 1993).

The Children Act 1989 is an important watershed in the development of legal concepts of parenthood, dealing as it does with private family law as well as the relationship between parents, children and state intervention. The private law parts of the Act were the result of a Law Commission inquiry which produced a report in 1988 (Law Commission, 1988b). An important principle embodied in the Act is that of 'non-intervention' (Section 1 :5). This lays down that the court should not make any order unless positively convinced that it is better than *not* making an order. The emphasis is on parents and other relevant parties reaching agreement between themselves, rather than resorting to the court. Nevertheless, orders can still be made under Section 8, relating to the child's place of residence, contact with specific individuals, specific issues, or steps which are prohibited without consent of the court. These replace the former custody, care and control, and access orders. The child may apply for a Section 8 order if the court is satisfied that this is appropriate in the light of her or his own understanding, and it was applications by children for (in particular) residence orders to live other than with a biological parent which caught the attention of the media in the early 1990s (see Harding, 1993).

The question of legitimacy versus illegitimacy is another aspect of private child law. These specific terms are no longer in legal use since the Family Law Reform Act 1987 (which followed three Law Commission reports in 1979, 1982 and 1986) came into force in 1989; this Act is modified and re-enacted by the Children Act 1989. Prior to this, the concepts of legitimacy/illegitimacy embodied the distinction between children born in and outside marriage, and constituted one way in which marriage was of considerable legal significance. Children could also be legitimated by the *subsequent* marriage of their parents, or through legal adoption, from 1926. The legitimate/illegitimate distinction had its roots in the need to have clear rules of inheritance (Hoggett, 1980) and to uphold particular standards of sexual morality and the institution of patriarchal marriage. The common law regarded the child born out of marriage as *filius nullius*; the child's position was severely disadvantaged and stigmatised. The approach was especially punitive in the latter part of the nineteenth century and the early part of the twentieth.

The position is now dramatically different. The disadvantages of illegitimacy were reduced by a number of Acts prior to 1987; for example, the Affiliation Proceedings Act 1957 (mainly concerned with maintenance); the Family Law Reform Act 1969 (mainly to do with inheritance); and the Guardianship of Minors Acts 1971 and 1973 (dealing with custody and other disputes). These made the situation of the illegitimate child less 'different', less disadvantaged. In the 1980s, following the various Law Commission reports, there were debates about bringing the legal situation of unmarried fathers and their children further into line with marriage. The Family Law Reform Act 1987, as amended by the Children Act 1989, does not give unmarried fathers quite the same status as married fathers (this was the Law Commission's original proposal, but it met with

various criticisms). The Act represents rather an attempt to
remove legal disadvantages from formerly illegitimate *children*,
rather than from the fathers. The position of those born out
of marriage is now very close to those born inside marriage,
with a few differences which relate to succession to titles and
citizenship. The position of unmarried fathers remains different from the married in that they do not have automatic parental responsibility. But under the Children Act they can achieve
it by order or by agreement with the mother under Section 4;
they can also apply for a Section 8 order for residence, contact and so on; and wherever the Children Act refers to a
'parent', that indicates an unmarried father whether he has
acquired parental responsibility or not.

Prior to the Family Law Reform Act 1987, maintenance for
the out-of-wedlock child could only be obtained under the Affiliation Proceedings Act 1957 (a procedure which carried various problems and restrictions). The 1987 Act replaced this with
new proceedings under the Guardianship of Minors Act 1971,
with these in turn being replaced by Schedule 1 of the Children Act. The maintenance position became very similar to
that relating to children and divorcing parents. The relevant
legislation is now the Child Support Act 1991, which makes no
distinction between children born in and out of marriage in
terms of liability to maintain. A parent does not have to have
parental responsibility to be deemed liable. For children born
in marriage, child maintenance before the Child Support Act
could be paid as a result of a private agreement, or enforced
under a court order in divorce or separation proceedings. The
Child Support Act now replaces all other means of *enforcing*
maintenance, for all children, with its own procedures (see,
for example, Dewar, 1992; Garnham and Knights, 1993). Under
this Act a fixed formula is applied which results in *more* being
demanded of most absent parents, and an Agency has been
set up to calculate and enforce payment. Compulsory maintenance is out of the hands of the courts except for a few specific
matters, such as disputes about paternity. The Agency has a
range of sanctions it can deploy in the process of enforcing
payment. The full effects of the Act are not yet known, but
two features which can be stressed are the tougher approach
being adopted to parental responsibility in a financial sense,

and the inescapability of this however tenuous the relationship between the biological parents of the child. The Act caused a storm of protest by absent fathers when it began to come into force in 1993. (For the effects of the Act, see, for example, Garnham and Knights, 1994.)

The question of access by an absent parent to their children was settled under separation or divorce legislation or the Guardianship of Minors Act prior to the Children Act 1989. Under the Children Act there is a presumption of non-intervention, with parents being expected to make their own arrangements; but, failing this, the Act has orders available under Section 8 for what is now called 'contact' by the parents. The guiding principle is still the child's welfare. In principle maintenance and contact are supposed to be separate issues. The Children Act deals with contact, the Child Support Act with maintenance; and the payment of maintenance does not imply any 'rights' to contact. One of the reservations about the Child Support Act, however, is that absent parents compelled to pay maintenance, or more maintenance, would demand contact more aggressively, which is not necessarily in the child's interests.

Reference may be made briefly to the legal process of adoption. Dating from an Act in 1926, the adoption process enables the full status of parenthood to be irrevocably transferred by means of a court order, with safeguards built in for the welfare of the child and for the consent of the original birth parent(s) (usually in practice the mother only, as most children given up for adoption were until the 1970s infants born out of marriage). Ever since the beginning of legal adoption, however, there has been provision for *dispensing* with consent under certain conditions, so adoption *could* take place against the biological parent's will.

Prior to the first Adoption Act informal 'adoptions' took place but had no standing under the law; and, unless the case were covered by some other part of child welfare legislation dating from the late nineteenth century (for example, the Custody of Children Act 1891), birth parents retained their rights and could reclaim the children. Thus legal adoption put the position of non-parental caretakers on a secure footing; and it was usual for the process to sever relationship and contact with the biological parent(s) altogether. Subsequent acts since 1926 have elaborated the procedure of adoption further, facilitating it in some ways, although regulating it more closely. Changes have occurred in adoption practice, notably the increased adoption of older children, and the reduced availability of babies, because of changes already discussed involving the easing of the position of unmarried mothers (see, for example, C. R. Smith, 1984).

At the time of writing a review of adoption law has been published and is being considered by government (Department of Health, 1992 and 1993). The new approach favours a less exclusive form of adoption, emphasising the benefits of contact between adopted children and their biological parents so that after adoption contact would not necessarily be lost (as it was in most cases in the middle decades of the century). More openness has been a trend in adoption practice in the 1980s and 1990s. These proposals remain an area for debate, however (see Dewar, 1992).

Further complications are introduced into the legal definition of parent–child relationships by various reproductive technologies and surrogate motherhood. These developments complicate the decision as to who is a 'parent' in a full legal sense, and in particular as to who is a *mother* (the question of who is a father has always been more problematic). This is an area where the law has had difficulties in catching up with the complexities produced by new methods of procreation, although some progress has been made (see below).

The law has extensively regulated parent–child relationships, and increasingly so where children are born out of marriage. Looking at a longer timescale, two trends have been noticeable: greater equality for women as parents, and greater protection for the welfare and rights of children. More recently, there has been an emphasis on parents making their own arrangements without recourse to the courts, and (under various provisions of the Children Act 1989) on children asserting their own rights independently: for example, by taking legal action on their own behalf. However the law still perceives children as being in need of special protection. Another recent emphasis is on parents' *responsibilities* rather than their rights, and particularly in the financial sense (under the Child Support Act 1991). This emphasis is almost regardless of the type of relationship between the two biological parents.

Equal opportunities law

Although not part of family law as strictly defined, a cluster of measures with considerable significance for gender may be briefly referred to here. These are the Equal Pay Act 1970 (implemented in 1975), the Sex Discrimination Act 1975, and the Employment Protection Act 1976. The Equal Pay Act made wage discrimination between workers of equal 'worth' (that is, doing the same work) illegal, but did not tackle differences between male and female labour market experience, such as differences in hours of work, training, work experience and so on (Lewis, 1992). The Act does, nevertheless, appear to have had a slight impact on the male–female earnings differential in the mid-1970s (Joshi, 1989). The Sex Discrimination Act outlawed discrimination on grounds of gender in employment, education, the provision of goods and services and so on (but not in social security and tax), and covered both direct and indirect discrimination: that is, where conditions are imposed which make it more difficult for one sex to comply, as well as explicit discrimination against one sex (Lewis, 1992). The Employment Protection Act provided for a minimum amount of paid maternity leave and right to re-instatement in employment for up to 29 weeks after the birth. In 1983 the Equal Pay Act was amended to bring it in line with European Community regulations, whereby a woman could show that her work was of equal value to that of a man in the same establishment doing a different job, although 'material difference' might mean that her argument for equal pay was still not accepted (Lewis, 1992).

While widely criticised as inadequate, these measures have had some effect in protecting women's formal rights in the public sphere and in reducing gender inequality. However, as Lewis comments (1992, p. 119): 'The legislation assumed that the position of women in the labour market is susceptible to improvement by treating like individuals equally. It did not address the broader issue of systemic inequality arising from the unequal division of unpaid work and the fact that a majority of women workers enter the labour force on different terms from men.' In other words, 'equal treatment' in a formal sense is hardly sufficient to achieve equality.

Other areas: homosexuality, abortion, and reproductive technology

In the fields of homosexuality and reproduction a general trend to liberalisation of the law may be noted, associated with what Weeks (1981, 1985) has called the 'permissive moment' of the 1960s. Following the Wolfenden report of 1957 on homosexual offences and prostitution, the law on homosexuality was changed with the 1967 Sexual Offences Act, which legalised homosexual acts between consenting male adults in private (homosexual behaviour between women had never been illegal). 'Adult' in this context meant aged 21 and over, and the age barrier remained at 21 despite the subsequent reduction of the age of majority to 18, until the 1990s. In 1994 Parliament lowered the homosexual age of consent to 18 (still two years higher than for heterosexual consent). Weeks (1981, p. 267) comments on the 1967 Act: 'Homosexual law reform did not legalise homosexuality as such; it narrowly decriminalised certain aspects of male adult behaviour in private, in England and Wales.' In fact, prosecutions for homosexual offences *increased* after the Act.

In the area of abortion, the 1967 Abortion Law (Amendment) Act made termination of pregnancy legal up to 28 weeks gestation under certain conditions. These were: a risk to the woman's life or of injury to her mental or physical health which was greater with continuation of the pregnancy than if the pregnancy were terminated, or a substantial risk that the baby would be born seriously handicapped. Account could be taken of the woman's environment and her existing children. The agreement of two doctors was normally required, and thus access to abortion was effectively determined by medical discretion, and became in practice variable in different parts of the country, although there was a general rise in abortions after the Act (Greenwood and Young, 1976). Despite numerous attempts over the years via private members' bills, abortion law has not been made more restrictive again, with the exception of the reduction in the upper time limit from 28 to 24 weeks in 1990 under the Human Fertilisation and Embryology Act (in recognition of the increased possibility of viability in foetuses of this age).

Reproductive technology and 'unorthodox' means of reproduction were the subject of the Warnock Report of 1984 on human fertilisation and embryology (Warnock, 1984), which paved the way (after a White Paper in 1987) for the Human Fertilisation and Embryology Act 1990. There was concern about the development of technology in reproduction such as egg or embryo donation and *in vitro* fertilisation, which confuses the issue of who are the 'parents' of a child (see Harding, 1987; Stanworth, 1987). There was also a concern about other practices which blur questions of parenthood, such as sperm donation and 'surrogate motherhood' (whereby a woman carries a man's child with the intention of handing it over to him and his partner). *Commercial* surrogacy was banned by the Surrogacy Arrangements Act 1985. The Human Fertilisation and Embryology Act 1990 enabled *married* 'commissioning parents' in a surrogacy arrangement to obtain a 'parental order' in respect of the children born to the surrogate mother (Section 30): this was the functional equivalent of adoption. The Act also stated that a woman *carrying* a child from a donated egg or gametes was normally to be treated as the legal mother (Dewar, 1992). Thus full legal parenthood may be achieved in some cases by individuals who are not necessarily the genetic, or automatically the legal, parents of the child.

In a sense individual freedom was enlarged by these various acts, and the state's restrictive regulation of sexuality and reproductive behaviour reduced. However, homosexuality continues to be regulated in a different way from heterosexuality. The age of sexual consent remains different, and the provisions governing heterosexual marriage and cohabitation do not apply to homosexual partners. Abortion is not available 'on demand' and may be quite difficult to obtain, dependent on the attitude of individual doctors, and on whether a woman can afford to use the private sector. The use of reproductive technology and surrogate motherhood as means of achieving parenthood in a full legal sense has been eased, but remains subject to considerable state regulation, indeed, in some ways the 1990 Act *elaborated* the regulation by introducing more control over infertility treatments and embryo experimentation, for example. Only *married* commissioning parents can obtain a parental order under this Act. Furthermore, all these areas are the subject of debate and controversy, and those who take a traditionalist or 'moral lobby' position on family change would wish to see greater restriction re-instated (see, for example, Durham, 1991).

Assumptions and influence in family law

A useful comment on family law comes from Dewar (1992, p. 71).

> There is now less emphasis on the exclusivity of the legal status of marriage and evidence of a move towards constructing status-like relationships around new organising concepts. The primary aim, it was argued, is to construct a set of legal-economic relations among family members that are clearly demarcated from, and thereby reduce the financial burden on, the state. In this process, the legal concept of marriage is logically, and is *de facto* becoming, redundant.

In other words, family law is moving towards the construction of a number of status-like relationships to prevent a drain on the state. The concern about the financial burden on the state is clear in the Child Support Act, which attempts to redefine family relationship, so that the increased dependence on the state which has resulted from shifts in patterns of sexual and parental relationships is thrown into reverse. This is clearly more important to the state than matters of legal status, let alone sexual morality. Government has now accepted, as social reality, sequential marriage and reproduction out of marriage.

The law embodies certain assumptions, indeed, it makes them explicit. Marriage is monogamous in the sense you can have only one spouse at any one time, but is terminable under what are now (in practice) quite wide conditions. Married parents have both responsibilities and rights in relation to their children and each other; the position of parents not married to each other has increasingly converged with the married parent–child relation. Certain rights and responsibilities remain after divorce, in respect of spouses and, more particularly, children. Parent–child relationships are primarily defined by biology, but are not wholly dependent on biology since they can be artificially created, in a legal sense, through a 'parental order' and through adoption; although adoption seems to be moving away from an attempt to exclude genetic relatives altogether. The financial responsibilities of parenthood are increasingly stressed. Spouses and children have certain claims in inheritance, so some rights and responsibilities continue after death. Heterosexual cohabitation does not have the same legal status as marriage, but is not altogether unregulated, and is moving closer to the status of marriage. In a sense individuals have the law's assumptions imposed on them, on pain of some kind of penalty (for example, for bigamy or non-maintenance), or because of the sheer impossibility of getting the law as it stands to behave in any other way (for example, homosexual partners cannot marry). However, laws can change, and have indeed changed over time. The divorce, homosexuality and abortion laws are striking examples. There is also a huge area of *interpretation* of the law; the law itself often states only broad principles such as the welfare of the child. Courts have discretion to apply the law in particular cases, and here individuals may influence the law's operation and effects.

In a sense, then, the law does promote a particular family form; but the influence of the law on families is complex and is, broadly, to set up a number of constraints and possibilities. Certain courses of action are allowed, encouraged or compelled, while others are prohibited, punished or disadvantaged. Within this framework, however, there is a degree of latitude *as far as the law is concerned* as to how people live out their family relationships until a formal termination of relationship occurs. Laws may influence ideology about family life, although not in a straightforward way, and this uncertain relationship between law and ideology enters the debate when change in the law is proposed, because it may be either wished or not wished to change people's ideas, values and assumptions through change in the law. It may be argued that people receive 'signals' from the law about what is or is not socially acceptable; the law may thus act to influence further change. For example, the virtual ending of the legal disadvantage suffered by the one-time 'illegitimate' may send a strong message that births outside marriage are no longer a socially disapproved pattern. However, ideological messages are contested and subject to challenge and change.

Incomes policy and families

Two aspects which should be considered here are taxation of incomes and the provision of a cash income from the state through the social security system. While these aspects of government policy have been administered separately – and tax reliefs have not been regarded as a part of public expenditure – both systems have a role in maintaining, or indeed decreasing, family incomes. While social security provides a direct cash income, taxation determines how much of nominally received income, earned or otherwise, can be retained. (For a good recent source on social security relevant to families, see Baldwin and Falkingham, 1994.)

Taxation

Income tax has treated married couples as a unit since the system was first introduced at the end of the eighteenth century, with the married man receiving a tax allowance in acknowledgement of the supposed situation of 'having a wife to support', regardless of the wife's actual resources or dependency. A wife was regarded as a dependent solely because she was a wife. The wife's income was regarded as part of her husband's for the purposes of taxation, and he was required to make a return and pay tax on it, until relatively recent times. The continued treatment of married couples as one unit for tax purposes, with that one being the husband, constitutes an intriguing survival of a set of essentially Victorian assumptions into the latter half of the twentieth century. Wives were granted an earned income allowance of their own only during the First World War, which was then reduced in the inter-war years, but became equal to the single person's allowance during the Second World War (Robinson, 1989). Without such an allowance, all their income was liable to tax, the husband's allowances being deemed to relate to both of them. Robinson (1989, p. 60) comments: 'When married women are wanted in the workforce they are offered more generous personal allowances against tax, when they are not wanted they are treated less generously than other individuals.' A separate allowance for earning wives, along with the married man's allowance, also

meant that two-earner couples were treated favourably relative
to one-earner couples.

The possibility of separate taxation of earned income was
not introduced until the early 1970s. This enabled high income couples to avoid the higher bands of tax while forfeiting
the married man's allowance. Full independent taxation, with
separate treatment of *un*earned income and greater privacy
for wives in their tax affairs, did not arrive until 1990. Wives
were not formally responsible for completing their own tax
returns until this time; they had not usually received communi-
cations from the Inland Revenue relating to their tax affairs
(these had usually been addressed to the husband: see Robinson,
1989).

Married women could claim the married man's allowance in
the place of their husband only if he was not in employment,
or too poorly paid to benefit from it himself; this was paid for
the full tax year regardless of change of circumstances. The
renamed married couple's allowance, which was instituted in
1990, did not have even this flexibility, but reverted to the
husband immediately he had sufficient earned income to benefit from it in whole or part. (This change also altered a rather
intriguing anomaly whereby wife earner-only couples had benefited from more tax allowance – the wife's earned income
allowance plus the married man's allowance – than husband
earner-only couples.) Therefore, from 1990 (to 1993) there was
no right of choice for couples, or even for men acting independently, as to which partner should claim the allowance; it
might be more beneficial if the man's earnings were irregular
for the wife to claim permanently, but the system did not allow this. However, this rule was again changed in 1993 (possibly due partly to the amount of administrative work the 1990
rules must have created for the Inland Revenue) when couples
could choose which of them should claim the married allowance, or split it between them, thus allowing more equality.
(The allowance had, however, been frozen since 1990: see Child
Poverty Action Group, 1992a.)

Movement towards treatment of married women as separate
units has therefore been very gradual. Even post-1993, an allowance for *being married* continued, and it might be anticipated that this would usually be claimed by the man. There

has been pressure over a number of years, particularly from the Child Poverty Action Group, for abolition of this allowance and redistribution of the cash raised through social security benefits such as Child Benefit. This would leave childless couples worse off, however, and intensify hardship for some low-income couples.

A tax allowance worth the same as the married allowance payable to single parents was introduced in 1976. Known as the additional personal allowance, it was created to meet the costs of running a single-parent household, which are very similar to those of a two-parent family, but must be met by only one breadwinner who is also the only resident carer. This change was in response to campaigns on behalf of single parents in the 1970s. From 1988 the allowance could only be claimed where there was indeed just one adult/parent in the household, and could no longer be claimed where two single parents were cohabiting. (This allowance was also frozen from 1990.)

Tax relief on mortgage interest payments has been an important subsidy to owner-occupiers. Cohabiting and married couples were treated differently until 1988, in that each partner in a cohabiting relationship (but not in a marriage) could claim separate tax relief on mortgage interest payments, thus doubling the ceiling up to which this relief could be claimed. This gave a distinct financial advantage to cohabiting house purchasers, or indeed any non-married copurchasers. After 1988, however, the ceiling on mortgage relief was applied to the *property*, rather than to each purchaser individually, thus removing the non-married copurchasers' advantage. Mortgage interest relief is now split between copurchasers, married or not.

These rules, which allowed two single parents together to claim a tax allowance each, and which allowed cohabitees to claim mortgage tax relief separately, had been felt to discriminate unfairly against the married and two-parents units. This was certainly the effect, if not the intention. The changes in the late 1980s removed the advantages that parents and couples outside marriage had experienced.

Another form of tax allowance relevant to families was the child allowance. Re-introduced by Lloyd George in 1909 (an early form of it had existed a century before), this was paid according to the number of children, again to the married man, and initially to those at the lower end of the income scale. The amounts were not large at first, but the principle was established. In the 1960s and 1970s (and indeed well before this: J. Brown, 1988, refers to a Royal Commission in 1920) arguments were raised in favour of amalgamating this allowance with the cash benefit paid for second and subsequent children since 1946, known as Family Allowance. The argument was that poorer families below the tax threshold could not benefit from the child tax allowance, but *would* benefit from an increased cash payment. This integration was achieved, with some difficulty, in the Child Benefit Act 1975 (implemented 1977–79: see Field, 1982). Child Benefit, which incorporated the child tax allowance, will be discussed separately below as a cash payment belonging with the social security system. While child tax allowance had usually benefited fathers in families, Child Benefit – like Family Allowance before it – was normally paid to mothers.

The taxation system has allowed for family responsibilities in the shape of allowances paid (normally) to the married man, reflecting the concept of wives and children as dependants. While only those over the tax threshold benefit from these, during the post-war decades the tax threshold has dropped markedly, so these allowances have come to be of widespread significance. The privileging of marriage is noticeable in the married allowance, but not in Child Benefit, the additional personal allowance or mortgage interest relief.

Child Benefit

The new Child Benefit of 1977 took the form of a larger cash benefit, now payable for the first child as well as for others, unlike the old Family Allowance of 1946–77, but payable, like Family Allowance, to *mothers*; the child tax allowance from which fathers had benefited ceased to exist, being phased out between 1977 and 1979. There was an also an extra cash amount paid – although not on a per child basis – to single parents, in response to pressure for better benefits for this group in the 1970s. This was known initially as Child Benefit Increase and later as One Parent Benefit. The switch to a single cash benefit for children involved a redistribution of resources from fathers to mothers, and it was this redistributive aspect, and the feared male reaction (particularly from trade unions at a time of wage restraint), which almost caused the scheme to founder (see, for example, Field, 1982; J. Brown, 1988). The larger cash benefit, paid to all those with dependent children, benefited those without earnings sufficient to take up the child tax allowance, and indeed this had been one of the main arguments for merging the two benefits. However, those below the tax threshold had been a diminishing group because of the fall of this threshold in relation to earnings.

Child Benefit remains a central cash benefit in the state's financial support of all dependent children. It is universal in that it is paid for all such children, not being dependent on either a record of insurance contributions or a test of means. However, the amount of Child Benefit *is* deducted from the safety net means-tested benefit for those not in (full-time) work – that is Income Support – leaving families on this benefit no better off. The benefit is very small in relation to the total cost of keeping a child (£10.20 for the first child, £8.25 for others, plus £6.15 additionally for single parents in 1994), and at various periods in the past it has been held behind inflation. In the 1950s and 1960s, for example, Family Allowance lost in real value; in the 1980s Child Benefit also did so, and in fact the cash value of the benefit was frozen for the three years 1988–90 inclusive (before a modest rise in 1991, and a commitment to index-link the payment in 1992). Nonetheless, Child Benefit is unique in that it recognises the cost of rearing children *unconditionally*, and, though small, it is an essential element in the incomes of many mothers. Various government plans to abolish it at different times have repeatedly been fought, and not just by women on the left; for example, the Conservative Women's Association has supported the principle of Child Benefit payable to mothers.

Other child and dependants' payments

Other cash benefits are also paid in respect of children. Most National Insurance benefits, based on a record of contributions and payable for certain contingencies such as sickness, maternity, invalidity, retirement and unemployment, since their inception and until the 1980s included a certain amount for dependent children (as did some of their precursors in the pre-war period); they have also included an amount for wives (but not for husbands except in certain defined circumstances). The practice of paying dependants' additions was based on the principle, embodied by the Beveridge Report, that National Insurance benefits were intended to provide a subsistence level income, and the costs of subsistence rose with the number of 'dependants'. In practice, National Insurance benefits did not reach anything like a subsistence level for all who claimed them, and were overtaken by the level of basic means-tested subsistence benefit intended as a fall-back for those not in work, National Assistance. Where National Insurance payments did *not* bring claimants to the Assistance level, National Assistance, later Supplementary Benefit, was also paid as a supplement.

In the 1980s the principle of dependants' additions was significantly eroded for short-term National Insurance benefits. The children's additions with Unemployment Benefit, for example, were phased out by 1984, although the wife's addition remained. In 1983 short-term Sickness Benefit was reorganised and 'privatised' in that it was paid by employers for the first six weeks, with (at first complete) reimbursement from the government through reduction in employers' National Insurance contributions. The benefit was now known as Statutory Sick Pay. But the additions for wives and children were dropped. In 1986 the employers were made to pay for the full 26 weeks of the benefit's life. Reimbursement dropped to 80 per cent in 1992 and to nil for some employers in 1993. Maternity allowance – a National Insurance benefit for women in the latter stages of pregnancy and for a short period after the birth – was 'privatised' in a similar way in 1987, and the children's additions were lost.

With the long-term National Insurance benefits – that is, widow's benefits, retirement pension and Invalidity Benefit – the dependants' additions remained in place. Again these included payments for children, and usually for wives rather than husbands. (Retirement pensions for a spouse based on a working spouse's contribution record are not paid for a *husband* unless he has been *incapable* of work.)

Additional amounts for dependants were also paid from 1948

with National Assistance, following the tradition of public assistance before 1948 and Poor Law outdoor relief before that. In this case, where the benefit was a minimum safety net, recognised by government as a 'floor' for those not in (full-time) work, the logic was that the amount should cover the minimum needs of each individual. The *adequacy* of the amount is clearly a matter of dispute, and the original calculation of need, particularly for children, had a dubious basis which has never been fully put right (see Field, 1978; J. Brown, 1988). Under various circumstances, such as when deductions are made, or in 'voluntary unemployment', an income which is below this basic level may be paid. But where the principle of subsistence is recognised, along with the interdependency of family members, then the logic is that an amount is paid for each member (family being defined here as the couple plus their children still in education).

National Assistance was renamed Supplementary Benefit in 1966, and Income Support in 1988, with certain changes to the benefits being made on each occasion, but the principle of dependants' additions was maintained. While the assumption had been that in a husband–wife (or cohabiting) couple the male would claim for the woman and the children, modifications to this principle appeared in the 1980s. At first, in 1983, in line with an EC directive, the female partner could claim for the couple/family unit under certain stringent conditions, and then, from 1988 the woman could claim on the same terms as the man although, as it was for the couple to decide, this meant that the man was in a position to influence (veto?) the decision.

Other means-tested benefits carrying dependants' additions or allowances on the same sort of principle include Family Income Supplement, introduced in 1970 and becoming Family Credit in 1988, which is a benefit for families in full-time work (as this is defined, and the definition has varied) but on low wages; Disability Working Allowance, a benefit based on a similar principle but not restricted to those with children, introduced in 1992 for the disabled in work but on low wages; and Housing Benefit.

Means-tested benefits, then, tend to include additions for 'dependants': that is, partners (usually wives) and children. Some

National Insurance benefits still carry such additions, but not all. The principle of family responsibility is partially recognised, more so in means-tested benefits which function as a 'safety net' when other income sources fail.

This section has not discussed private and occupational benefits (that is, those deriving from for-profit companies and employers' schemes) but the importance of these for better-off groups should be noted. Some of the benefits in this sector include allowances for dependants.

Maternity benefits

Maternity benefits have been mentioned above, and will be referred to briefly again. Under the National Insurance scheme a maternity grant, a one-off lump sum, was claimable on a husband's contribution record, or on the woman's own. In 1988 this grant was abolished, although women on Income Support or Family Credit could now make a claim from the Social Fund. A maternity allowance (that is a benefit payable on a weekly basis for a period of time before and after the birth) was claimable only on the woman's own record. Greater rights to maternity pay from an *employer* were enshrined in the Employment Protection Act 1976. The National Insurance maternity allowance became in most cases an employer-administered benefit in 1987. This was now known as Statutory Maternity Pay. Various conditions, including length of service, surround employer benefits. Benefits for pregnancy and the period after childbirth are inadequate, reflecting the assumption that women have the support of a male partner. If all else fails, however, Income Support is available to a woman without a partner or other resources in the latter stages of pregnancy and once she is a mother. In the early stages of pregnancy she must normally show herself 'available for work' in order to claim this benefit.

Assumptions and influence in incomes policy

The first point to be drawn from this brief review of income maintenance provisions in relation to families is that government does recognise up to a point (and has in fact recognised since the Poor Law) the legitimacy of certain family claims.

Indeed, as government also negatively recognises and sometimes attempts to enforce the *duties* of family members to support each other (rather than being supported by the state), it
is only logical that when a family member claims benefit, their
duty to support their dependants should be *positively* recognised by the payment of an additional amount for those dependants (having said which, government policy does not always
adhere to this sort of logic!).

The spouse–parent–child unit is recognised, and to some
extent treated as one; so there is an assumption that it is a
unit of consumption in which resources are shared, but that
more extended family units, even if coresident, are not economic units bound by such mutual obligations. For income tax
the unit has been the nuclear family, but with children's *incomes* on the whole treated separately (apart from a brief period in the 1970: see Robinson, 1989). With the ending of child
tax allowances in the late 1970s, the unit for tax purposes was
clearly only the husband and wife. Here the assumptions about
the identification of spouses in one unit might be seen as ar-
chaic, but with recent moves towards more independent treatment, the tax unit is becoming much more the individual (except
that the married couple's allowance remains).

Nuclear family members may also claim benefits independently: for example husband and wife may independently be
entitled (if both have contributed) to certain National Insurance benefits, or to non-contributory disability benefits. The
independent entitlement of wives to contributory benefits has
been an increasing trend as, first, women joined the labour
market in increasing numbers, and second, they began to pay
a full National Insurance contribution rather than the 'married woman's' lower rate introduced by the Beveridge plan.
The latter option was decreasingly favoured, and in 1977 was
abolished for new entrants to the workforce. It will be less and
less the case, therefore, that those married women who work
above the minimum threshold to contribute to National Insurance will lack entitlement in their own right. However, many
married women *do* work below the qualifying threshold (in terms
of hours and/or income), and *are* therefore excluded from
the scheme as beneficiaries in their own right. Married women's
broken work record and therefore broken contribution record

also reduces their entitlement to certain benefits such as retirement pension, although (since the late 1970s) 'credits' can
be granted for years spent out of the labour market caring for
children or others, which enable some rights to be preserved.

The second point is that the income maintenance system
has been essentially patriarchal in its assumptions, and to an
extent remains so. Married women were quite explicitly seen
as dependent housewives by the Beveridge Report; in a now
(in)famous quote Beveridge (1942, p. 53) said: 'In the next
thirty years housewives as mothers have vital work to do in
ensuring the adequate continuance of the British race and of
British ideals in the world.' There was an assumption that
marriage was, in the vast majority of cases, lifelong; that women's
subsistence needs would be taken care of by, and be under
the control of, their husbands, in return for women's domestic and child-rearing work. Where husbands were sick, disabled,
or out of work, they would claim a benefit which would include a wife's (and children's) additions as well. The assumption was therefore that the husband – whether actually in work
or not – was responsible for providing for his wife and children.

The possibility of married women working and building up
their own record of entitlement was not excluded, however.
Beveridge has been rightly criticised by feminist writers on the
welfare state for what are now seen as his anachronistic assumptions, in terms of what post-war marriage was to be like;
but married women's participation in the National Insurance
scheme was not made impossible, it was just not assumed. Also,
Family Allowances were paid to mothers: carrying the patriarchal assumptions to their logical conclusion would have dic-
tated that they should be paid to men.

With the means-tested safety net National Assistance, however, it was only possible for a married or cohabiting couple
to claim as a unit, and until the 1980s it was the man who
claimed; this was also the case with the benefit for working
poor families from 1971, Family Income Supplement (Family
Credit post-1988). The married man's tax allowance went to
the man except in exceptional circumstances, until 1993. The
wife was therefore clearly treated as the man's dependant. The
system caused hardship to some cohabiting women who were
treated as wives – that is, as a man's dependant – and therefore

denied benefits, when they were not in fact being maintained by their partner and perhaps did not wish to be (and could not enforce maintenance from him). The specific case of cohabitation may be cited as an extreme example of assumptions of female economic dependency on men. The conditions on which widows' benefits are provided constitute another example: paid work is *not* a bar to receiving the benefit, but marriage or cohabitation *is*.

Gradual change towards women's equality in social security has come about particularly in the 1970s and 1980s, although it is certainly not complete. The increasing inclusion of women in the National Insurance scheme, and their ability to claim some benefits on behalf of the couple/family, has been referred to. A benefit which was previously denied to married and cohabiting women, the Invalid Care Allowance (introduced in 1975), became available to them after a test case in the European Court of Justice in 1986; and a former highly discriminatory non-contributory benefit for long-term disability, the Housewives' Noncontributory Invalidity Pension, was replaced with something less blatantly discriminatory in 1984, the Severe Disability Allowance. Yet women remain in practice disadvantaged within the social security system, at the very least because of their more broken work histories and part-time patterns of work. The assumption that they would be provided for in retirement by their husband's pension has left some divorced women facing old age without a full pension. (They are entitled to a proportion of the basic pension corresponding to the years of marriage; but the husband's State Earnings Related Pension cannot follow them in this way after divorce, although a portion of it may do so after widowhood; neither do a husband's occupational benefits follow a woman after divorce.) Many National Insurance benefits still remain unavailable to women because their work record has been too part-time, too low paid, or not sufficiently long, or they have paid the married woman's contribution. It is also more difficult for women to register as unemployed, and therefore claim benefits on this basis, as they must show that arrangements can be made immediately for any children or other dependants for whom they care. This has been the case since the mid-1980s.

There is also the key point that women are over-represented among certain groups of social security, and particularly Income Support, claimants; especially among the elderly, and single-parents. Indeed, women represented over 60 per cent of Income Support claimants at the end of the 1980s (Oppenheim, 1990). The greater number of women claimants arises from the inadequacy of other sources of income for women who are single parents, or older widowed, single or divorced pensioners. Women are therefore more dependent on the effective functioning of the social security system for their survival, and in particular more dependent on the means-tested minima. Any reductions in the scope or level of benefits therefore bite disproportionately into *women's* living standards. Women also have a different relationship with the state due to this dependence. This is one of the ways in which Walby's shift from private to public patriarchy may be argued for (Walby, 1990). The state remains largely controlled by males at the higher levels and may be seen to operate largely in male interests; its assumptions and ideology remain largely patriarchal. Women are therefore more subject to the patriarchal practices of the state as they avoid, or are less subject to, private patriarchy in the shape of an individual male.

Children are the other major group whose dependence is assumed, and this is the third point to be made. Children are not 'entitled' to claim benefit in their own right until they are 16, and even then not if they are still in full-time education. Further qualifications are that since 1988 the right of unemployed 16 and 17 year olds to receive benefit has been severely curtailed: those who are childless can only claim an income if they are on a Youth Training Scheme, with some exemptions for hardship cases. In the late 1993 budget it appeared that restrictive provisions of this sort would be extended to 18–25 year olds, yet by this stage their parents are no longer formally responsible for maintaining them. The main point, however, is that 'children', as defined, are seen as the financial responsibility of their parents, as dependants who would not normally receive an income in their own right. Therefore all the benefits intended for the support of children are paid to one or other of their parents or carers. The concept of children's economic dependency, and the responsibility of adults to maintain them, is so deeply ingrained in our culture that it might be thought scarcely necessary to draw attention to this feature of the benefits system. However, this aspect of the status of childhood *has* been questioned, most notably by those writers of the 'child liberation/children's rights' school, who argue for children to be accorded a more adult status (for example, Holt, 1975). A salutary reminder is that through most of the nineteenth century a similar dependence for married women – indeed, a worse one – was assumed and enforced by the law. It eventually gave way, at least partially, to arguments about women's rights and equality. The financial dependence of children might be similarly questioned.

Central to the benefits system is this assumption: since families are seen to be units of consumption, income can be channelled to one member who will then distribute to all. What happens after this point has traditionally not been much concern of the state's, although parents may be prosecuted for not maintaining their children, and spouses for not maintaining each other. Feminist criticisms of both the notion of a 'family wage' – paid to a male breadwinner for his wife and children as well as himself – and the family benefit, paid similarly, sought to draw attention to the internal distribution of resources in families, but little research was available until the 1980s. Studies suggested a varied pattern, but a general tendency by men to consume more than their 'fair share' of resources (Brannen and Wilson, 1987; Pahl, 1989 and 1990).

What has been the influence of family benefits policies on families? Certainly the assumptions constrain family patterns, but not absolutely. Where spouse and child additions are normally paid to husbands, but only to wives under very restricted conditions, then 'role reversal' – that is, the woman acting as breadwinner and the man as domestic labourer – is made more difficult because it is financially disadvantageous. Neither is sharing of roles assumed by the system. Until 1993 the tax allowance system also made role reversal difficult in some ways because of the obstacles in the way of the wife claiming the married allowance, although paradoxically where she *did* manage to claim, she could until 1990 benefit from the wife's earned income allowance *as well*, and therefore do better out of the tax system than more conventional couples. From 1993 the couple could allocate or split the allowance between them, so role reversal or role-sharing was allowed for.

Where benefits for the family unit are in principle or in practice claimed by men, women remain subject to male economic power. One of the effects of the system is thus the reinforcement of patriarchal power within families. Where female economic dependency on a male is assumed and benefits to women are withheld, restricted, or never instituted in the first place, then such economic dependency may be the only practical option. Thus women's weaker power position in the family is reinforced by social security policies, but the situation could be much worse for women than it is, and has been worse in the past. The fact that women *can* claim some benefits independently, and can claim them more freely than in the past, has eased the exit from unhappy partnerships, or made it more possible to avoid them in the first place, and has given women some independence *within* partnerships.

Cuts to social security benefits in the 1980s affected women disproportionately because of women's greater dependence on them. Freezing of Child Benefit, and reductions in widows' and maternity benefits in the late 1980s, specifically affected women. The coming of the Child Support Agency in 1993, the withholding of some benefits to single parents on the assumption that maintenance from the other parent is being paid, and a benefit penalty for 'non-cooperation' in pursuing the absent parent, can affect some women badly, although the new system also impoverishes many men (and their current dependants). The government's motives in cutting back on social security spending in these ways have been to cut public expenditure; but there is also an ideological sub-text concerned with reinstating earlier patterns of obligation to maintain, in a situation where clearly an increasing number of women with children have been without a male breadwinner. Government policy is thus moving women back into the 'private dependency' arena.

Tax and benefits systems have acted in some ways to reinforce female dependency and male power. But the picture is not unified or straightforward, and both tax allowances and cash benefits have in some instances enhanced *women's* power and made independence more possible. There are also differences in assumptions in different parts of the system and a lack of clear objectives. Further, many of the assumptions have been contested and challenged, particularly regarding the treatment of women.

Housing policy and families

A somewhat different set of considerations arises with housing policy, where another type of benefit is consumed by individuals and families, in part through the mechanisms of the state. Policies have historically operated to offset some of the difficulties which the market creates for the achievement of adequate accommodation, particularly by low income groups. These policies may take the form of subsidised 'bricks-and-mortar' in the public rented sector, or other kinds of direct or indirect subsidy in the private (rented and owner-occupied) sectors. The role of each sector in the provision of housing in relation to families will be considered.

Low-cost working-class housing was provided by voluntary housing bodies in the nineteenth century, and then, increasingly, in the late nineteenth and twentieth centuries, by local authorities. Rents were effectively subsidised by being set below market levels, so that they were affordable on a working-class income. In the inter-war years standards of local authority housing rose, and there was an attempt to house families adequately, in terms of the space for the number of family members, and the actual physical standard of the dwelling. Although standards fluctuated, the pursuit of good quality local authority housing continued in the post-war years (Malpass and Murie, 1987). Many families in public sector houses thus had better quality homes, although there was more construction of high rise flats in the late 1950s and 1960s.

The local authority housing sector expanded greatly until the 1970/1980s; for example, Malpass and Murie give a figure of 17 per cent of housing being rented from local authorities in 1951 and 29 per cent in 1971, though with a fall-back to 25 per cent by 1984. This was related to two other trends: the growth of owner-occupation, and the decline of private renting. Malpass and Murie (1987, pp. 20–1) comment: 'There has been a long transitional period (which is not yet over) from the overwhelming predominance of private renting to the new predominance of owner-occupation.' Historically the demands of organised labour were for control of private renting and for local authority housing rather than for owner-occupation. However, this had changed by the post-war period, and owner-occupation increased, from 31 per cent of housing in 1951 to 63 per cent by 1984 (Malpass and Murie, 1987). The increase extended to better-off working-class families while, as the private rented sector declined, poorer working class families moved into council housing.

Local authority renting, after its earlier expansion, declined in the 1980s, because of a drastic slowing of new building due to cuts in government subsidy, and the massive selling-off of property, at below market prices, to sitting tenants, with assistance with mortgages. This policy had begun cautiously in the early 1970s, but it became mandatory on local authorities under the Conservative governments from 1980 onwards. Houses were sold to longer-standing tenants, with generous discounts. The local authority sector then shrank as over a million council homes were bought by existing tenants by the late 1980s who therefore became owner-occupiers. By the early 1990s the smaller local authority housing sector provided for those who *must* rent (those excluded by low incomes from home ownership). In the 1980s government had also legislated for ways by which local authority housing could pass into other hands, such as private landlords, Housing Action Trusts, tenants' cooperatives or Housing Associations, although only a small amount of stock did transfer in this way. This policy was likely to lead to rent rises in a situation where local authority rents had already risen, due to a number of policy initiatives. There has thus been a significant change in the role of local authority housing.

Local authorities have considerable autonomy, within certain constraints, as to how they allocate housing. With regard to families, preference is given to families in the sense of units with children. Large families in particular were given preference under the 1957 Housing Act (Malpass and Murie, 1987). Priority for families with children characterised the public sector until the 1970s, when other groups, notably the elderly and disabled, became targets for the provision of 'special' housing by local authorities, although only on a small scale. Some tenants who had been allocated housing at a relatively early, family-

building stage in due course became elderly, and so a number
of one- and two-person households were in practice accommo-
dated by local authorities before this time; but the housing
built in the earlier part of the twentieth century and the early
post-war period was overwhelmingly of the two, three and four
bedroom kind and was allocated to couples with children.

Childless couples were a lower priority, although younger
couples might be given tenancies on the assumption they would
in time have a family. Single people were barely catered for at
all until the 1970s (see, for example, Watson, 1987), and then
only in a few instances and often in 'hard to let' properties;
they are still usually only given local authority housing if they
fall into the category of 'vulnerable' under the 1985 Housing
Act as a result of old age, mental or physical disability (see
Sexty, 1990). The Housing (Homeless Persons) Act 1977 had
also defined as priority groups such vulnerable single people,
as well as families and pregnant women. The exclusion of most
single childless people from local authority housing bears most
heavily on single *women* who, because of their lower earning
power, find it more difficult than men to become owner-occupiers or to rent in the private sector.

Single-parent families have tended to be given a lower priority under the council house 'points' system used to determine
priority for housing allocation, because of their geographical
mobility and the smaller number of adults in their households.
They tended to be placed in the worst housing, and unmarried
mothers were allocated poorer quality dwellings (Finer Report,
Department of Health and Social Security, 1974; Watson and
Austerberry, 1986; Watson, 1987). Yet single-parent families are
more dependent than two-parent families on the local authority sector to meet their housing needs. The Finer Report of
1974, and other sources since (see, for example, publications
from the National Council for One Parent Families) found single
parents more likely to be council or private tenants than other
households, and this is associated with their lower incomes.
Sexty (1990, p. 35) comments, quoting Strathdee (1989): 'Over
twice as many two-parent families own their own homes as single parents. Conversely, over twice as many single parents as
two-parent families are council tenants.' Crow and Hardey (1991,
p. 47) comment, quoting Harrison (1983), that lone mothers:

'tend to get very much worse council housing: older rather than newer; flats rather than houses; higher floors rather than lower'. The authors quote the Finer Report as having found discrimination against single parents in the allocation of council housing, and refer to the 1950s designation of single mothers as 'unsatisfactory tenants' (Rose, 1985), and their more recent classification as 'problem' or 'difficult' tenants (Karn and Henderson, 1983). They comment that the sale of council housing and the curtailment of new building in the local authority sector have contributed to a social polarisation in which single parents, along with other groups, have been caught up. Lone mothers, because of their low incomes and dependence on social security benefits, are unlikely to benefit from the policy of selling council housing to sitting tenants. Crow and Hardey (1991) note that lone parents are prominent among homeless households and, following this route into the council sector, tend to be given poor quality accommodation. (See also Simmons, 1993.)

The preoccupation of government Ministers in the late 1980s and the 1990s with young unmarried women deliberately becoming pregnant to jump the council housing queue (see, for example, Sexty, 1990, and Chapter 2) has to be seen in the context of the difficulties lone parents face with local authority housing, although, yes, they are regarded as a higher priority than a single person or a couple *without* children. A survey commissioned by the National Council for One Parent Families found that housing was rarely considered by young pregnant women, and none of those interviewed saw motherhood as a passport to it (quoted by Sexty, 1990). Crow and Hardey (1991) quote Holme's finding (1985) that young single mothers had a history of housing instability and stayed with their parents; local authority housing is only likely to be achieved after some time.

The preference for couple-plus-dependent child nuclear units in local authority housing may be seen positively or negatively (see Land and Parker, 1978, who are critical). Where housing is in short supply, an argument may be put that households with children should be allocated units first, because of the special social claim of the needs of children. Discrimination against single-parent families, however, is not in line with this emphasis on children; indeed, arguably children in these families ought to have a *higher* claim because of their special vulnerability. Where children *are* given priority, there is effective discrimination against childless people, which may be objected to on the grounds of their rights (and single women without children are particularly vulnerable). However, some childless adults, such as the elderly and disabled, are also recognised as a priority. Where individuals, because of low incomes or need for specially adapted housing, are disadvantaged in the housing market, then a strong case may be put for allocating them subsidised rented housing. Non-disabled, non-elderly women without male partners arguably fit into this category, but are not a priority in local authority housing, although there has been some Housing Association provision in the 1980s and 1990s. (The housing problems facing spinsters in earlier decades are noted by Simmons, 1993.)

An intermediate and smaller sector of the housing market is provided by Housing Associations, which are partly government funded but outside direct government control, although regulated by (a quasi-autonomous non-governmental organisation), the Housing Corporation. Based on the voluntary housing movement of the nineteenth century these bodies, a growing sector since the 1970s, aim to provide subsidised rented housing at affordable rents to low income and vulnerable or disadvantaged groups. While more provision for special groups of childless people has been made by these associations (Malpass and Murie, 1987), the voluntary housing movement builds mostly family housing.

The private or for-profit rented sector has declined dramatically in the late twentieth century. Malpass and Murie (1987) show that while in 1914, 90 per cent of housing in England and Wales was rented from private landlords, this had dropped to 52 per cent in 1951, 19 per cent in 1971, and 9 per cent by 1984. Once the primary provider of housing for the working class and for better-off groups, the private rented sector fell victim to reduced profitability, the expanding local authority rented sector, and the gradual move to owner-occupation as the favoured form of tenure for those who could afford it. The letting of housing became more unfavourable to landlords, due partly to government attempts to control rents at below market levels and protect tenants' security, and partly to slum clearance, maintenance costs, the desire for home ownership, and subsidies and tax allowances to the public rented and owner-occupied sectors (Balchin, 1985). Formerly rented property was gradually sold off into owner-occupation. The introduction of rent allowances for low income private tenants in 1972 seemingly did not arrest the decline.

By the late 1980s privately rented dwellings accounted for less than 10 per cent of the total; from figures given in *Social Trends*, 1994, it appears there were only about two million dwellings in this category. Government policies in the latter 1980s attempted to revive the sector by reducing tenant security and allowing rents to rise (under the 1988 Housing Act), making the prospect of letting more favourable to potential landlords, but the sector remained small. In contrast to the public sector, the private sector has tended to discriminate *against* families with young children, partly because of the link between accommodation and ability to pay (see, for example, Wynn, 1971; Land and Parker, 1978). Children's presence in a household may also be disadvantageous to landlords. Neither is a market-orientated sector obliged to make provision for families or any other special or needy group as a high priority, since the criteria for letting are ability to pay the rent and look after the property, rather than need. This might also favour two-earner couples over one-earner or single-parent families. There is no distinctive 'family policy' here, then, but a set of commercial considerations which tend rather to disadvantage families. Nevertheless poorer families and single-parent families may have to depend on this sector, which includes a high proportion of the oldest and poorest dwellings (Balchin, 1985).

Regarding the third major housing sector, owner-occupation, it may be said that at the beginning of the twentieth century dwellings owned by their occupiers were in a small minority; even the wealthy might rent houses, as the rented market was large and diverse. But after the First World War, the purchase of houses by the middle class and some of the better-off working class became more common, and this pattern gradually filtered down the income scale in the post-Second World War period. Malpass and Murie (1987) give a figure of only 10 per cent of housing being owner-occupied in 1914, 31 per cent by

1951, 52 per cent by 1971 and 63 per cent by 1984. Sexty (1990) gives a figure of 66 per cent of households being owner-occupiers by 1989, and the latest figure available is 67% (OPCS, *General Household Survey*, 1994). The process was assisted by the greater availability of mortgages and tax relief on the payment of mortgage interest, and by the extensive sale in the 1980s of council dwellings to their sitting tenants at a discount, with provision of local authority mortgages.

Owner-occupied tenure therefore became the commonest, and until the 1990s the most esteemed and valued tenure, with numerous seeming benefits: control, autonomy, security, and an appreciating capital asset. This was assumed by government to be the tenure people aspired to, whatever their financial situation or social class. By the late 1980s the impossibility of attaining owner-occupation for all households was more understood, and the government took steps to revive the private rental sector. By the early 1990s the housing market had gone into a serious slump, and some owner-occupied houses had become liabilities rather than assets, and were difficult or impossible to sell. Mortgages raised to buy property when prices shot up in the late 1980s (in 1988, particularly, when there was a rapid rise in prices caused partly by a rush to buy before the abolition of multiple mortgage relief) were someimes larger than the current value of the house, giving rise to the phenomenon of 'negative equity', where even the sale of the house would leave the owner with a debt to the lender. Mortgage arrears, repossessions of homes by lenders, and homelessness all increased (see Baker and McGarry, 1992; Child Poverty Action Group, 1992b and 1993b). Loss of the owner-occupied home, followed by homelessness, sharing with others or being placed in bed and breakfast accommodation while waiting for rehousing by the local authority, is extremely damaging to families with young children. For example, there are hazards to children's health from bed and breakfast accommodation (S. J. Smith, 1989; National Children's Bureau, 1991).

The implications of the growth (and then the crisis) of the owner-occupied sector have thus not been altogether favourable for families. As with private renting, this was a sector governed primarily by market criteria, although with a subsidy via the tax system for the cost of mortgages. The prime considerations were economic ones, not housing need, and those who did best were high earners and households with two earners. Young families with high outgoings and lower earnings (perhaps only one earner) were therefore disadvantaged. Because of their general material disadvantage, there were particular difficulties for female single parents in getting into the owner-occupied sector, or in remaining in it after separation and divorce (Sexty, 1990). Jointly owned matrimonial property would often be divided, leaving a single-parent mother with a low income and a little capital at a disadvantage in purchasing again or buying the other partner out. In some cases no-maintenance or 'clean break' deals were struck, in which wives were given the husband's share of the property in return for waiving their right to maintenance, thus acquiring sole possession of the matrimonial home. But the coming of the Child Support Act 1991 makes such deals less likely, as a mother on benefit cannot forgo her maintenance rights in this way. Should she claim Income Support or Family Credit at some time in the future, her side of the 'clean break' bargain is difficult to honour, as she will be put under pressure, under pain of financial penalty, to apply for maintenance after all. Husbands are thus less likely to consider such deals in the future, and this has adverse implications for the wife's housing situation.

Sexty (1990, pp. 34–5) comments:

> Just 38 per cent of separated or divorced women are home-owners compared to 50 per cent of men in similar circumstances ... This serves as an indicator of the disadvantage women face when relationships break down and the fact that many women will move out of the owner-occupied sector on the break-up of a relationship because they cannot afford to keep up mortgage repayments alone.

The position of women as single parents has therefore been uncertain in the owner-occupied sector, although the possibility of retaining the property or a share of it after the breakdown of a relationship has improved due to changes in matrimonial law. Both single mothers and other lone women are disadvantaged in obtaining a mortgage by their weaker earning power. Also, until the Sex Discrimination Act of 1975, it was not unlawful for lenders to discriminate against women solely on the grounds of gender, by refusing mortgages or only allowing them on more unfavourable terms than for men: for example, by requiring women to produce a male guarantor. Women, including single women with steady middle-class incomes, could be effectively cut off from the owner-occupied sector unless they could buy outright or inherit. When it became unlawful to discriminate on grounds of gender, women could at least obtain mortages on the same terms as men at given income levels, but women's lower incomes still disadvantaged them, and hidden discrimination might have continued. (Discrimination could also apply in the rented sector until it was outlawed.)

The housing situation for some women has eased since the 1970s, due to practice on divorce, anti-discrimination legislation, and women's greater opportunities in the labour market. It may be that this improvement in housing chances made it more possible for women to exit from partnerships or avoid them in the first place, and to bear children without a resident male; it has become slightly easier than it was to guarantee some sort of secure home base. However, the likely tendency of the Child Support Act to work in the other direction for separated and divorced women (because maintenance cannot be effectively swapped for property) has been mentioned; and government housing policy since the beginning of the 1980s, tying housing opportunities more closely to income, does generally disadvantage women, as their incomes are generally so much lower than those of men.

Owner-occupation has not given greater security and better housing to all families; and the loss of an owner-occupied home is all the more serious where the alternatives have been shrinking. Because the private sectors are based on market criteria and ability to afford rents/mortgages, they have discriminated *against* families. However, most housing in the owner-occupied sector is of the three and four bedroomed family housing type because it is based on assumptions about characteristic household size.

A final aspect of housing policy is Housing Benefit. This is a subsidy paid to tenants on lower incomes, enabling them to meet rents which they otherwise could not afford (and therefore perhaps keeping rents at a higher level than they would otherwise be). Housing Benefit was instituted under the Social Security and Housing Benefits Act 1982 to combine a number of existing benefits: rent rebates for those in public sector housing, rent allowances for private tenants, the rent element in what was then Supplementary Benefit, and rate rebates. All these benefits were means-tested and therefore went to those on low incomes, either on other benefits or low wages or some combination of the two. It was argued that the new system of a combined Housing Benefit would simplify administration and cut costs. A difference with the new, amalgamated benefit was that it was paid through local authorities, and this caused a certain amount of administrative chaos at first. At central level the Department of Health and Social Security was responsible (see Malpass and Murie, 1987).

Like other means-tested benefits, Housing Benefit allowed amounts for the recognised family dependants – spouses and children – and thus acknowledged family commitments. In the 1980s the government favoured this form of benefit subsidy for rents, targeted on those with low incomes, rather than sub-sidising buildings and therefore rents from the supply side. There were significant cuts to Housing Benefit, however, in the mid- and late 1980s; and problems arose both about what might be judged a reasonable *rent* to be subsidised in this way, and what might be reasonable *accommodation* for family units of a given size. Families deemed 'over-housed', or whose rents were judged unreasonably high for the property, would not receive their full entitlement. Both of these criteria were tight-ened, and in the former case – being suitably or 'over' housed – some rather rigorous assumptions were made about the amounts of space families of different sizes required. Arguably this approach did not favour or facilitate family life.

Assumptions and influence in housing policy

Asssumptions underlying housing policy are not easy to dem-onstrate because of the diversity of this sector and the signifi-cant influence of the private market on housing opportunities and provisions. In *public* housing, it has been assumed that family commitments should be provided for and children given priority, but children have been in practice more favourably treated in a two-parent than in a single-parent unit. This suggests that it is mainly legal marriage which has been supported, as well as childhood and parenthood, so women without a male partner were seen as less deserving. The historic trend to favour the marriage-based family has perhaps been attenuated in recent decades, with single and cohabiting parents given better treatment (though not necessarily as good treatment as the married), and discrimination on the basis of sex becoming formally illegal, while children remain an important priority in public policy. However, the housing opportunities of women, whether as single parents or otherwise, remain disadvantaged compared with those of couples and men. Watson (1987) argues strongly that patriarchal familist assumptions are embedded in all housing tenures, with non-family households marginalised and excluded in housing provision. Most dwellings are constructed for the nuclear family and are planned and designed by men. Units are privatised and self-contained. The centrality of family housing reinforces dominant notions of family and non-family households, and 'the only route to home ownership for many women is through association with a male breadwinner' (Watson, 1987 p. 135), thus reinforcing women's dependency. Various verbal assaults by government ministers on single parents in the 1990s looked by 1994 as though they would be followed by restrictions on homeless families' rehousing rights (see, for example, *Guardian*, 19 July 1994).

The private market sectors do not necessarily make it easier, and in some ways make it harder, for families with children to gain access to adequate housing. Also single-earner units are disadvantaged in comparison with dual-earner units, and this may favour childlessness. It certainly disadvantages couples where one partner does not do paid work, and single-parent families. It is not altogether accurate, then, to claim that non-family households are consistently disadvantaged throughout the housing market. Wealthy single individuals or childless heterosexual or homosexual couples where both are high earners may purchase excellent housing.

The ways in which the various sectors respond to family dissolution through separation and divorce is instructive. The public sector strives to accommodate the parent with the children, usually the woman, and the divorce court is also concerned with the children. But in the private housing sector the male's (usually) higher income opens more doors for him. After divorce, even if the equity of an owner-occupied home is split, the man, whether he has the children or not, is likely eventually to be better housed because of his higher earning power. Sexty (1990, p. 34) comments: 'Policy makers and popular perceptions see the family as a nuclear unit, in which all members benefit equally. However, policies constructed around such perceptions do not make allowances for what happens when the family unit breaks down and the disadvantage some members of the unit face in obtaining individual access to income, housing, and other resources.' Assumptions about families lasting till old age no longer match the reality. Shifting family patterns have given rise to increased mobility, both between housing units and housing sectors (Sexty, 1990). Where women are favoured in housing terms only because they are mothers, this leaves them vulnerable when their children grow up. For example, in divorce settlements wives have sometimes been allowed to remain in the matrimonial home only while children were young.

A further assumption is that the nuclear, not the extended, family is recognised in public housing; units were rarely built large enough to accommodate other relatives beyond the parent–children unit. This may pose some difficulties for, for example, Asian families who do live as extended units. And in rehousing policies, the post-war construction of new towns and outlying estates and so on, families were usually displaced as *nuclear* units. Extended families could thus be separated by distance. Larger-than-usual, complex step-families may face similar problems to extended families. In the private sectors, the ability to obtain units large enough to accommodate a family extending beyond the usual parent–children nucleus would depend on purchasing power, but most dwellings are of the three or four bedroom type.

Housing deprivation, and most particularly homelessness, have detrimental effects, especially on children; and housing provision with its diverse elements is not altogether well-designed for families with children. There are great inequities: income is a large determinant of the type of housing occupied and the terms on which it is occupied, and children do not necessarily come first. However, the argument can be put that *public* sector housing provision is biased *towards* conventional nuclear families with children, to the disadvantage of other groups; also that women are more likely to be housed in their role as wives and mothers than otherwise, but are disadvantaged in all sectors when they head households, including when they are elderly women living alone. The category of marginalised groups might thus include single and (currently) childless people, especially women, and families who do not correspond to the two parent–children nuclear norm.

Policy is ambiguous, therefore, and open to attack on both sorts of grounds: that is, it is insufficiently, or too much, 'pro-families with children'. In so far as market-orientated systems provide housing, however, one can expect greater disadvantage for poorer groups, including many families with children and women of various ages without male partners.

Community care and families

Another area of welfare state policy which is relevant to state–family interaction concerns social care for adults who are dependent due to age or mental or physical disability. The complex of services in this adult care area, provided largely by local authority Social Services departments, and by voluntary and private bodies, is often described as 'community care', a term which has had a shifting meaning over the post-war years. (For a good recent source on community care, see Bornat *et al.*, 1993.)

In the 1960s, when it first came into common usage, 'community care' tended to be construed as meaning care outside hospital, or outside a *large*-scale residential institution, these institutions being seen as having adverse psychological and social effects on their inhabitants; but it *was* seen as including care in a smaller and more informal residential home. Later meanings, in the 1970s, put more emphasis on care in a private household, and by 'the family' (which might mean just one family member). A distinction between 'care *in* the community' and 'care *by* the community' was seen by some to contrast the idea of support by formal services in a community setting with a fuller degree of social integration (see Bayley, 1973). But by the early 1980s this dichotomy was taken by the Conservative government to indicate something more like care by the formal services (and therefore by paid staff), contrasted with (preferred by government) unpaid care by neighbours, friends, and, particularly, family. 'Care in the community must increasingly mean care by the community', according to the Department of Health and Social Security (1981, p. 3). Government was seen by its critics as attempting to shift care of dependent groups from the funded services of the welfare state to the apparently 'free' services of informal carers in the home who, it was argued by feminist writers, were invariably women (see, for example, Finch and Groves, 1980). 'Community care' thus appeared to critics to denote informal care, family care, female care, less care, or even no care.

Certainly this objective accorded with government's general aim of reducing public expenditure and cutting back the activities of the state and what people expect from it. However, it was impracticable and politically impossible to dismantle all local authority social services, and in any event local authorities in the 1980s protected these services against cuts in central government funding by giving them priority (Hayes *et al.*, 1989). In addition, a further twist to the history of 'community care' developed over these years. Government ideology favoured provision by the private or commercial sector, and put this preference into practice by making relatively generous 'board and lodgings' payments to (then) Supplementary Benefit claimants who wished to enter private or voluntary sector residential homes. Amounts allowable for fees under this system were soon curbed, but the limits were not sufficient to stop enormous entrepreneurial activity particularly in residential homes for the elderly. Key features of what occurred were: first, that any Supplementary Benefit claimant could have their fees met (up to a certain limit) in such a home, provided that they did indeed qualify for Supplementary Benefit, so while there was a *financial* assessment no assessment of their actual *need for care* was made; and second, the budget was perforce open-ended, as it was part of the means-tested safety net system which it is virtually impossible to cap without creating gross inequities and destitution.

By the mid-1980s the government was deeply concerned about the wildly escalating cost of this provision. Also, despite the rising overall cost, families and charities often had to make up a shortfall between social security payments and actual fees. Some elderly people entered residential homes unnecessarily; the system gave a 'perverse incentive' to do so. A report by the Audit Commission (1986) which drew attention to the problems of cost and the 'perverse incentive', was followed by a special inquiry headed by Sir Roy Griffiths (Griffiths, 1988). 'Community care' was again commonly taken to mean care *outside hospital*, and therefore the concept included residential homes as well as other community-based alternative forms of care. This interpretation was in line with another arm of government policy, which was to discharge large numbers of long-stay patients in mental hospitals into other forms of care, and then close (at least some of) the hospitals. The alternative forms of care available for ex-patients ranged from residential homes to minimal or indeed non-existent care, but the term 'community care' was commonly used to embrace them all. (For community care developments in the 1980s, see, for example, Hunter and Wistow, 1987; K. Jones, 1989; Baldwin and Parker, 1989; Langan, 1990; Walker, 1993.)

The Griffiths inquiry reported in 1988 (Griffiths, 1988), but was not acted on by government immediately. However, after a White Paper in 1989, *Caring for People* (Department of Health, 1989), an Act followed in 1990 and was implemented by stages, with the main changes taking effect in 1993. The essence of the new system was that there would no longer be an uncapped budget for (now) Income Support claimants to enter residential care, but that all clients seeking publicly-funded care would be channelled through local authorities, who would assess the individual's needs, consider alternative ways of meeting them, and meet the cost of care (though also making a financial assessment of the client's ability to contribute). To this purpose a fixed amount of money was transferred to local authorities from the social security budget. The authorities were expected, however, to be *purchasers* rather than sole providers of care services, and to make extensive use of both private and voluntary sectors, using the majority of their budget for this. The private sector would not necessarily go into decline, therefore, but would face more rigorous screening of its potential customers, and a different mechanism of funding.

The interaction of care policy with family units is the important point for this discussion. The implications are complex and somewhat contradictory. When residential care for elderly and disabled people becomes more widespread, family care is less in demand, although family members do not necessarily forget about and abandon their relatives. When residential care is less common, the demands are potentially greater, although not necessarily met by families: dependent adults could, for example, be more neglected, or they could be cared for by 'community care' in the earlier sense (that is, provided with formal support services at home). While much criticism of government community care policies in the 1980s – the rhetoric about informal care, the attempt to cut back on local authority services, the 'decarceration' of mental hospital patients into the community without adequate support – was rightly concerned that demands on families (and women) would be increased, the dramatic growth of the private and voluntary residential sector must surely have had the opposite effect, reducing care demands (although not necessarily financial demands) on families. At the same time, however, the more rapid movement of mental hospital patients out of hospital, including some of the more severely impaired, potentially created *more* demands on families.

Most care for dependent adults *is* provided by family members and other informal carers (see Chapter 1), rather than by the organised, formal services, and being an 'informal carer', to some degree, is a common experience in British society. For example, the *General Household Survey*, 1985 (Green, 1988) found that one adult in every seven was a carer, this being 6 million people; although the magnitude of the group has been disputed on the grounds that the definition of carer was too broad (Redding, 1991). Fifteen per cent of women and 12 per cent of men were found to be carers; four out of five cared for relatives; only 4 per cent of *all* adults looked after someone living with them (however, this was 1.7 million people). Eight per cent of adults, about 3.4 million people, carried the main responsibility of looking after someone; 10 per cent looked after someone *not* living with them. Women were more likely to look after someone outside the household, and to carry the main responsibility of caring, but there were no differences

between the proportions of men and women caring for someone living with them, or spending more than 20 hours per
week caring (with a quarter of carers spending this amount of
time). Women constituted 58 per cent of all the carers, which
is not an overwhelming majority, and is partly accounted for
by the greater number of women in the older half of the population (the age group more likely to care). Only about a third
of carers with a dependant in the household received regular
visits from health/social services or voluntary groups.

While the boundary between state and family caring is contested, and arguments are put on both sides for a shift – that
is, *either* towards greater state care (usually from feminism and
the political left) *or* towards greater family care (usually from
family 'traditionalists' and the political right) – it is clear that
in this area, in practice, the responsibilities of families are considerable. They are not, however, clear-cut. As Finch (1989)
shows, family responsibilities are essentially negotiated between
individuals, are dependent on reciprocity and a number of other
factors, and cannot be simply read off from the degree of biological relationship between family members. Rules of responsibility in the field of personal care are not legally based
as in income maintenance, partly because it is more difficult
to define and quantify such care than in the case of financial
support, and partly because it is harder to enforce it. Money
can be taken forcibly from family members (for example, through
attachment of earnings or deduction from benefit), but how is
a person to be *forced* to care for a dependent relative, and how
could such forced care ever be desirable? It may be better than
no care at all, but it also opens up the possibility of severe
neglect and abuse, both physical and financial.

The state has an interest in maximising family care as this
saves expenditure, and the pressure to maximise such care will
be greater in times of economic recession, general public expenditure constraints, and the dominance of right-wing ideology (see Finch, 1989). So while the trend in the twentieth
century, particularly in the post-war era after the ending of
the Poor Law, has been to *increase* the scope and quality of
state service for adults through various Acts and the expansion
of the personal social services, from the late 1970s onwards
there have been distinct attempts to lessen state input and re-

emphasise family care. The specific exception to this is the expansion of independent sector residential care financed by social security in the 1980s. This occurred largely for ideological reasons, but (as shown) was eventually curtailed. There are considerable difficulties facing a state which wishes to enforce family care so that state services can then withdraw. One approach is to withdraw state services in the expectation, belief or hope that more family care will materialise. This creates a degree of moral pressure on family members but also puts dependent individuals at risk. The problem of a lack of an agreed definition of responsibilities is particularly acute in this area (see Finch, 1989; Finch and Mason, 1993).

Assumptions and influence in community care

In this uncertain area it is difficult to pinpoint what exactly the state's assumptions are since they are ambiguous, and both vary over time and are subject to variability at the micro-level. For example, different local authorities and even different divisions within authorities may make different assumptions about what people should and can do for their elderly and disabled relatives, and when it is justified to provide services and when to withhold them. Feminist writing has argued, with considerable justification, that here (as in income maintenance policy) women have been assumed to be the dependents of males, to be out of the labour market – or easily able to leave it – and therefore available for caring duties at home. There is also evidence that female carers receive less support from the formal services at given levels of dependency than do male carers (for example, Charlesworth *et al.*, 1984; Wright, 1986). In this sense the assumptions are patriarchal; however, men, especially husbands, may also be assumed to be available to care in some circumstances (Pitkeathley, 1989). Expectations of family care are not narrowly focused on the spouse–dependent child unit but, most obviously, take in the elderly parent–adult child unit, and possibly range more widely than that. But as there are no specific legal rules about such obligations, much will depend on the relationships between the individuals concerned, as well as factors like geographical distance and other practical demands made on potential carers. What is significant also is the set of criteria that family members *themselves* adopt in deciding on the legitimacy of demands on them as carers. These criteria may not correspond to those assumed in government policies or adopted by professionals and practitioners on the ground. As Finch and Mason (1993, p. 179) comment: 'It makes little sense ... to build public policies which assume certain types of assistance will be given more or less automatically.'

Family responsibilities are assumed therefore in community care policies, but cannot be precisely defined or relied upon in any clear-cut, legalistic way; and similarly there are no formally defensible *rights* to family care; indeed, as Finch and Mason (1993, p. 180) say, 'policies which rest on the assumption that people have a right to expect assistance from their relatives ... will not align with the realities of family life'. Much is variable, negotiable and unpredictable; and where family helping is assumed by state agencies to be functioning well, but is not, vulnerable adults could be left to face neglect, suffering, even death. It is worth recalling the case of Beverley Lewis, a very severely disabled adult neglected by her mother to the point of death in the late 1980s. The systems for intervening and protecting *adults* are much less developed than for children, and the alternative care provisions are usually less available and favourable. For example, while attention to elder abuse appears intermittently in the field of social care, and is believed to be a significant although largely hidden problem (see Pritchard, 1992), the systems for responding to this are nothing like as developed as those for child abuse.

What assumptions are made about the need to *help* family members care for one another? Employment practices tend to be insensitive to the needs of employees who are also carers; they could be, but currently are not, regulated by statute (for example, through protection of rights to 'family leave'). Some rather minimal financial support for carers is given through the income maintenance system (for example, Attendance Allowance, now Disability Living Allowance, and Invalid Care Allowance); and if all else fails, there is Income Support to maintain the carer, which has included a carers' premium since 1990. Housing policies tend to favour nuclear rather than extended units, and have thus not made coresident caring particularly easy, although the idea of 'granny flats' built on to public sector houses found some favour at one stage. Rehousing after slum clearance often took younger families out of the inner cities, and left their older relatives behind. The policies of Social Services departments and related agencies have tended to substitute for families where family caring was inadequate, rather than to support families in their caring roles with *supplementary* services (Moroney, 1976), although there was more provision of supportive services, such as respite care, in the 1980s and 1990s (see Chapter 5 for further comment on substitutive and supportive services). However, a policy of *de facto* encouragement of residential care, as happened with independent sector care in the 1980s, tends towards family substitution rather than support. Policies are not very sensitive to family care and its complexities, services tend to be rigid, and 'interweaving' of formal and informal services is problematic (see, for example, Bulmer, 1987).

The influence of community care policies on families is mixed. Sometimes family members have a huge burden of care, while scarce services are targeted on those who have no one to care for them (Wright, 1986; Lewis and Meredith, 1988). Often 'family care' is given by one family member who is on duty 24 hours a day and whose own health and welfare is imperilled. There is also evidence of some very young carers looking after parents or grandparents (see, for example, M. George, 1992; Aldridge and Becker, 1993). And the need for a carer can reinforce gender roles in families because of the perception that women's paid work is more dispensable. Caring places constraints on family life in general, although it may have its rewarding side as well (see Clifford, 1990).

Fears that family members will withdraw from helping roles, because of a superabundance of state and other formal services, are found on the political right and among family traditionalists. From another viewpoint, family care can be so burdensome, because of the dearth of supporting help, that individuals may avoid it wherever they can. However, it is very hard to predict the effects of variations in the provision of services. The whole gamut of responses is possible, from total abandonment to 24 hour a day nursing care with little or no support. The effects of any particular framework of care on the family are hard to predict. A more restrictive system may force families to care but also break them apart. More generous provision, on the other hand, may leave more space for the development of affective bonds (see Finch and Mason, 1993, on the maintenance of affective bonds at a distance, and Jamieson, 1991, on affective ties in Denmark where family care is not assumed), or alternatively may give family members the feeling that they have no role. These considerations have to be seen in the context of the family's likely reduced capacity to care in the future, due to the family changes described in Chapters 1 and 2.

Child care and families

Another vulnerable group who have been the target of various care services from, and protective interventions by, the state, is obviously children. Again, it is mainly the local authority Social Services departments who are the relevant agency, backed up in some cases by the courts; a number of long-established voluntary organisations are also active in different aspects of child care work. (For child-care policy generally, see, for example, Frost and Stein, 1989; Fox Harding, 1991b.)

The protection of children from abuse and neglect by means of legislation and statutory action has a long history, going back to the first prevention of cruelty Act in 1889, which enabled maltreating parents to be prosecuted and children to be removed from them and cared for by someone else. Substitute care for children who were deemed destitute was provided under the Poor Law and was usually of poor quality, although it improved over the late nineteenth and early twentieth centuries. Voluntary organisations and, increasingly, local education authorities had a child care role and met somewhat better standards. As well as institutional care, some foster family care was used, with improving standards from the late nineteenth century.

In the post-Second World War era the aim was to provide high quality care for any children who were not living in their own families, whether this was under a court order for reasons such as cruelty or neglect, or whether the reason was parents' inability to care and/or wish for the children to be cared for elsewhere. Foster or adoptive family care was favoured, although some children were cared for in residential homes. The child's well-being and best interests were an important consideration (Section 12 of the Children Act 1948); and, as well as good quality substitute care, this was also taken to mean that children should be returned to their original family whenever possible. These family bonds were more recognised in the post-war period as important: wartime experiences with evacuation and children placed in nurseries had been influential and had shown the importance of early bonds. This emphasis on the original family contrasted with the pre-war view, which had favoured a 'clean break' for children who came into care.

In time, the emphasis on the child's original family resulted in a bias in policy and practice towards 'prevention': that is, preventing children entering full-time care in the first place, by means of help and support to their birth family. This was backed up by legislation in 1963 (the Children and Young Persons Act). The 1960s was largely the decade when work with families was favoured to avoid children needing to enter care, and also to help families in deprived areas in a broader sense. Where children did enter care, the most favoured option was, in general, for them eventually to return home again. Some children in fact remained in care for considerable lengths of time, because of the wish to hold the door of 'rehabilitation' open; or they bounced like a yo-yo between care and the parental home.

However, by the mid-1970s a very different emphasis was becoming predominant. This was largely because of the highly publicised death in 1973 of Maria Colwell, at the hands of her step-father. She had been in care at an earlier stage, and was then returned by Social Services and the court, against her obvious wishes, to her mother's home (see Secretary of State for Social Services, 1974). In the light of this and other serious child abuse cases, policy now emphasised prevention of further abuse by keeping children away from their abusing families, finding them permanent adoptive and foster homes, and stressing the welfare of the *child* as a separate entity from the original family. Child abuse inquiries followed thick and fast throughout the 1970s, with much criticism of social workers for exposing children to risk in their birth family homes. Biological bonds were by now counting for less, and secure emotional bonds with substitute caretakers for more. The object was to avoid abuse and achieve 'permanence' for the child, over-riding biological links if necessary.

The 1980s may be seen as a mixed decade. While a 'backlash' pressure for more respect for the rights of birth parents was visible at the beginning of the decade, further child death inquiries brought forth criticisms of social workers for being excessive respecters of parental liberties. The most famous of the abuse/death inquiries in the mid-1980s concerned Jasmine Beckford, Tyra Henry, and Kimberley Carlile; these children died after Social Services either did not or could not take action to remove them from the parent(s). Yet almost immediately after this Social Services were criticised for the opposite reason: for over-riding birth families' rights by taking children away where it was unnecessary. In the suspected sex abuse cases in Cleveland in 1987, parents fought a rearguard action to defend themselves against accusations of abuse and to reclaim their children from care. (For Cleveland, see, for example, Campbell, 1988; Secretary of State for Social Services, 1988).

All these events fed into a government inter-departmental review of public child-care law which had been ongoing since 1984 in response to a report from a Parliamentary select committee (House of Commons, 1984; Department of Health and Social Security/Law Commission, 1985). A review of the 'private' side of child care law was being undertaken around the same time by the Law Commission. These reviews bore fruit in a White Paper in 1987 and a Law Commission report in 1988 (1988b), and they culminated in the Children Bill 1988 which became the Children Act 1989.

This was a large consolidating piece of legislation, embracing both public and private law, which attempted to balance the conflicting considerations and formulate new principles. It aimed to protect children further from abuse by making *likely* significant harm, as well as actual harm, a ground for legal proceedings, and by making it easier to investigate suspected abuse. However, it also tried to protect family autonomy and give parents *more* rights by making the emergency provisions for removing children less weighted against the parents; by giving parents more contact (that is access) rights and more say generally when children were in care; by replacing the notion of voluntary care (that type of care not based on a court order) by something even more favourable to the parents called 'accommodation', which was firmly construed as based on partnership with the parents; by empowering local authorities to give more help to families and children 'in need'; and in a variety of other ways. Backing this up was a general statement of principle: that the courts were not to intervene and make an order at all, unless it was clearly better for the child; this is the non-intervention principle referred to when discussing private family law. The bias was towards letting families/parents sort out their own disputes and difficulties. There were also enhanced rights for the child concerning, for example, where he or she wanted to live, and children could initiate certain legal actions themselves concerning their care in both 'public' and 'private' law.

It is difficult to sketch a general picture of the Children Act without over-simplifying (see Fox Harding, 1991a), but it appears to support and maintain original family units rather than enhance the compulsory powers of the state to separate parents and children. The greater powers to help families and children 'in need' seemed to carry further the 'preventive' principle so favoured in the 1960s, but there were fears that these would be jeopardised by the cutting of local authority expenditure in the early 1990s. On paper local authorities were also given more power to provide day care, but lack of resources suggested that little more was likely to be done.

The respect for the *child*'s autonomy had appeared in a more muted form in previous legislation, notably the Children Act 1975; but it was more strongly present in the 1989 Act, and has already given rise to some rather unexpected cases where children challenged their living arrangements and sought court backing for decisions they had made themselves (see Harding, 1993).

The areas of interaction between family and state in this field are rather dramatic. The state, acting through local authorities and courts, has the power to sever parent–child bonds, possibly permanently and legally. Where children are under a Care Order most parental rights and responsibilities are lost; children in care may be kept away from their parents permanently and may be adopted against the parents' wishes. The extreme powers of the state were experienced in a raw form by parents in the Cleveland sex abuse cases, and later in similar cases in, for example, Orkney and Rochdale. Children were removed from their homes suddenly by force, and parents were often denied contact; in some cases these children never returned home.

Children may be under statutory supervision at home following a court order, or may go into what is now called accommodation (previously voluntary care); and although parents are supposed to be fully consulted and in 'partnership' with the local authority, and to have contact with their children, some of the day-to-day control over the child is ceded. A local authority may also have control through informal supervision and support of families, and much was made from the 1960s onwards of help to families in a supportive rather than a coercive mode. This theme has re-appeared strongly in Section 17 of the Children Act, which requires services to children in need (although in practice this is subject to the availability of resources). But 'help' that is on offer can be withheld, and this gives social workers considerable power over parents. Indeed, the authority's powers to take cases to court and obtain an order in respect of a child also constitute a powerful sanction even before the situation warrants it.

All this power exists in principle for the child's welfare and safety, and has evolved in response to concern about children's health and well-being and the accumulating knowledge of child development and of adverse parental care and its consequences. Yet there are unresolved debates as to what actually *is* best both for children in general, and for any individual child. And, as the suspected sex abuse cases and the action taken by parents in response have demonstrated, state intervention can seem the most brutal over-riding of parental civil liberties and destruction of the family unit; indeed, it may damage the children. The forcible separation of parent and child may be one of the harshest interventions of the state in any field of life; yet the consequences of *not* so intervening may be tragic, as the various highly publicised child abuse and death inquiries have graphically highlighted. This is an area where huge and perhaps unresolvable conflicts of principle appear.

With regard to the supportive interventions of Social Services departments and voluntary organisations, one specific area of service provision that may be discussed briefly is day care for younger children. This may be seen as a means of preventing children needing removal from their families, or as a service in its own right to help families and children. Publicly provided day care is not currently in Britain seen as anything like a standard or universal service to all families, or as a service to assist mothers to enter the labour market. (For day care in general see Cohen and Fraser, 1991; S. Jackson, 1993; see also Chapter 1.)

As is well known, during the Second World War, when women's labour was needed both in the armed services and to take over jobs previously done by men, extensive day care provisions appeared (Lewis, 1984 and 1992). These were clearly to meet a specific need, however, and rapidly closed down after the war. For example, in July 1943 there were over 1300 day nurseries in England and Wales; by 1947 this number had halved (Frost and Stein, 1989). The earlier history of day care and under-5s education had shown patchy and fluctuating provisions; some nursery provision in schools, for 3–5 year olds, occurred earlier in the century (Cohen and Fraser, 1991), and in the inter-war years nursery education was favoured by contemporary educational theories (Hardyment, 1983). But post-Second World War thinking about child care did not favour daytime care for very young children, for another reason besides the initial drop in demand for women's labour. The popular theories of Bowlby, referred to in Chapter 1, about attachment and the adverse effects of separation from the mother figure for young children, militated against systems which involved children under five being away from their mothers for a large part of each day. At its extreme this was interpreted to mean that babies and toddlers should not be parted from their mother at all. This ethos was in marked contrast to pre-war thinking on child care, which had emphasised emotional distancing from the child, the independence of children from their caretakers, cognitive development and rigid routine (Hardyment, 1983). The 'Bowlby era' stressed the child's need for love and constant attention, preferably from the primary caregiver. The demands placed on women from this philosophy were considerable, and by the 1970s a feminist critique of this approach was developing which challenged the arguments about child development and argued for greater provision of day nurseries, either to free women for paid work or to give them opportunities to develop their own lives (see, for example, New and David, 1985, who also quote Rutter, 1972). Bowlby's ideas were challenged directly, and it was argued that young children did not need to stay with only one caretaker to preserve their emotional security, but might actually benefit from some exposure to other adults, and to other children in a group setting, if care was of good quality. Some recent research supports this. (See National Children's Bureau, 1993, which quotes McGurk *et al.*, 1993, and other sources.)

More nursery education was briefly favoured by the Conservative government of the early 1970s (for example, a White Paper in 1972 was called *Nursery Education: A Framework for Expansion*), but this was affected by public expenditure cuts later in the decade. Nursery education and public day nursery provision did not therefore advance greatly in the 1970s and 1980s, although voluntarily-run playgroups developed in the 1970s. Day nurseries in the public sector (which actually decreased in the late 1980s according to the National Children's Bureau, 1993) remained a special service for priority groups of children (for example, those at risk of abuse). There were only 29 000 local authority day nursery places in England in 1987, when there were three million children under five (Frost and Stein, 1989). Potentially wider provisions for day care under Section 18 of the Children Act have to be seen in the context of lack of resources and the unlikelihood of any development of a universal service for children in the pre-school years, or indeed for out-of-school times for older children.

There is a small amount of voluntary sector and employer provision, but many working mothers have to make private arrangements. (See Chapter 1 for findings from the General Household Survey, 1991, which found that over 50 per cent of under-5s' parents used unpaid informal care, private or voluntary schemes, or a child-minder/nanny.) Private child-minding or family-based day care increased during the 1980s (Frost and Stein, 1989; National Children's Bureau, 1992). Private sector nurseries have been an increasing area of provision (National Children's Bureau, 1993); other alternatives have been nannies and relatives. Demand for all forms of provision grew in the 1980s and 1990s with increasing numbers of mothers returning to work, despite access to full-time and affordable day care remaining difficult. The government placed its emphasis on private and employer, rather than state, provision. Britain compares badly with other European countries in this respect (S. Jackson, 1993), although tax relief on workplace nurseries, abolished in 1984, was reinstated in 1990 (Cohen and Fraser, 1991); and in 1993 a child-care allowance was introduced for certain parents claiming Family Credit and related benefits (Lister, 1994).

Assumptions and influence in child care

What are the assumptions on which the state operates in the field of child care policy? As in other areas, assumptions are problematic. The importance of children being cared for in their own birth families, and parental responsibility for children, are stressed, *but* the state's powers to intervene are considerable. Exactly how these powers are used has varied over time and by court and local authority. The state, acting through local authorities, may also intervene to help and support families with children with various kinds of services (social work help, financial assistance, family centres, day care, advice, holidays and so on). Such supportive services are not provided on a universal basis and are not even widespread, but are minority services for some families who are deemed vulnerable (for family centres in this respect, see Cannan, 1992). With day care as a specific example, the assumption is that families (usually meaning mothers) will make their own arrangements, except in cases where children are clearly at risk. In a sense, then, the state's role in child care is minimalist – it stands back until there is clear evidence of a need for help or control – but its powers can be very sweeping, although some have been curtailed by the Children Act 1989.

The importance of care by *some* kind of (nuclear) family unit is another assumption which should be noted. Only in a narrow sense do the child-care interventions of the state challenge 'the family' as an institution. For most children, and certainly for younger ones, a nuclear family setting in a private household is thought to be the optimal environment; that is, where children are not with their *own* family, then foster and adoptive *families* are usually preferred to group settings. This prejudice in favour of nuclear families also affects the willingness to provide group-based day care. There is also the assumption that the family is not just a biological unit but a social/psychological one as well: that is, the important characteristics of family care can be created between adults and children who are not biologically related. Where children are adopted just after birth, the relationship between them and their adoptive parents may be a parent–child relationship as in any other nuclear family. However, there is debate about how important genetic links actually are, and there have been moves since the 1980s towards a more 'open' form of adoption where some genetic family links would be preserved. Adoption law and practice, under review by the early 1990s, explicitly moved towards this. While some authors have argued that it is exclusively 'psychological parenting' which is important (Goldstein, Freud and Solnit, 1973 and 1980), there is evidence that links with biological relatives are valued, that their severance is experienced as a loss, and that there may be a wish to find out about one's original family, and possibly establish a relationship with them, even much later in life (see, for example, Howe *et al.*, 1992). This search became easier under the Children Act 1975.

While some support of a 'voluntary' or non-coercive kind is offered to original birth families with difficulties, this is insufficient, and the state may be doing too little to keep the institution of the (disadvantaged) biological family afloat (see Fox Harding, 1991b). The situation is ambiguous, however, since it is not clear what effect the supportive interventions of social workers and others actually have; whether, for example, any erosion of the family's autonomy might in some ways damage its internal relationships.

What of more general help for parenting through the policy of the state? Statutory maternity leave and maternity benefits may assist parenting, as may paternity leave, and parental leave to extend maternity leave, or to deal with childhood illnesses, for example. These latter ideas developed largely from the 1980s, but were only minimally established in Britain by the early 1990s, and the British government vetoed an EC directive on parental leave from the mid-1980s. The proliferation of social security benefits to support children has been mentioned in the section on income maintenance; these benefits, however, are insufficient to cover the full cost of rearing children (see, for example, Oldfield and Yu, 1993) and are mostly selective, not universal. General government policy and the practices of employers are not particularly supportive of parenthood; that is, they do not go far enough in allowing for and offsetting its demands and costs. This may be seen as positively anti-family, as well as anti-natalist (discouraging reproduction).

Finally, the issue of day care throws into relief the underlying ideological debate about family responsibility, and especially maternal responsibility. The day care debates highlight a struggle over the state–family boundary and over what is properly a public/private area of responsibility. Broadly, the state's expectation in Britain is that parents/mothers will care for young children during the day, and this is conveniently reinforced by post-war theories of child development which suggested that day care outside the family was damaging. However, recent research indicates that much depends on the *quality* of day care; it is not adverse *per se* (National Children's Bureau, 1993). Nevertheless, publicly provided state care is construed as a 'welfare' provision for a minority of families with special problems, for whom it is seen as helpful; otherwise mothers will care (or make their own arrangements). The effects of this are that working parents/mothers must turn to a range of other (possibly unsatisfactory) non-state alternatives, or indeed leave children alone: a situation beginning to attract media attention and public concern in the early 1990s. The assumption that day care is a 'private' matter may be highly damaging to children.

The universal services of health and education, and families

Health and education services, although both have important effects for families, will be dealt with more briefly, as they are not explicitly targeted at families in the same way as the others. These are 'universal' services (in principle) for, in the case of health, the entire population, and, in the case of education, all children up to the age of 16, and a proportion of young people and indeed older adults in further and higher education. While services are not specifically designed with families

in mind, or explicitly based on family assumptions, their existence has considerable implications for the nature of family life,
and they may also be argued to embody some assumptions about
family life.

The development of modern medicine, along with the appearance of publicly financed health care, available post-war
(at least notionally) to all, has taken much care and treatment
of the sick out of the immediate family arena. Modern health
care systems have been seen by some sociologists as one means
by which the family has lost some of its traditional' functions'
of nursing and medical care. However, much care of the sick
and disabled continues to be carried out within the family.
This has been increasingly the case from the 1970s onwards,
as policy has favoured earlier discharge from hospital, especially
of the mentally impaired. General policies of community care
for the elderly, disabled and mentally impaired, along with the
ageing of the population, have also meant that an *increasing*
rather than a decreasing amount of caring work has needed
to be carried out in the home. Also, modern medical intervention, by saving lives which would previously have been lost but
preserving them with some disability or need for ongoing treatment and care, and by generally keeping people alive longer,
has *increased* rather than reduced the amount of care needed
by family members at home. The development of modern medicine and state health care, then, has been ambiguous for the
family, and it cannot be claimed that it has simply 'reduced its
functions' in any straightforward way.

With child health, medical intervention through treatment
and immunisation, and improved procedures in pregnancy and
childbirth, have vastly reduced the child mortality and illness
rate, revolutionising the experience of parenthood. Less time
has to be spent caring for sick children, and, above all, their
survival can be largely assumed. Again, however, life may be
preserved with a disability, as in the saving of brain-damaged
infants who need more than the usual amount of care. The
effect on parenting experience is not all in one direction, therefore, and while the assumption of the child's survival is a more
reasonable one, it may occasionally be survival with an ongoing need for care. (For a general recent source on child health,
see Woodroofe *et al.*, 1993.)

Provisions for contraception, abortion and reproductive technology have reflected changing assumptions about parenthood, specifically motherhood, and the appropriate contexts for sex and reproduction. For example, contraception became more widely available to the unmarried, but a woman's circumstances are relevant to whether she is granted an abortion or not; while only married commissioning parents in a surrogacy arrangement can obtain a parental order, and infertility services for single women are discouraged. The provisions for abortion, contraception and infertility have also had a marked *effect* on sexuality, family life, and women's lives in particular. In general there has been a widening of choice.

A further point to be made about health services and their interaction with families is that services are often mediated through families. This is particularly so where children are concerned, where parents largely control their children's access to health care, and here there is a possible area of conflict between the state and parents: for example, where parents refuse to let children have important, even life-saving, medical treatment (see, for example, Freeman, 1983). Another aspect is the effect which family life itself has on the need for health care, through, for example, healthy or unhealthy behaviours and lifestyles, the distribution of resources within the family, ideologies and practice relating to the use of health care services, and, more dramatically, directly health-damaging behaviour such as violence and neglect. Health care systems and families thus interact in complex ways. (For the general issue of the relationship between family life, gender and health, see, for example, Graham, 1984.)

With education, clearly the coming of a universal state service made a great difference to family life. When compulsory education for all children, initially until the age of 10, was instituted in 1880, parents were deprived of their children's full-time labour and wages to that age, and this caused hardship for some working-class families. Children's paid labour was a necessity for poorer families throughout most of the nineteenth century, although children's hours of work and working conditions had been progressively restricted from the 1830s. It was, however, the coming of universal compulsory education which fundamentally changed the child's economic position within the working class family. Although children might still work part-time, their contribution was not what it had been (Fyfe, 1989), and the age of compulsory schooling was also progressively raised, taking them out of the full-time labour market for longer periods. Children were thus less available for paid work, for domestic work and for the care of their younger siblings. The extent of their economic and practical dependence therefore increased considerably over the period of a century, making children far more of an economic liability and less of an asset in the family. This effect was more marked for the working class, who had depended on their children's labour and were now forced to maintain them for longer. But this shift may have had far-reaching effects on the general attitude to children, particularly where more emphasis was being placed on their development and on standards of child-rearing. And Walby (1990) suggests that the transformation of children from an asset to a liability has contributed to a 'flight from fatherhood', in which the care and maintenance of children has been left increasingly to women.

There is a view that, as with health care, the coming of universal state education removed a long-established 'function' from the family; that the family in earlier times was the context in which education took place, whether delivered by parents or by paid tutors and governesses, and that with industrialisation and the proliferation of state services this role was lost. To make sense of this sort of position, account clearly has to be taken of a vast variety of practices and of the wider field of child socialisation beyond formal education. The upper class and, increasingly, the middle class, did send some of their children, especially sons, away to school for some of the time in earlier centuries. Conversely, a few parents continue to educate their children at home today, as this is still allowed with certain safeguards (see, for example, Skeens, 1994). Also, schools do not substitute completely for the broader educational role of parents. Teaching of children takes place at home before formal schooling begins, and continues throughout the child's school life; indeed, the variations between families of different social groups and classes in performing this role are recognised to be a major factor in educational inequality (see, for example, Reid, 1986). Education in a broader sense *is* still the responsibility of the family, and there are particular areas where the boundary between the state and the family is contested, most notably sex education, but also general morality and discipline. (For a general source on family and education, see David, 1993.)

Thus no straightforward transfer of the educational function has occurred. However, laws which say that from 5 to 16 children must spend a large proportion of each day at school – and the detailed conditions, such as the timing of schooling, the location of schools, and the need to prepare children for school – have a considerable impact on family life and set certain limits within which families must operate. The mismatch between school hours and normal hours of full-time work is one obvious example of the constraints and problems which arise for families because of the way in which compulsory education is organised.

Education may also be seen to have a role in the transmission of gender roles, divisions and inequalities through the different educational experiences received by girls and boys. However, while education may play a part in reinforcing traditional divisions, it may also assist girls and young women to escape the most oppressive aspects of these by providing a route into better-paid employment, although women's position in the labour market is not commensurate with their educational achievement.

The education system in general assumes that children have family homes to return to where their emotional and physical care is provided for; exceptions to this are 'boarding schools' or children's homes with education on the premises, which, for part of the year at least, combine the education and care functions. This may occur simply because parents wish to pay for boarding education, but occurs also for groups of children who are in special need, including some under Care Orders where it is thought necessary to keep them in a secure environment. In general the care/general socialisation/education boundaries are never totally clear-cut.

It is concluded from this brief discussion that state health care and education systems have a considerable impact on families, although there has not been a straightforward and total transfer of functions from family to state in these fields; that there is an important area of interaction between family and state in both health and education; and that while what the state does affects families in a variety of ways, family behaviour also has consequences which feed back into the workings of the health care and education systems: there is a two-way relationship.

Conclusion

This chapter has examined state–family interaction in the fields of family law, social security and tax, housing, care for adults and children, and (more briefly) health and education. In these various policy areas some assumptions are made about how families operate and the patterns of obligation between family members, but these are not always clear-cut or uncontested. The assumptions are gendered, and somewhat (but not altogether) traditional as far as women are concerned. The policies and their underlying assumptions constrain families in various ways (and in some cases may involve coercive action), but may also support families and enable family roles to be more easily carried out. Policy is ambiguous therefore; and in many fields the state–family boundary is problematic. As Wicks (1987, p. 4) comments, policies affecting the family are muddled, and 'there is a sense in which relationships between families and the state are less clear cut today than in former times'. There is uncertainty about both rights and responsibilities, while family changes have produced new needs and ambiguous commitments focusing round employment, (re)marriage, family diversity, child care and ageing.

Chapter 5 will now consider a number of models which might help to describe different relationships between families and the state.

Chapter 5

Models of the Family–State Relationship

The last chapter looked at how family and state interact in key areas of social policy in Britain and considered the assumptions which policies appear to make about families, and the influence that policies might be argued to have on families (constraining, supporting, or facilitating forms of family life). The focus was on the areas in which state and family tend to interact, in the field which is broadly concerned with welfare. The state both controls and supports families, and the effects of various services on family life are mixed, setting parameters, facilitating certain patterns, making others more difficult, releasing family members from some burdens but adding and enforcing others, making certain options possible and others not possible, assuming patterns which may or may not be the case, reinforcing some ways of living but penalising others. Boundaries between state and family are often confused and contested, with ambiguous areas of responsibility. Where defined family 'responsibilities' are not met, the state may respond in a variety of ways. There is a power relationship between family and state, but the direction of influence is not just one way: families can affect how the state behaves, as well as being on the receiving end of its actions. For example, families change how relationships are defined, who lives with, supports and is maintained by whom. Different arms of the state may treat families in different ways and make different assumptions; while families are very varied in form and include social units such as adoptive and step-families as well as biological units. Neither

'family' nor 'state' is a unitary concept, therefore (see Introduction).

This chapter will now move the discussion on by setting up
a number of generalised models for the overall relationship
between the state and families in order to distinguish different
ways in which this relationship could in principle operate.

First, two extreme models will be outlined, which are not
found in reality in any country in their pure form, and which
may well be incapable of actual achievement, but which are
put forward as ideal types in order to elucidate different principles on which the state–family relationship may be based. The
two extreme models are one where the state is highly authoritarian and *dirigiste* in its attempts to control family form and
behaviour; and, at the other extreme, a model where no sort
of position on what families should do or what they should be
like is taken at all, the stance of government and the various
organs of the state being one of libertarian *laissez-faire*. These
two extremes illustrate that the state can have clear defined
objectives for families which it can seek to enforce rigidly, or
can have no objectives whatever and can regard family life as
an entirely private area of activity beyond the state's legitimate
concern.

It is intended that the account of the two extreme models
will illustrate what these principles might look like if taken to
their logical conclusion. *Prescriptions* for directions for families
and family policy have implications for a more controlling role
for the state which, it is implied, should intervene more vigor-
ously in family life. This is regardless of what the particular
direction favoured is (whether it is less or more patriarchal,
for example). The diametrically opposed position of 'keeping
the state out' of people's private family lives suggests a very
minimal state in this area, with no prescriptions for family life.
The latter model leaves unanswered the question of how families would in fact behave in the absence of any policy at all,
although those who advocate *laissez-faire* may think that they
know this.

In between the two extremes are intermediate models which
approximate more closely to the real world of actual state policy:
models which are more or less controlling, which set more, or
fewer, constraints on how people might live their family lives,

which operate on more, or less, limiting assumptions, and which use greater or lesser means of reinforcement or discouragement for particular patterns. While an infinite number of such intermediate models could in principle be sketched out, five possibilities are outlined, ranging from the more to the less authoritarian. These are introduced in more detail when the two extremes have been discussed.

An authoritarian model of family–state relationship

The first model describes a situation where the state is extremely *dirigiste* in its approach to family life, with the clear intention of enforcing certain preferred behaviour patterns and family forms, and prohibiting others. Such an authoritarian model would only be likely to be found within a society and form of government which was itself authoritarian rather than democratic, where ideals and objectives formulated at the top as clear goals could effectively be passed down and enforced on the vast majority of the population. This would be done by a variety of means, but certainly, overall, by limiting personal freedom quite severely, and by restricting or excluding popular participation in the formulation of policies or discussion of them or feedback of their effects. The political culture of the society would therefore be relevant (see Zimerman, 1992; also Chapter 6).

The directions from those in power would be supported by a range of numerous, and possibly draconian, sanctions. These could be instituted formally through the criminal or civil law; or by means of material penalties (for example, by depriving those who did not conform of certain economic benefits or services); or through manipulating more informal means, such as social exclusion, disapprobation, stigmatisation and allocation of low status; or by otherwise altering the structure of rewards and sanctions to make alternatives to the favoured patterns extremely unpleasant. Means of enforcement might also include the forcible separation of families/removal of some members. Some of these means of control may also be expected in less auhoritarian models of the family–state relationship, but it is posited that an authoritarian state would use most or all of them. A particular ideology about family life is also likely to be imposed by the authoritarian state, using a variety of means such as the partisan presentation of policies, the control of information, and generally the mechanisms of propaganda.

The intention in the authoritarian model is to achieve uniformity of family patterns in accordance with the prescribed objectives. These have been decided by those in power to be, for whatever reason, the most desirable options. Scope for individual or family choice is thus heavily constrained or non-existent, or is certainly intended to be so by government. The effects of such authoritarian policies, however, will not necessarily be precisely what those in power wish to achieve: there will be problems of enforcement. (The issue of side effects and unintended consequences will be discussed also in Chapter 6.) Even under a very coercive regime people may manage to evade or subvert policies. Nevertheless, experience of the family–state relationship under such an authoritarian model is likely to be oppressive. Individual and family interests, needs and choices are largely over-ridden by the implementation of the goals of those with power.

There are various key areas of family behaviour to which this model might be directed; most obviously, perhaps, the target may be more or less fertility (see Douglas, 1991, for fertility policies). Governments may seek to control the size of their populations in either direction, by limitation (for example, China) or expansion (for example, Romania in the Ceauşescu era), or, perhaps, to increase the size of certain ethnic groups at the expense of others (for example, Germany under the Third Reich). The challenge for a government with clear fertility objectives is how to affect people's behaviour in a most intimate area of their lives, an area of behaviour which is notoriously difficult to oversee and police. A less authoritarian solution is that a variety of inducements, including the financial, can be offered to pressure individuals in the direction of the desired behaviour pattern (that is, to produce more, or fewer, children). A battery of other means, both punitive and non-punitive, could also be used to shift reproductive patterns in one direction or the other. In a movement to a more authoritarian solution, stricter investigation and severer penalties including the criminal would be expected for non-conformity (for example, action on suspected abortions in Romania: see Douglas,

1991, who cites the *Guardian*, 24 January 1990), with certain options effectively ruled out. If the elimination of one particular ethnic group were intended, for example, prison camps or other institutions could be set up where people from that group were physically prevented from reproducing. This may seem an extreme example even for the authoritarian model, but it should be remembered that in the early twentieth century in Britain, when eugenicist ideas were prevalent, this sexual segregation was effectively imposed on many people with learning difficulties (see, for example, Taylor, 1986). An obvious way of achieving fertility *growth*, which an authoritarian government might adopt, is to make most forms of contraception and abortion illegal and unobtainable (examples would be the Republic of Ireland and the more extreme case of Romania: see Douglas, 1991). Even then, however, some form of 'black market' is likely to grow up, particularly where there is contact with other countries with less strict policies.

Reproduction is obviously linked with sexuality, and the state may also attempt to make and enforce rules governing the expression of sexuality in its own right, its approved forms and contexts, either because it wishes to control reproduction or for other reasons. Again this is difficult to enforce, but authoritarian governments may have some success in preventing the opportunity for (non-approved) sexual relations, and in exacting penalties where these occur, using the law and other institutions. An extreme example from some Muslim countries would be the punishment of adultery and fornication by death, imprisonment or lashes (Mumtaz and Shaeed, 1987). Societies where religious and political institutions are closely interpenetrated might provide the best examples of states which succeed in controlling sexuality to a very high degree.

An authoritarian model may also imply rules, strictly enforced, about who can – legitimately – live with whom; who is responsible for whom and in what way; who is related to whom; and marriage and parenthood as formal, legalised institutions. Through the law the state can allocate to certain relationships, and not others, a particular status, backing this up with a range of penalties. Certain groups defined according to family status (for example, the illegitimate, the divorced, the unmarried mother) could be barred from particular activities: for example,

from inheriting, voting, holding particular offices, or from receiving certain forms of state assistance. In this way certain
behaviour patterns and institutions, and not others, would be
upheld.

Even the most authoritarian government is likely to find that
in areas where they are not constantly surveyed people will
sometimes behave in ways that deviate from the ideal, whatever the sanctions against them. However, where the state can
succeed in altering people's *internal* controls, so that they effectively police their own behaviour, the chances of success in
imposing particular patterns would be greater. It is here that a
religious state, or a state with an extremely efficient propaganda
machine, may have more success. In so far as individuals develop a strong conscience about the moral rightness or wrong-
ness of particular family forms and behaviours, there is a greater
chance that the approved forms can be promulgated, and indeed reproduced through the socialisation of children. Where
one of the approved norms is that children should indeed *be*
strictly socialised into the established patterns, then the whole
system can become self-reinforcing to a degree. Examples might
be religious societies which practise strict and all-encompass-
ing child socialisation. Nevertheless external conditions may
change and upset the stability of the pattern.

To restate the main contours of the authoritarian family–
state relationship: the relationship between state and citizens
is marked by extreme power exercised rigidly and harshly against
individuals and families to ensure conformity. This leaves the
actual *direction* of the objectives which the state has for families unsettled: the direction of an authoritarian policy could,
for example, be feminist or anti-feminist, right- or left-wing
(not that these terms apply to the family arena in a simple
way), towards deeply 'traditional' or towards revolutionary family
forms, towards larger or smaller families, towards families that
are always biologically based or that are purely social units. In
the authoritarian model there will be *a* clearly defined and
rigorously enforced direction for families (or at least for certain key aspects of family behaviour, such as fertility).

A *laissez-faire* model of family–state relationship

The second model describes a situation at the other end of the control continuum where the state seeks to exercise *no* influence over what families should do or be like; the position of government and the other institutions of the state is libertarian, in that family life is regarded as an area of complete individual freedom and choice. There are no objectives as far as the state is concerned for family behaviour, no preferred forms, no imposed ideology or values relating to family or sexual morality; and therefore *prescriptions* for the direction that families and family policy might follow have no place in this model. Indeed it cannot by definition contain any 'family policy': the policy is 'no policy'. The family is a private arena, contrasted with the public areas of government, economic life and work, and various other institutions. The state has no legitimate concern with what occurs in 'the home'; the power of the state stops at the portals of this entirely personal terrain of citizens' lives. This pattern might fit more easily with a state which was minimalist in general, restricting its activities to, say, law and order in the public arena, external defence, and enforcing the rules of contract. A state which is very minimalist in general is less likely to get in the family's way inadvertently. This model of the family–state relationship fits best perhaps with an anarchistic model of society where the coercive power of the state is kept at an absolute minimum, and individuals have territories which they control, where they can do as they like, and where the state does not go.

As the position of the state towards the family in this model is 'hands-off', there would be no need for the legal regulation of marriage, parenthood or other family relationships, and no assumptions built into any policies that individuals had family responsibilities. There would therefore be no need for sanctions of any kind supporting or penalising particular family forms, or for any state-promoted ideology as to what family behaviour should be like. The state would relate to individuals in their private lives only *as* individuals. This would mean, for example, the complete disaggregation of tax and social security policies so that individuals were taxed, and given allowances and cash benefits only for themselves (assuming that taxation

and benefits did indeed exist). While individuals would presumably be free to make contracts with each other regulating
their relationships, these would be upheld by the state only in
the way that any other contract would be, and the terms of any
initial contract would be for the individuals concerned to determine; there would be no standard pattern or approved model.

How people would in fact behave in families is left unanswered in the *laissez-faire* model. In a sense it should not matter; people would do as they wished within the confines of the
(minimal) law. But where calls are made for a more *laissez-
faire* approach to families, there is sometimes an assumption
made that, left to themselves, individuals will in fact manifest
certain family patterns. For example, the right-wing thinker
Mount (1982) sees the spouse and parent–child bonds as in-
herently strong and resisting all attempts by church and state
to mould and control them; in conditions of *laissez-faire* these
bonds would presumably flourish. The child-care writers
Goldstein, Freud and Solnit (1973 and 1980), who advocate a
form of *laissez-faire* in the state's approach to children – although
nothing as extreme as the model posited here – believe that
in the vast majority of cases parents provide a loving environment for their children and the children's interests lie in remaining with their parents (see Fox Harding, 1991b). Again,
presumably this pattern would flourish in conditions of minimum state intervention. Some neo-traditionalist writers on the
family tend to assume that *really* everybody wants the conventional family form which they themselves favour, and therefore left to themselves would pursue it; at other times, however,
these writers may be extremely authoritarian in their wish to
impose this form (see, for example, Fletcher, 1988b). The point
to be made here is that any implicit assumptions about family
behaviour within a *laissez-faire* approach do require examination, since there may be a hidden agenda in the advocacy of
laissez-faire.

That there are problems and contradictions in this model
should be readily apparent. For example, how would the general criminal law relate to families? Presumably as families had
no special status or protection, the law would apply as it would
where any offence had been committed by an individual against
another individual, with no consideration of family circumstances.

And in the civil law the state's position is that it will uphold contracts made between consenting individuals, but go no further in intervening in family life. But particular problems arise regarding vulnerable groups who are not able to make contracts or act effectively in their own interests, and who are dependent on their families. These groups include, most obviously, children, but also mentally impaired adults and those who are physically weak and dependent on family caretakers.

As soon as the state starts to make particular rules for particular categories, however, it begins to step into the family arena. Again, the most obvious example is children. It is a tenet of this model that no specific family statuses or relationships are recognised or protected. In cases of child abuse, there should be no problem with penalising abusing parents under the criminal law. But the question of alternative care for the abused children sits awkwardly in this model, since it might still be argued it is no business of the state's to arrange this as it is up to the children themselves to find alternative caretakers. This appears to be the line taken by some 'child liberationist' authors such as Holt (1975). Similar problems arise where vulnerable and dependent adults are in fact being cared for within some kind of family unit. As soon as the state starts to intervene at all it faces questions about what to do when existing family caring breaks down. It is difficult for the role of the state to stop at criminal prosecution or upholding contracts if this means that vulnerable people are then left living with an abusive carer or with no care at all. A wider version of this problem is that power in family units in actual societies tends to be unequal, with the balance of power tilted towards adults in relation to children, men in relation to women, and able-bodied people in relation to disabled people. *Laissez-faire* proposes to leave this power imbalance untouched. In this sense it is not neutral towards families but reinforces pre-existing patterns which may be very adverse for some groups.

To restate the characteristics of the *laissez-faire* model: the relationship between state and citizen is marked by a withdrawal of the state from the family and an absence of prescription as to how individuals should conduct their personal lives. Sexual and reproductive behaviour, patterns of living together and mutual support, would be matters of personal choice; the state would neither support nor penalise any one form. The state's relationship with individuals is not mediated through any kind of family unit. The only way in which the state would intervene would be to uphold contracts and the criminal law, but family groupings would be treated no differently from any other relationships. This approach leaves existing institutions as they are in a policy of non-interference in family privacy, and raises questions about the care of vulnerable groups.

It is more difficult, perhaps, to point to actual states as examples than with the authoritarian model, although the USA has been influenced by this type of ideology. It may be that no state which is recognisably a state can be as *laissez-faire* as this model supposes; that there would always in fact be demands for *some* control over patterns of family life.

Introduction to the intermediate models

The authoritarian and *laissez-faire* models have been presented as ideal types or two ends of a control continuum for the purposes of analysis. In the real world such models are unlikely to be found in a pure form. In most cases an intermediate position is occupied by the state in relation to families, with some (but not draconian or totally limiting) control exercised over how families operate. It is somewhere in this intermediate area that British policy in relation to the family can be placed. Britain is said not to have a family policy as such with clear objectives for family life (Kamerman and Kahn, 1978), but it is certainly very far from a *laissez-faire* model which does not attempt to mould family life at all. It is suggested that elements of all the intermediate models which will now be proposed can be found in British policy, with variations over time and between different policy areas.

Five possible intermediate models are posited, ranging from the relatively more authoritarian to the relatively more *laissez-faire*. It is difficult to place these precisely on a continuum of control, but in general terms the sequence here represents a shading from a clear attempt to control families, at least in particular areas, to a more reactive stance which responds to family patterns and changes but does not attempt explicitly to influence, let alone direct, them.

The first intermediate model involves the enforcement of family responsibilities in specific areas, in line with certain objectives; the second the manipulation of incentives (both penalties and rewards) in order to create specific family behaviours and forms; and a third and much less controlling model deploys constraining assumptions which, while they may be correct or incorrect, in practice limit the boundaries of family variation, or at least make some patterns easier and others more difficult. The next two models (which are essentially reactive rather than proactive) involve, first, substituting for or supporting those roles which are normally carried out in families, where families fail or malfunction in some respect; and second, simply responding – through various benefits and services – to needs and demands that arise from families. Again, these are presented as hypothetical models, but are reflected in actual policies to a greater degree than the more extreme models.

The enforcement of responsibilities in specific areas

The model suggested here lacks the totality of control implied by the authoritarian model, although certain objectives for family life may be implied or even specified. Enforcement of particular patterns here is directed to specific circumscribed areas, such as the obligation to maintain financially, or to care for, certain relatives in certain defined circumstances. Enforcement may be by means of the criminal and/or civil law and by the use of financial and other penalties imposed when the defined obligations are not met. Where individuals do not behave as the state says that they should towards family members, they could therefore be prosecuted, forcibly separated from them, financially penalised, or otherwise punished. Here the state is putting its coercive power behind the creation of particular patterns of responsibility. Where these are not fulfilled, there are serious consequences.

Liable relative provisions in British law provide an obvious example, and it can be noted that child maintenance obligations are now being stringently enforced under the Child Support Act 1991. This measure is significant as a development in a more authoritarian direction. In some cases there is a penalty (a benefit reduction) for the parent who does not comply with a direction to help enforce the responsibilities of the *other* parent, as well as penalties imposed on the other/liable parent himself. The theme of more rigorous enforcement of parental responsibility has been apparent in a number of areas of Conservative policy in Britain (see Fox Harding, 1994). The pursuit of parental responsibility builds on earlier provisions, but may be seen as a kind of family policy in its own right developing in specific areas. There is an attempt to promote a particular ideology of parenthood and family responsibility, with the aim of reducing public expenditure and strengthening the social order.

The exclusion from certain preferred statuses (for example, legitimacy), may be used to enforce particular patterns, as may the withholding of various benefits and services; in fact, the range of sanctions mentioned when discussing the authoritarian model. In this model, however, the use of penalties and sanctions is less all-embracing, and the objectives to which they are directed less comprehensive. On the other hand, the model is more heavy-handed in approach than intermediate models two and three (manipulating incentives/working within constraining assumptions). In specific areas of life individuals may find that they confront the power of the state and its considerable array of weapons if they do not conform.

We should note the consciousness of intention in this model. While the state's objectives for the family are not as over-riding as in the authoritarian model, there are still clear policy objectives such as the strengthening of parental responsibility, or the strengthening of marriage. As with the authoritarian model, enforcement problems are encountered, with individuals finding various ways to evade the responsibilities which the state attempts to impose on them. Penalties and sanctions do not necessarily achieve the effects intended; most obviously, relatives may 'disappear' from contact with those for whom they are supposed to be responsible, or leave the country, or even commit suicide, as has been claimed in relation to the Child Support Act.

The manipulation of incentives

In this model both penalties (up to a point) *and* rewards are consciously manipulated in order to encourage preferred patterns of family behaviour and to discourage those which are not favoured by the state. This is seen as a somewhat less authoritarian approach than the preceding model, but the objective is still to control or influence aspects of family life in particular areas, if by slightly more gentle means. What is characteristic of the model is that positive means of reinforcement are used, as well as some deterrence through penalties. So individuals may be encouraged into particular family forms and behaviours by the advantageous consequences, and discouraged from others by the disadvantageous consequences; these consequences are consciously designed by the state to achieve this effect.

The most obvious way in which this may be done is through economic incentives. That is, structures can be created where individuals stand to gain financially from pursuing particular family patterns and to lose from pursuing others. The state may therefore, for example, organise the tax and benefit system in such a way as to produce a particular structure of rewards. This serves the purpose of both actually rewarding approved patterns, and signalling to all citizens what the approved patterns are. For example, as in Britain, a tax allowance may be given to the married but not to the cohabiting (a reward), while the cohabiting share with the married the 'penalty' of being required to maintain each other under social security law, and are not paid all cash benefits on the same basis as the married. There may be pro-natalist or anti-natalist financial incentives (see Douglas, 1991). Other types of incentive would be favoured and unfavoured legal statuses such as the distinction between legitimacy and illegitimacy which makes the status of birth within marriage more favourable in various ways. As noted in earlier chapters, this distinction has in fact been diminished over time in British family law and is now negligible. A government which was neo-traditionalist in its perspective on family life might wish to restore it.

Although the effect of policies under this model may be to give certain family forms preferential treatment, questions arise as to whether a particular structure of incentives is *always* the result of a conscious intention. A system of tax allowances and benefits, for example, may look as though it is set up to reward a particular type of family relationship, and therefore penalise those that deviate, but the intention of government was perhaps not so clear-cut. Other objectives may have been in mind; the structure might arise incrementally or by default; or policy-makers may *assume* a particular pattern, correctly or not, and therefore set up systems to allow for it. (This type of 'constraining assumptions' model of the state-family relationship will be discussed below.) So a given direction for the structure of incentives does not necessarily indicate that the state's *objective* is to send messages about approved behaviour patterns.

For example, in the decades since the Second World War in Britain, tax and benefit policies have tended to work to disadvantage families with young children relative to the childless or those whose children are independent (see, for example, Field, 1978). Were these policies consciously ani-natalist? It is difficult to interpret them as a general signal from government that having children is on the whole an undesirable behaviour and they wish citizens to avoid it (though it might be thought, cynically, that government does wish certain groups at the bottom of the social structure to cease to reproduce). The reasons for the growth of the considerable material disincentive to have children are connected with the pursuit of other objectives by government: the reduction in the tax threshold in order to finance state spending, and later the wish to drive down public expenditure on cash benefits. Other examples from the tax system are that spousal role reversal was formerly 'rewarded' by the wife's having two tax allowances, as was cohabitation under the mortgage interest relief scheme with each cohabitee claiming tax relief separately. Presumably government did not consciously want to reward these behaviours, and indeed in the late 1980s the rules were changed.

The 'messages' or 'signals' communicated by structures of incentives may, then, convey ambiguous judgements about preferred patterns. This is particularly the case where widely agreed objectives for family behaviour are not established in society or government. This model is best understood as *not* representing a situation where there is an all-out attempt by government to impose specific, approved family forms through deliberately altering the balance of incentives across the board. There will be areas of inconsistency, contradiction and anomaly, with 'loopholes', policies which offset or conflict with other policies, and so on. Incentives are manipulated at times; the message concerning approved patterns is there, but it is mixed. The question of what might be referred to as 'temporal lag' is also of interest here. Certain structures of rewards and incentives may date from a time when it *was* clearly intended to favour and disadvantage respectively particular patterns of family relationship but, with the passage of time, the general societal view of these patterns may have changed. The existing structure of incentives may thus become culturally out of date. The idea of a tax allowance for married couples is perhaps anachronistic in this way, although it has not yet been abolished. It favours marriage at a time when cohabitation has become almost equally acceptable, and assumes financial dependency of wives when this has been at least reduced.

However, when systems of reward *are* changed to keep pace with social reality, this may in itself react back on change and reinforce or accelerate it.

Working within constraining assumptions

Less authoritarian and controlling still, but likely to have a powerful influence on family forms, is a model of the family–state relationship where the state's actions are based upon certain assumptions about how families operate, and these are built into policies. Having adopted these assumptions, the state in effect limits and constrains families because the effect of the assumptions is to reinforce them; it becomes more difficult to behave in a way that is out of line. It has been said that this is broadly how family policy in Britain has operated (see, for example, Land and Parker, 1978); while there has been no specific family policy, no officially adopted over-arching goals for families, the building of assumptions into policies has in practice determined how families function, making certain patterns easier or more difficult. In particular, feminist criticism of social policy in Britain has argued that assumptions about female dependency have served to reinforce it. It becomes difficult for women to be independent, for example, if systems of tax and social security assume that they are not and treat them accordingly. Flexibility of roles between husband and wife may be blocked by the system's insistence that husbands are the main breadwinners and women are economic dependents at home. For example, role reversal may be disadvantaged when a man can claim certain benefits for his dependent partner but a wife cannot (see the section on incomes policy in Chapter 4).

However, while assumptions mould family behaviour and tilt the balance of advantages one way or the other, they do not actually prohibit, or always penalise, behaviour which is different from the assumed pattern. Beveridge's social security scheme, for example, assumed that married women would be maintained by their husbands, but did not severely penalise wives who worked; the opportunity was present for them to join the National Insurance scheme as independent workers, although on less favourable terms than men. The effects of not complying with assumptions are not necessarily seriously disadvantaging.

An important point to note about assumptions concerning family relationships is that they may be more or less correct/incorrect in terms of how families do in fact behave; and, like structures of incentives, they may be out-of-date in terms of social reality. There might be no particular problem with assumptions which *do* accurately reflect social reality, although they would militate against change in the future. If, for example, all married women were in fact totally dependent economically on their husbands, then a policy which reflected this by allocating cash benefits to husbands *for* wives but with no benefits for wives in their own right would arguably not be a particularly oppressive one, but would merely reflect and extend the status quo, although the policy would make change in the pattern more difficult and would therefore be constraining. The assumed dependency of children, and the withholding of benefits to them in their own right, paying them instead to their parents, is not a 'problem' if children are in fact usually maintained by their parents, although this dependency on parents in itself might still be objected to in principle.

On the other hand, a policy which made an *inaccurate* assumption would tend to distort behaviour in the direction of the assumption, and in effect discriminate against patterns that were different from what was assumed. For example, if women who are not actually dependent on a husband receive no benefits at all on the grounds of female dependency on individual men, then, if not employed, these women would either suffer badly or effectively be forced to marry. While the position of women under social security in Britain is not as stark as this, it is broadly the case that female dependency on men is still assumed in the structure of benefits, and this tends to work to the disadvantage of those women who do not have a male bread-winner to support them. The inadequate provision of maternity benefits would be one example of this effect; the shortcomings of pensions provisions for women would be another; and the insufficient level of Child Benefit provides yet another. In all cases, a husband's financial support is in effect assumed (Family Allowance, the precursor of Child Benefit, was originally fixed on the assumption that most male wages would support a wife and one child; in other words it was assumed that there *would* indeed be a male breadwinner there: see Beveridge, 1942.) Similar problems face women who do have a male partner who is not in fact supporting them. The disqualification from some benefits in Britain due to cohabitation provides the most obvious example (the male cohabitee may not be suppporting the woman, and indeed may not be able to), but women may also get 'caught' in this way within marriages where a husband is not in fact maintaining them adequately. This may leave them facing hardship. With young people, since the late 1980s benefits have been withheld (for most unemployed 16–17 year olds, and for students) or reduced (for 18–25 year olds), apparently on an assumption of continuing parental support. Parents are not legally obliged to provide this, or necessarily able to provide it, and receive no benefits themselves to subsidise these young people. This inaccurate assumption-making has left some young people caught in the middle, impoverished, or even homeless and destitute (see, for example, Pollitt, 1989).

In other words, what can occur when inaccurate assumptions are made about maintenance being provided when it is *not*, is that individuals are maintained inadequately or not maintained at all. The same sort of pattern can occur when adequate care is assumed to be provided by families for dependent members, adults or children, which is not in reality being provided. The dependent person may be 'caught in the middle' with insufficient or no care, or with damaging care (see sections on community care and child care in Chapter 4).

It is, of course, possible in principle for assumptions to be inaccurate in the opposite direction, and to work to the individual's advantage. For example, this could occur where the state intervenes on the assumption of *no* help from families, when in fact some help is forthcoming. Most obviously, the system of social security benefits may assume that someone is *not* being maintained or helped materially by another person, when in truth they *are*, if only partially. Rules such as disqualification from benefit on grounds of cohabitation or the existence of a 'liable relative', or reduction of benefit in response to other income, are designed to prevent such situations. Maintenance paid by another party is thus likely to be unofficial and undeclared if there are rules which stipulate that its existence results in a loss of benefit. For example, single mothers on Income Support may receive undeclared help in cash and/ or kind from the absent father. The system may perceive concealment as fraud, but from another perspective it is merely rational common sense if one individual does indeed wish to help another, and not simply to assist the Treasury by enabling the helped person's social security payments to be reduced. Presumably a similar covert pattern may apply where care given by a family member, if known about, would result in a withdrawal of state care services. While a family member's existence and support is not known about by the official agencies, the dependent person may gain both ways: that is, help from the relative *and* the formal services. Individuals in need may thus either lose or gain where constraining assumptions are inaccurate in one direction or another; indeed, in some cases the inaccuracy of the assumptions may mean that they do not constrain at all.

In terms of the state's control over family behaviour, there is even more of a mixed message possible here than with the 'manipulating incentives' model. The effects of assumptions in policies are not clear-cut, and are not intended to be. They are after all only *assumptions*, not directions, requirements or prohibitions. Much depends on whether the assumptions are broadly accurate or not; and, if they are inaccurate, in what direction. Inaccurate assumptions may in fact open up new possibilities for individuals and families. In many cases, however, they will act to limit, somewhat, the boundaries of family variation, or at least make some patterns easier and others more difficult. This model is less controlling than the previous three, but it can still be a powerful influence over family forms.

The assumptions made by the state in welfare policy may arise in good faith, either because policy-makers believe them genuinely to reflect social reality, or because there is in fact a wish to limit family variation and mould the direction in which families should go. However, assumptions may not even be conscious or explicitly chosen, but based on taken-for-granted ways of looking at the world. For example, the Beveridge Report may be cited as having simply taken for granted that pre-war patterns of marriage would persist in the post-war world.

Substituting for and supporting families

The next model is placed much further towards the uncontrolling, *laissez-faire* end of the continuum, since here there is no conscious attempt to influence how families should function (though policies may still well do this unintentionally), but only to work with existing patterns, by supporting them or stepping in with an alternative when they fail. That is, established family roles are assisted to continue, or are taken over in whole or in part, by various supplementary services or by services which substitute for the family temporarily or permanently. While the general aim may be only to facilitate and strengthen existing family roles, the state's intervention may also cause these roles to be weakened (this is part of the problem of unintended effects, which will be referred to further in Chapter 6).

It should be noted first of all that two very different things are implied by this model: that is, supporting families on the one hand, or substituting for them on the other. These two activities of the state may be seen as in contrast and opposition to each other, rather than belonging together in the same general model (see, for example, Moroney, 1976, who distinguishes these two approaches). For instance, where the state more or less completely takes over the family's caring function by taking a child or dependent adult into 24 hour care it may be thought that it is doing something very different from providing services to help the family fulfil its caring role more

adequately in its own home. In the latter case the family relationships continue much as before with support; in the former
there is a major disruption of them, temporarily or permanently. Writing on child-care policy has distinguished supportive help to families which keeps the parent–child relationship
intact, from more controlling policies which remove children
from their parents and more readily place them with substitute families who may well be permanent (see Fox Harding,
1991b). It may reasonably be held that the latter approach is
coercive. However, while it is conceded that forcible removal
of a child from a family under a court order is indeed a powerful
sanction, and in a sense belongs with the more authoritarian
models described, less forcible removal of a family member
may be construed very differently: for example as relief for an
over-burdened family which cannot cope with the care, and as
a way of providing the person removed with better care. Indeed families may *request* that a child or dependent adult be
taken into care (or accommodation, in respect of children since
the 1989 Children Act). What is intended in describing this
model, then, is those situations where substituting for family
care is intended, broadly, to *help* the family and the dependent member. Removal to alternative care, temporarily or permanently, may be seen as part of a continuum of support services
ranging from minor forms of assistance to a major sharing, or
total carrying, of the care task. It is substitution understood in
this less coercive sense which is seen as belonging appropriately with this model.

The essential feature of the supporting/substituting model,
then, is not control or an attempt to direct or change the family,
but the support of families as they do in fact function, in a
non-judgemental and helpful way; this may include substituting for them at times. In general, with this model the state
does not seek to determine what the family should be like;
although it may take the initiative in identifying and seeking
out families who appear to need help. So far the discussion
has tended to relate to the field of care, but some financial
assistance for family commitments may also be seen as belonging with this model. Social security benefits, through additions
for dependents, may assist families to function and meet their
responsibilities, without specifying in detail how they should

do this. For example, Child Benefit is paid to mothers *for* children, but there is no surveillance or monitoring of how the money is spent, even to ensure that it *is* spent on the children. It is, however, difficult for any system of cash benefits entirely to get away from making some assumptions about how dependencies and responsibilities are worked out in families, about who should control money, and what exactly is the unit of consumption. Even supportive benefits may therefore work within assumptions which constrain to a degree, and belong more appropriately with the previous model.

One fear, which has already been referred to in Chapter 4, is that the presence of state help will cause family roles to wither, as family members see the convenience or superiority of state responsibility and withdraw. Even supportive benefits and services may lead family members to do less, to expect to do less, and to look to the state for progressively more. In this scenario, the model of the state–family relationship, based on the notion of helping families to continue as they are, in fact results in a degree of family change. It possibly produces greater dependency on the state and weakening of the family as an institution. Damage to the family is a risk of even non-directive, would-be helpful state interventions. This is only one scenario, however. Family members may in fact be *encouraged* to care for each other by the knowledge that state services will support, help, and occasionally take over from them, and that they will not be left with a crushing burden. Alternatively, the existence of state help may make no difference in either direction.

An alternative criticism sometimes made of British policy is that there is *too little* non-controlling help made available to families; that there is, for example, insufficient financial support for the cost of rearing children, too little day care and other services for children, too little supportive help to families with difficulties (see, for example, Holman, 1980 and 1988), and too little assistance to dependent people at home on terms which are sufficiently flexible and sensitive to be acceptable to them and their family carers. The result is *either* the overburdening of the family, *or* the finding of permanent alternative care. A more supportive style of intervention might enable the original family structure to continue, if that is what those involved want. It is this sort of supportive approach which this model embodies. Here the state's approach is facilitating and non-threatening, aiming to strengthen families in their existing structure rather than to separate or fundamentally alter them. However, it is suggested that policies and services might still be targeted at families or at families of particular types, and the agencies of the state might seek out families in need of help, as well as just responding to those who present themselves.

Responding to needs and demands

The final intermediate model is closer still to pure *laissez-faire* and involves a more reactive approach of responding to family needs and demands as and when these are made manifest. The implication could still be that extensive state services are required, but the initiative here is with families and not with the state; families are free to take up various provisions, which are made available not necessarily with families specifically in mind. The state simply provides a range of services and benefits which are taken up as and when need arises in families, and these services are sensitive to family change in the sense that changing families may start to make use of the services in a different way. The position is very far indeed from a formal 'family policy'; there are welfare state policies here but nothing much is assumed about families in the way services are organised, and families are not constrained. The services are largely for *individuals*; individuals who are in fact grouped in families may well make use of services in a particular way, but this is left up to them. Some family links may be recognised and responded to, but the assumption of family membership or of particular family forms is not built into the operation of the services.

Perhaps a useful example which comes fairly close to this idea is a universal state health service (see the section on health in Chapter 4). Despite the occasional use of the term 'family doctor', a health service is essentially a service for sick individuals; being part of a family – or not part of one, or part of a family of a particular type – should in general make no difference to the right to treatment or the type of treatment given. Assumptions about families are not in general built into the service; it is not a service to support families specifically and neither does it embody particular objectives concerning family life. The service is not planned round family needs, patterns or responsibilities; its objective is to do with curing the sickness of, and providing care to, individuals. There are some exceptions to this description, however: for example, assumptions about available family care in hospital discharges.

Education may also be cited as a policy area which is not itself specifically family-oriented (see the section on education in Chapter 4). While education is concerned with the needs of children and young people, the service is essentially one geared to the development of individual children, and does not embody to any significant degree family assumptions or objectives, and neither is it construed primarily as a supplementary service for families. Education and family life *are* closely inter-linked, in that family background is known to influence educational performance, as noted in Chapter 4; and both families and schools are concerned with the socialisation of the young. But education as a service essentially focuses on the educational needs of individuals outside their family roles. On the other hand, it *is* compulsory for those aged up to 16, and this has a constraining effect on family life.

It is constructive also to consider the role of financial benefits in simply responding to needs. While the social security system in Britain does in many cases respond specifically to family patterns, and indeed attempts to enforce particular family responsibilities, some benefits are primarily benefits for *individuals*. Some National Insurance benefits and disability benefits fall into this category, for example. There are also benefits which may be taken up by families more extensively when families change, without this having been a planned part of the system when the benefits were set up. The most obvious example here is the means-tested benefit structure, comprising notably what are now called Income Support, Family Credit and Housing Benefit. These benefits, while recognising family responsibilities, were never intended to be the major family support system that they now are ($2\frac{1}{2}$ million children were on Supplementary Benefit or Family Income Supplement in 1988: see Bradshaw, 1990; see also Chapter 2 for numbers of single parents on Supplementary Benefit/Income Support). Beveridge, indeed, had expected the predecessor benefit, National Assistance, to wither away! What has occurred is that an open-ended, demand-led system of means-tested benefits has been taken up increasingly by poor and unemployed families and single-parent families. It has therefore become a major system for the support of families in conditions of economic and family change, and it has been able to respond in this way just *because* it does not relate strongly to a specific 'family policy' but is a system designed to respond to those units who meet the criteria for the particular benefits. In this sense it has been 'sensitive' to family change, although the inadequacy of the existing benefit system as a provider of family income, and long-term income in particular, would surely support the argument that it is not sensitive enough (see, for example, Oldfield and Yu, 1993; Oldfield, 1993).

This example illustrates also how the 'responding to needs' model of the state–family relationship may *facilitate* family change: by responding to changing family forms, albeit inadequately, it may make more possible and reinforce such change. Arguably the existence of a social security system which was not designed with the intention of supporting large numbers of lone-parents, but which can do so and has in fact done so, encourages the further formation of lone-parent families. This is an argument which is heard from the political right and the traditionalist wing of the family lobby, who see great dangers in making provisions for single parents which may then make the choice of the single-parent option easier and more probable (the most notable exponent of an extreme form of this view being Murray, 1984 and 1990). The argument here is that welfare systems may facilitate family change in an unintentional way, where they are in practice *responsive* to family change.

The essential features of this model, then, are that it involves a responsive and reactive approach to demands from individuals and families, and does not attempt to direct or influence the form that families should take. It is close to the extreme *laissez-faire* model, although by no means identical to it; some provisions may be made for families and their obligations (and one can envisage this model including some legal rules about what 'families' are), but services and benefits are for individuals and families to take up; they are not designed to favour or reward particular family patterns at the expense of others, or to constrain families by making particular assumptions about them, and neither are families sought out, or services targeted specifically at them or at particular types of families.

Conclusion

Altogether seven models of the family–state relationship have been described. Two are at the extremes and are unlikely to represent accurately anything in the real world, although some highly totalitarian states will attempt to come close to the authoritarian model, and anarchists of both the right and left wing might dream seriously of the *laissez-faire* one. In between are five intermediate models which are more likely to appear in the behaviour of actual state policy, although not to the exclusion of each other. These five are not the only models theoretically possible, but have been selected as representing usefully the spread of possibilities. They are roughly ranged on the authoritarian–libertarian continuum and therefore in general terms shade from more to less control and direction. The seven models are listed below.

1. An authoritarian model.
2. The enforcement of responsibilities in specific areas.
3. The manipulation of incentives.
4. Working within constraining assumptions.
5. Substituting for and supporting families.
6. Responding to needs and demands.
7. A *laissez-faire* model.

In the real world of policy the models are not mutually exclusive: aspects of a number may be found in any actual state and its dealings with the family. For example, social security may be used to illustrate most of the models: enforcement of responsibilities in the pursuit of liable relatives; manipulation of incentives through benefits which favour particular family patterns but not others (for example, for a married partner but not a cohabiting one); constraining assumptions through reinforcing female dependency on a male by making indadequate provision for *non*-dependency; supporting family roles by off-setting the financial costs of children; or responding to demands through an open-ended benefit system for those who meet certain

criteria. Particular areas of the welfare state cannot necessarily
be slotted wholesale into particular models of the family–state
relationship, any more than an actual state will necessarily conform to just one model in its inter-relationship with the family. Even one individual benefit or service may be doing a number
of different things at once: for example, it may be authoritarian in relation to one family or if applied in one particular
way, and supportive or facilitating with another family, or if
applied in a different way.

There are problems, therefore, with the models and their
application, but what the framework outlined here may do, it
is hoped, is to make the nature of particular policies – and
arguments surrounding policies – better understood in terms
of the control which it is proposed to exercise over individuals
in their family settings. Where particular prescriptions and policy
directions are argued for, it is not always made explicit how
much directiveness in respect of family relationships is being
implied. One set of constraining assumptions may be criticised
for their control function, when it is proposed to replace them
with an equally constraining, albeit different, set (for example,
assuming female *in*dependence from men rather than dependence might also constrain). This problem may sometimes arise
because those advocating particular directions for policy do
honestly believe that 'this is what people really want'; although
this position can easily shade into 'this is what they ought to
want', followed by 'this is what we are going to make them
have'. Policies may also be directing and controlling in relation to one group in order to enhance the freedom of another;
for example, controlling parents in relation to children (in
order to improve things for children), men in relation to women
(in order to improve things for women), or, of course, vice
versa, controlling children in relation to parents and women
in relation to men (in order to improve things for parents
and men). In such cases a degree of authoritarianism/
directiveness in policy may be thought justified, but the degree
of control proposed ought, the author would argue, to be
exposed and debated.

This chapter's argument is essentially that the dimension of
control–no control is an important characteristic of policy and
the state which may be examined independently of the con-

tent and direction of specific policies. Where policy prescriptions are advanced, they involve a degree of control (just how much can be examined); and different policy prescriptions may resemble each other in seeking to enforce conformity, while the actual *content* of the prescription may vary enormously. Most obviously, policies which either seek to restore 'traditional' roles *or* to transform them might be equally authoritarian in their implications for the state–family relationship.

The next chapter will conclude the discussion by examining some questions relevant to the elusive notion of 'family policy'. It will consider the meaning of 'family policy', rhetoric and reality, 'family policy' as smokescreen, side-effects of policies on families, inconsistencies in policies, and whether policy can be value-free.

Chapter 6

The Quest for 'Family Policy'

The previous two chapters, considered, respectively, areas of interaction between family and state in actual British policy, and generalised models for the family–state relationship. This chapter will conclude the discussion of family and state by addressing briefly some aspects of the idea of 'family policy'. This phrase, which appears at intervals in the literature on family and state, and on social policy generally, has no clear-cut meaning, and is not perhaps susceptible to any definitive analysis. What this chapter attempts to do is only to raise some specific questions and issues relating to the concept of 'family policy'.

The first area to be considered comprises attempts to define family policy and to delineate what this has meant in different national frameworks. The main sources to be used here are Kamerman and Kahn (1978) and Moss and Sharpe (1979). Second, the question of *rhetoric* and 'family policy' will be addressed. In this field the distinction between rhetoric, and real policy and its actual effects, is particularly important. The third topic addressed concerns an important way in which the rhetoric of family policy can be used as a smokescreen for policies with quite other objectives, and, similarly, ostensible 'family' policies can be used as an instrument or means for policies with other aims (economic, miltaristic, ideological and so on). The fourth issue is the crucial one of 'side-effects' of policies which are not necessarily 'family policies' in any meaningful sense, or even social policies, but which have implications (sometimes drastic ones) for family relationships, functions and structure. The existence of family effects arising from policies across a wide range has given rise to the demand for some device for anticipating and monitoring these: for example, through some kind of 'family impact statement'. The fifth issue involves the way in which policies may (in combination) act in an inconsistent, contradictory way towards families, creating what are referred to here as policy 'holes' and 'knots', and the demand for a more coherent 'family policy'. The sixth question, considered briefly, is whether what might be regarded as 'family policy' can be 'value-free'.

Definitions of 'family policy'

Kamerman and Kahn (1978) considered 'family policy' in fourteen countries, and classified those fourteen into three groups: those with an explicit and comprehensive family policy (the examples of specific countries being Sweden, Norway, Hungary, Czechoslovakia and France); those with family policy seen as a field covering various policies (Austria, the Federal German Republic, Poland, Finland and Denmark); and countries where family policy was implicit and reluctant (the UK, Canada, Israel and the USA). Later the authors say that it was possible to classify countries on something of a continuum with regard to whether family policy was implicit or explicit, comprehensive or episodic, harmonised to a degree or uncoordinated, although this classification was nowhere completely unambiguous. It may be noted here that this continuum may to some extent relate to the continuum of authoritarianism suggested in Chapter 5, with the more explicit, comprehensive and coordinated policies being, at least potentially, more authoritarian.

Although the idea of family policy came to prominence in the 1970s, it was not a new concept; Kamerman and Kahn pointed out that the idea had been part of the European political scene since the 1920s. It was first used in the context of income policies favouring large families; and second in the context of population policies and concern about demographic projections. But although in some ways family policy was a longstanding concept, there was still a problem in defining it. Kamerman and Kahn suggest that family policy can mean *every-*

thing that government does to and for the family, but they go on to pose three divisions within family policy: explicit family policy with specific programmes and policies designed to achieve specified family goals; explicit policy with family programmes which deliberately do things to and for families but which have no agreed overall goals; and implicit family policy. With the latter, policies are not specifically or primarily addressed to the family, but have indirect consequences for it, including incidental or unanticipated consequences arising from policies designed to accomplish very different objectives, such as industrial policy, transport and immigration (see 'The problem of side-effects', below). The authors themselves defined family policy to mean *deliberate* governmental actions taken towards the family, such as day care, child welfare, family counselling, family planning, and some areas of tax, benefit and housing policy. Here an explicit definition of family policy (with or without overall goals) is being utilised, where the family is clearly the object of policy.

In addition to these distinctions, Kamerman and Kahn note the importance, in family policy analysis, of differentiating the interests of the family as a unit from the interests of particular roles and statuses *within* the family; and they note the use of family policy concepts to think about policies affecting children, and those affecting women. They also make the distinction between family policy as *field* and as *perspective*. Family policy may be seen as a (potentially broad but in practice usually modest) *field* of policies, where there are certain objectives regarding the family, and measures are developed to achieve the objectives. The field could include population policy, transfer payments, employment, housing, nutrition and health; also the personal social services, child care and policies for women. In fact the chapters in Part II of Kamerman and Kahn's work, which deal with 'Family policy as Field' and the countries where family policy is understood in this way, include the areas of income maintenance for families, family counselling, maternity provision, child day care, family law, women's policy and population policy; also, to some extent, education, employment, housing and health; a wide spectrum, although not all of the chapters on individual countries cover every area. As Kamerman and Kahn say (p. 496): 'As field, family policy at most usually covers a modest, if significant, domain.' Alternatively, family policy may be seen as *perspective* or criterion: that is, *all* policy could be examined for its effect on families and their well-being, and this could also be a criterion for policy choice. Interest in the *perspective* concept translates into the idea of operational-ising it through structured arrangements in government, which would monitor the family impact of policies and contribute to policy development with family interests in mind (to be dis-cussed under 'The problem of side effects' below). A family perspective requires knowledge, greater clarity about values, and political will.

Kamerman and Kahm also observe that the purposes of family policy may be manifest, or latent: that is, not made explicit, and not overtly declared. In fact, family policy may be an in-strument where some behaviour in families is required to achieve other societal goals; family policy here is a *means* to latent, even unacceptable, objectives. This sort of point will be ex-plored further under '"Family policy" as smokescreen and in-strument' below.

Schultheis (1990), cited by Hantrais (1993), applies another version of Kamerman and Kahn's categorisation to EC states. A few countries were seen as having had a long tradition of explicit, far-reaching and legitimated family policy-making which responds to a wide range of needs. Some have more implicit family policies which take account of family needs but without creating an autonomous area of policy. Measures used here are more selective and may lack overall coherence. Other states have what Schultheis describes as a 'negative family policy'. These countries are reluctant to intervene in family life and claim not to have a family policy, but do pursue actions likely to have an impact on the family. A measure of interest in fam-ily policy is how far family welfare is institutionalised in policy-making: for example, are there Ministers for the family, how is family policy funded and organised, and is the family enshrined in national constitutions, as it is in eight EC states cited by Hantrais? Here, then, family policy is seen as 'explicit', 'im-plicit' or 'negative', as compared with Kamerman and Kahn's division between between explicit policy with goals, explicit policy without goals, and implicit policy.

Writing, like Kamerman and Kahn, in the late 1970s, Moss

and Sharpe (1979) made some very similar points to those authors. They suggested various approaches to the problem of definition, the first being the very broad approach also put forward by Kamerman and Kahn: family policy as whatever the state does to affect people in their family roles. With this definition every country has some sort of family policy, as government policies always affect families in some way. The second approach is that family policy can be defined as a *field* which is definable in terms of objectives, programmes, policies and services; as noted above, Kamerman and Kahn also use this approach as one possibility. The 'field' approach, as Moss and Sharpe say, raises questions as to *which* objectives and programmes to include; where and why to draw the line that bounds the field. The authors say that family policy has been associated with goals in a wide range of policy areas including labour market policy; population policy; child health, development and socialisation; sex equality; and incomes. As they point out, there is a vast range of policies which *could* be included because they have some bearing on the functioning and welfare of families; but, in practice, countries that have attempted to assemble a set of programmes as an explicit family policy have actually come up with a modest range, including measures like child allowances, maternity benefits, child-care programmes, possibly abortion and contraception, and family counselling (that is, policies mostly to do with reproduction). Other policy areas which are also of crucial importance to families (tax, economic policy, health, social security, housing, education and employment) actually prove too much to be organised into a family policy field, not just because inter-departmental coordination is difficult, but because the goals and concerns of these other policy areas are not solely to do with families and their welfare, but include other goals as well. So, in practice, defining family policy as a field leads to a narrow field, although in principle the field could be extremely broad.

In criticism of the field approach, Moss and Sharpe say that it leads to discussion of what the field should include without offering any clear principles to guide selection. At best the result is a basketful of policies lacking overall coherence and lacking many items of policy which actually are important to family well-being. Moss and Sharpe also talk about a family *perspective* on policy, and again make similar points to Kamerman and Kahn. Here the key is the significance, for policy, of the family as a unit of welfare and behaviour. Evaluations of the impact of policies *on families*, and conversely of the impact of families *on policies*, are seen as essential to the development of more effective policies; the most appropriate government response is to *develop an approach* to the making and evaluation of policy based on an understanding of the complex interactions between policies, families and individuals. A family perspective on policy should have four premises: that the family–policy relationship is two-way; that family should be taken into account across virtually the whole range of public policy; that increasing family diversity should be recognised and respected; and that all types of family (broadly defined) should be taken into account. The latter points suggest an attempt at a value-neutral approach. Moss and Sharpe say (pp. 144–5): 'At its most basic and simplest, adopting a Family Perspective on Policy means increasing policy-makers' awareness of the family's impact on policy and vice versa, and therefore "thinking family" as a matter of course when considering any policy.' These two sets of authors, then, are in agreement that family policy can be defined in different ways, and that a field/perspective distinction is useful.

Later writing on the theme of family policy is found (in an American context) in the work of Zimmerman (1988 and 1992). In fact, back in 1979, Zimmerman had envisaged the criterion or perspective sense of family policy, saying (p. 492): 'The concept of family policy ... incorporates the criterion of "family well-being" which may be used as an objective, goal or standard for formulating and evaluating policy, as well as the assessment of public actions and decisions in terms of their consequences for families or particular categories of families.' That is, 'family well-being' may guide policy and be a measure of its effects. Zimmerman went on to talk about family impact analysis, which would analyse the effects of policy change on families: 'Family impact analysis of pending legislation, policies, regulations, and guidelines, would make explicit their potential negative or positive effects or outcomes, and their potential lack of coherence or consistency vis-à-vis families' (p. 493). This kind of prior analysis of policy might lead to some consensus about the goals of an overall family policy.

In her later work the author returned to the same theme. In *Understanding Family Policy* (1988, p. 13) Zimmerman comments that while the USA does not have an explicitly stated family policy, 'almost all government policies affect families directly and indirectly, intentionally or not'. In defining family policy she makes the by now familiar distinction between family policy as perspective and family policy as field of activity. Under 'Perspective', Zimmerman says that the problems of families relative to society are the concerns of family policy. Family policy may be regarded as a sub-category of social policy, but may also be as broad as, or even broader than, social policy. In incorporating family well-being as a criterion for policy, family policy introduces family considerations into the (whole) policy arena, whether in establishing policy objectives or measuring policy outcomes. Policy objectives may be explicit or implicit; outcomes of policies for families may be intended, unintended, direct, indirect, manifest or latent. Under 'Field of Activity' Zimmerman suggests that as a field, family policy includes various programmes, of which she gives American examples. A very wide variety of programmes is listed here; in fact, Zimmerman says (p. 21): 'In other words, as earlier definitions suggest, family policy connotes all activities promoted or sanctioned by government that affect families, directly or indirectly.'

Under her 'Concluding Observations' in Chapter 1, Zimmerman says (p. 22): 'Thus while family policy may be nothing less than social policy, . . . its emphasis on families in contrast to individuals is its differentiating characteristic', and 'family well-being represents a value that when operationalized can be applied in assessing and evaluating policy in all areas'. Family well-being, then, is a criterion in making judgements on (all) policies. In the final chapter of this book, Zimmerman makes the distinction between the explicit/manifest and the implicit/latent (p. 176): 'Policy choices into which family considerations are deliberately structured are known as explicit or manifest family policies . . . policy choices into which family considerations are not deliberately structured but [which] affect families nonetheless are known as implicit or latent family policies.' Thus even where family considerations are not deliberately incorporated into policies, there may be family effects: there is a latent policy. In order to protect families from the

unintended consequences of policies, and to shape policies so
that they meet the standard of family well-being, there is a
need to understand policies in relation to families and vice
versa, and to influence policy accordingly.

In her latest work, *Family Policies and Family Well-Being* (1992),
Zimmerman makes similar points. She distinguishes between
'family policy' and 'family polic*ies*', stating how she uses the
terms (pp. 3–4):

> *family policy* refers to a perspective for understanding and
> thinking about policy in relation to families. I use the term
> *family policy* in the singular as a policy perspective and also
> as a way of conveying the idea of a cluster of policy measures
> with identifiable family content that then find expression in
> family-related program activities. I also use the term in the
> plural to refer to all the individual policies that affect fam-
> ilies, both directly and indirectly. (Italics in the original)

'Family policies' denotes a broader range of policy, then. Family policy is also discussed as a field of activity. Zimmerman's
summary includes the statement (pp. 18–19): 'Family policy is
choice in the pursuit of family well-being as its goal. It is both
a *perspective* for looking at policy in relation to families and a
field comprised of many different kinds of family-related pro-
grams' (italics added).

Mention may be made briefly of the contribution of Quah
(1994), writing in the context of child care in Singapore. Referring to the large variety of interpretations of family policy
in vogue, Quah states that family policy 'may be defined as a
comprehensive plan of action formulated to reflect shared social
values and to attain defined social goals concerning the nation's families' (p. 125). Examples of comprehensive policy are
rare, she notes, and what is more common is an array of poli-
c*ies* that affect the family directly or indirectly. Quah also refers to the controversy over the role of government intervention
with families. At one extreme is the position that intervention
is harmful to families; Quah here cites, *inter alia*, Lasch (1977)
and Donzelot (1980). At the other extreme is the view that
only the state can solve serious problems affecting families; Quah
cites Kamerman and Kahn (1978) as advocates of family policy

in this sense. In between are moderate views about policies having a role in the well-being of families, but not interfering too much: 'in order to avoid blunders and excesses, the limits of state intervention should be clearly demarcated' (p. 126). Authors cited include Berger and Berger (1983), who envisage non-intrusive, supportive policies. As Quah notes (pp. 126–7): 'A number of studies have documented the unexpected and negative consequences of even the best planned welfare policies' (see 'The problem of side effects' below). The similarity of these various views to the continuum of control versus *laissez-faire* posited in Chapter 5 may be noted.

In conclusion, it seems that family policy is a confusing idea, and no clear definition of the concept emerges. Both the field and perspective or impact approaches have their value, but the fragmented, piecemeal and pragmatic nature of policy in general, and the complexity of the interaction between family and policy, perhaps make clear concepts of a 'family policy' (with definite objectives, assumptions and predictable effects, or even as a perspective on all policies) difficult to grasp. Neither is there a consensus on what the state's role and family policy should be.

The specific case of family impact statements will be discussed in a later section, as will the case for a more unified 'family policy'.

Rhetoric and ideology versus reality and implementation in 'family policy'

In the field of family policy, it is important to distinguish rhetoric from reality, because this area seems particularly prone to the use of rhetoric which is somewhat detached from reality by both government and pressure groups. Conservative governments of the 1980s and 1990s in Britain have been prone to the use of emotive 'family' rhetoric for its supposed popular appeal and political advantage, without, in any clear-cut way, backing this up with actual policy (see Durham, 1991). In 1990, for example, the slogan which adorned the Conservative party conference was 'Working to keep the family together' (Lister, 1994). Yet it is hard to point to any solid policy evidence that this was what the Conservative government was doing or had done (and, of course, huge questions arise as to what this phrase might mean), unless the reference was to the ongoing review of policy on single parents which eventually resulted in the Child Support Act 1991, though this was hardly to do with keeping the family together in anything but a financial sense. The attractions of this rhetoric were, presumably, that government, rightly or wrongly, believed it to tap into an area of popular anxiety; that it enabled government to appear to respond to pressure from some moral lobby groups associated with the right wing; and that it did indeed reflect a concern within government with self-sufficient and cohesive families (not a concern that would necessarily over-ride other policy objectives when they conflicted, but one that was compatible with certain aims, such as the reduction of public expenditure).

Rhetoric is one thing, detailed policy another. While a few Conservative measures were in line with neo-traditionalist 'pro-family' rhetoric (most notably the notorious 'Clause 28' which in 1988 prohibited local authorities from intentionally promoting homosexuality), other policies did not proceed in the direction which the 'pro-family' rhetoric would have indicated, and some moved clearly in the opposite direction: for example, changes in family law, and the drive to lower wages and benefits for families. While much was said by politicians about supporting the family, actual policy did not present a consistent, supportive line or pursue clear, over-arching, 'pro-family' objectives (see Durham, 1991).

In 1978 Kamerman and Kahn categorised Britain as a country without an explicit family policy, where the idea of a comprehensive family policy had in fact been rejected. This remained broadly the position in the 1980s and early 1990s, despite the surfacing of the theme of 'parental responsibility' in a number of areas such as child-care legislation, juvenile offending and income maintenance (see Fox Harding, 1994). Kamerman and Kahn did see Britain as a country which, on a broader definition, had a family policy: that is, policies were based on certain assumptions about responsibilities and dependencies in families which were implicit in the legislation. Chester commented similarly in 1983 (p. 99):

Societies vary in the extent to which they formulate an explicit 'family policy', and in Britain there has tended to be
a rhetoric of public support but not an articulated policy.
However, since social policies inevitably entail *some* assumptions about patterns of dependency between the sexes and
the generations, family policy can as well be formed implicitly,
or by omission and indirection. (Italics in the original)

Abbott and Wallace, writing in 1992, re-iterated the theme, saying:
'The Conservative administration under Margaret Thatcher's
leadership developed no explicit family policy' (p. 117). It may
be argued that the reluctance to adopt an explicit family policy
in Britain is connected with ideas of a non-interventionist state
in a liberal democratic culture (see, for example, Dingwall *et
al.*, 1983), and the connected idea of the family as a private
arena, sacrosanct from the state (see F. R. Elliott, 1989). Arguments for and against a unified policy will be explored below.
   The point here is, therefore, that government's public statements on desirable patterns and objectives have to be disen-
tangled from actual policies and their effects; and while this
caution would probably hold for all policy areas, it seems to
be particularly apt in the field of family policy where strong
emotions and ideals are involved, 'moral panics' and wild statements are prone to appear, and a more detached and realistic
approach seems more difficult to achieve. As Kamerman and
Kahn (1978; p. 482) said: 'Family rhetoric is attractive, family
policy politically dangerous.' They note the discomfort in some
countries – such as the USA – about explicit discussion of fundamental values and goals for families.
   Actual policies have to take into account a variety of objectives, and the interests of particular groups with their varying
degrees of organisation and lobbying power. Clear anti-female
equality policies, for example, would have to run the gauntlet
of something over 50 per cent of the electorate being female,
although it is the case that women understand their interests
in different ways and they certainly do not vote as a block.
But, for example, repealing the Sex Discrimination Act 1975,
as some of the traditional and 'pro-family' lobby might wish
(for example the Conservative Family Campaign in its early
days of 1986–7), could well face large-scale opposition from

women who would see their interests threatened by this. There are various pressures on government, even right-wing government, and rhetoric should not be swallowed wholesale as government actions may follow a very different path.

'Family policy' as smokescreen and instrument

As well as being out of line with the reality of actual policy, 'family' rhetoric can be used as a deliberate mask for policies which are really to do with other matters and which have objectives not in fact primarily related to family at all. Here 'family policy' rhetoric is a convenient smokescreen or camouflage for other things. Kamerman and Kahn (1978) point out that family policy can be an instrument, where some behaviour in families is required to achieve other societal goals which do not relate directly to families. 'Family policy' here is essentially a *means*; it may be defined as a rationale for achieving latent, 'perhaps even unacceptable objectives' (p. 6). This may all sound rather sinister, and the most extreme illustrations are probably from totalitarian regimes such as the Third Reich (see Caplan, 1987, who discusses Koonz, 1987).

One example of representation of this kind is a policy which is pro- or anti-natalist, which may be presented as to do with families (and certainly has significant implications for families), but where preferred family size is a means to another end: the expansion or contraction of population in the service of other objectives. These objectives may be valid in themselves, and indeed may be openly declared, but the policy may also be presented as a *form* of 'family policy' when its origins, although impinging considerably on families, actually lie outside the field of family. Another illustration might be situations where objectives are essentially economic: for example, where a shortage of labour, or a shift in the nature of the labour market, gives rise to a need to incorporate women (including wives and mothers) into the paid labour force. This has an effect on the role of women, and may give rise to various provisions to facilitate their working, such as maternity leave/allowances and child day care. The absence of a male 'family wage' may also be used to compel women/wives into the labour force. Such policies, although they may be represented as 'freeing' women and as beneficial for children, are not unequivocally to women's advantage, restricting the choice to be at home full-time, and enforcing a double burden of paid work and domestic labour; neither are they necessarily in the interests of children who must experience alternative care of variable quality. Here family structure and functioning is subordinated to other ends.

Policies may be represented in a number of ways; and of course the true reason for the policy, such as that wartime conditions require paid labour from almost all, may well be declared. People, then, may be fully aware of the nature of the policy, and not necessarily see it as to do with *family* objectives as such. On the other hand, family rhetoric/ideology may be used by governments to 'sell' or conceal the actual policy. An interesting British example would be the title of the 1990 White Paper which preceded the Child Support Act: the title was *Children Come First* (Lord Chancellor *et al.*, 1990). The true objective, as study of the proposals and the subsequent Act makes clear, was the containment of public expenditure, not the welfare of children. The slogan 'community care' – which has considerable family implications – has been used in a similar way, to disguise expenditure containment policies relating to dependent adults; these policies often seek an essentially cheaper form of care. Thus 'family policy' terminology may serve to mask, sanitise, legitimise or make respectable and acceptable policies with other objectives.

The problem of 'side-effects': the case for 'family impact statements'

Under 'Definitions of "family policy"', family policy as a perspective on all policy was referred to: that is, the position that *all* policies could be examined for their family effects. Many types of policy, across a broad range going beyond social policy as conventionally construed, have family effects which are not always anticipated or thought through, or seen as being of overriding importance even when they *are* recognised. A striking example would be war. Military mobilisation and participation in combat, mutliple deaths and injuries, imprisonment in wartime, attacks on civilian populations and so on, have dramatic and traumatic short-term and long-term effects for families (and potential families), disrupting relationships, producing long separations, creating disability, bereavement and single-parent families, to mention just a few effects. Another example would be economic policy; a specific case within this field is the deliberate creation and tolerance of high (male) unemployment. This may be argued to be a major factor in the transformation of 'traditional' family life, with its conventional gender roles of male breadwinner/female housekeeper, because men have increasingly lost their 'breadwinning' role, causing families to depend on female earnings and/or benefits (see Chapters 1 and 2). At the same time the casualisation of the labour market and the growth of part-time and short-term employment, which has increasingly drawn women into the labour market but on highly disadvantaging terms, has again altered earlier gender roles, with women still being largely responsible for domestic work, still in part dependent on a male partner, but taking on paid work as well (with various consequences for family life following from that). And the growth of low pay has made the feasibility of families surviving on one earner's wage increasingly improbable, and has further undermined the notion of the male 'breadwinner'.

Policies which *are* seen as social, or even family policies, may also have unintended effects, which may alter, among other things, family and relationship bonds. For example, some aspects of social security policy in Britain may make certain family members into an intolerable economic liability. This happened with the household means test before the war. The modern case of 16–17 year olds is relevant where they have no benefit income, and no benefit is claimable *for* them either (a situation which has arisen for some since 1988); the cost of maintaining them within the family may cause them to leave or be forced out (see, for example, Pollitt, 1989). 'Cohabitation rules', which deprive claimants of benefit on the grounds that their cohabitee is supporting them, may also put an intolerable burden on relationships at an early stage. And with either marriage or cohabitation, the rule that where one partner works 'full-time' (which has been defined variously) *no* Income Support is claimable for *either* partner may make the economic cost of continuing to live with the non-working partner a high one, particularly if earnings are low, and/or there are no children so that Family Credit cannot be claimed either. Liability to pay a non-working partner's community charge (1990–3) would have intensified the effect of their dependency.

What these specific cases illustrate is that policy may cause the continuance of a coresiding relationship to carry a heavy price tag; it might be expected that at least some of these coresident relationships would end, perhaps weakening families in an institutional sense. Clearly some relationships are set up with a pattern of economic dependency in mind, some are strong and established enough to carry it, and in some households resources are sufficient to accommodate this dependency comfortably; but where households are poor, where there was not the expectation that this particular person would be an economic dependent at this particular stage, and where relationships are problematic or fragile anyway, then it may be expected that some bonds will fracture, certainly as far as coresidence is concerned.

Other examples of adverse family effects of social policies might be housing policies which take no account of *extended* family links or family visitors; or the 'availability for work/actively seeking employment' test for the registered unemployed, which may put pressure on would-be workers to seek and accept jobs at a distance from home, regardless of child-care commitments, marital/cohabitation relationships, or other family links and responsibilities (such as the care of elderly family members). Policies of 'community care' which have in practice put intolerable burdens on relatives, or have pressured them into 'topping up' fees in private residential homes, might similarly be argued to weaken family relationships in some cases (see Chapter 4).

Where policies have effects which are unintended or widely viewed as undesirable in terms of their effects on family links, and which are in conflict with family forms and ideals which government does supposedly wish to promote, it may be argued that they should be scrutinised more closely for their actual family effects. Here the notion of family policy as perspective, referred to in discussing definitions of family policy, is helpful. Zimmerman's (1979) idea of family impact analysis was also mentioned. Zimmerman (1988, p. 183) talks about 'family frameworks' and the need 'to protect families from the unintended consequences of policies formulated for other purposes and to shape policies such that they meet the standard of family well-being'.

Arguments have also been advanced, since the late 1970s, for 'family impact statements'. These have been seen as similar in concept to statements mandated by federal legislation in the USA for proposed policies as they affect the environment. Kamerman and Kahn (1978) say that family impact statements were seen as statements to be submitted in connection with proposed legislative or administrative actions; to be useful they should involve attempts at rigorous scientific projection in the light of available knowledge. A booklet from the Family Policy Studies Centre, *Family Issues and Public Policy* (Craven *et al.*, 1982), suggested that statements were appropriate at the *second* stage of the policy process, as they defined it: that is, when policies were being processed in Parliament. This stage involves more public debate than earlier stages. The authors argue (p. 35) that: 'The hope for family impact statements is that they would lead to policies which are more in tune with contemporary family life, which take more account of family functions and which meet family needs and aspirations.' The statements should encourage civil servants and politicians to take family considerations into account, and stimulate public debate, creating heightened public consciousness. They should also be published, and could appear at the beginning of a Parliamentary Bill. In addition to statements, later family impact *analysis*, for evaluating the effects of policies *once implemented*, was seen as important. Whitfield, a supporter of the neo-traditionalist or 'pro-family' approach, in *Families Matter* (1987) suggests that each government department be required to produce family impact statements on both existing and suggested policies, which would 'pay particular attention to the position on intact families containing married men and women and their dependants, as well as to other household groups' (p. 227). Here there is a clear concern to protect the married two-parent family as a priority.

Deakin and Wicks, in another Family Policy Studies Centre pamphlet, *Families and the State* (1988, p. 35), note that: 'just when the interest in family impact statements seemed to have withered into social history, President Reagan in 1987 issued

Executive Order 12606 on The Family. Designed "to ensure that the autonomy and rights of the family are considered in the formulation and implementation of policies by Executive departments and agencies"', the order listed various policy-making criteria, such as the strengthening of family stability, the marital commitment and parental responsibility; helping the family to perform its functions; and the message sent concerning family status and social norms. While certain values of the neo-traditionalist kind appear to be present here also, the Order does, as Wicks notes, provide an opportunity for clearer debate about family issues and public policy.

Other mechanisms besides family impact statements for monitoring the effects on families of policies have been suggested from various sources: for example, presentation by each political party of their own family policy, to enable the electorate to evaluate more clearly how their own families would be affected; an annual Family Policy Review which would evaluate and monitor policy changes from a family viewpoint; a Minister for the Family (or for Women, or for Children); Family Ministr*ies* in the plural; an inter-departmental body, quango or purely voluntary body with an overview of family and policy; family lobbies on specific issues and a general family lobby or movement; and *Child* Impact Statements, which have actually been deployed in Childright, the bulletin of the Children's Legal Centre. Whitfield (1987) also suggests, more daringly, that the role of promoting marriage and family life be located in the office of the Prime Minister, and that a permanent Royal Commission on Marriage and the Family report directly to Parliament. However, he thinks that a special *Ministry* for the family would marginalise family issues further.

While the case for mechanisms of this kind can be cogently put, no systematic attempt to monitor policy in this way has been instituted by governments in Britain. It may be speculated that political problems would surround such mechanisms because of the lack of consensus about families, family change and the role of government, and because of government's need to achieve other objectives than family well-being. Similar difficulty surrounds the notion of a unified, consistent 'family policy' which will be discussed below.

Inconsistencies, anomalies, contradictions: a coherent family policy?

Connected with the problem of unforeseen and unintended effects is the question of inconsistencies, anomalies and contradictions in policy, and whether a more unified, coherent and harmonious policy could – or should – resolve these. In Britain there has been a lack of a coherent and consistent approach to families in the span of government policies. Family assumptions are not always congruent with each other while, as noted above, family rhetoric may not be borne out in action.

Examples of inconsistency and incongruence include assumptions about certain 'obligations' being carried out where there is no mechanism in either private or public law to enforce them. The case of 16–17 year olds who are unemployed and who have no right to Income Support has already been quoted to show how policies may have unintentionally adverse effects on family relationships. It also illustrates an anomaly in policy, whereby it is assumed parents will financially support young people, yet there is no legal liability of a parent to maintain a 16 year old who has left full-time education, and therefore no means of enforcing this support, or of forcing the parent to allow the young person to remain in the parental home. And a parent who did attempt to support their child in these circumstances would receive no Child Benefit (after the end of the short 'Child Benefit extension period') or other cash allowance for the young person, even if that parent were on benefits such as Income Support themselves. The parent is thus being expected to meet an obligation which cannot in fact be enforced on them, and for which they are not reimbursed as they would be for a younger child.

Under the 'cohabitation rule', there is similarly an expectation that cohabitees will support each other, but no means of *enforcing* maintenance from a cohabitee. Neither do they receive a tax allowance as a married partner does. No legal liability to maintain a cohabitee exists under private family law (as opposed to social security law). This has been the case even when one has children by a cohabitee (although the Child Support Act changes this for separated former cohabitees, bringing maintenance for the 'parent with care' into the formula, as well as maintenance for the child). The treatment of cohabitees as a unit affects those (usually women) on Income Support, Family Credit, widow's benefits, Housing Benefit and Disability Working Allowance, and also the payment of the community charge when that was in force. The rationale for the cohabitation rule has been that if a heterosexual couple are living as 'man and wife' they should be treated as such (see, for example, Lister, 1972(?)). The fact is, however, that they are *not* living 'as man and wife' according to rules found in other parts of the system.

Another example of unenforceable expectations would be assumptions about provision of family care to dependent adults (see the section on community care in Chapter 4). This cannot be required in law and, as Finch and Mason's (1993) work makes plain, there are also strongly held norms in English culture about help to relatives being given voluntarily rather than being a rigid expectation, still less an enforceable right, and the existence of familial help and support cannot be 'read off' straightforwardly from genealogical relationship; yet more formal services may be withheld or withdrawn, or people may be discharged from hospital or other institutions, on the assumption that the family care is present. The moral pressure is on family members to fill the void left by the absence of formal support services; but neither the dependent person nor the state has any legal mechanism available to them to ensure the provision of this care (which is not to suggest that such an enforcement mechanism would be *desirable* from the point of view of the dependent person and their care).

There is a contrast here with the care of children, where evidence (or even suspicion) of inadequate care may cause action by state agencies, and possibly the child's removal to other caretakers. Here there is much greater readiness to intervene where family members are unable or unwilling to care well; it has been recognised since the first child cruelty legislation in the late nineteenth century that the mere *presence* of parents should not signify a complete state withdrawal. In other words, children are not left at risk on the basis of an untested assumption about family behaviour to quite the same degree. The difference in approach links with general attitudes to childhood, the greater willingness to commit state resources to the care of children as opposed to adults, and (it has to be said) the greater availability of alternative, relatively cheap quasi-parental caretakers for children (foster and adoptive parents).

Where families are of the single-parent type, another type of incongruence is apparent. Parents are supposed to care for their children to a certain standard, yet single parents are, in the policy thinking developed by Conservative governments in the late 1980s and 1990s, also encouraged to be engaged in paid work. At the same time, there is little subsidised state child day care to cover the need for care of younger children whose one parent works. Neglect of the child in order to go out to work will call forth a punitive response from the state, as 1990s 'home alone' cases illustrate. As Lewis (1989) shows, the state in Britain has had difficulty in deciding whether single mothers should be regarded primarily as mothers or as part of the labour force. The inconsistencies of these expectations, in a situation where child care needs are not met by the state, leaves single parents in an anomalous situation where almost any option they choose can be criticised. This incongruent situation has been carried further in some American states where aid programmes may enforce a form of 'workfare' on single mothers with very young children (though usually not under the age of three). They must be workers *and* mothers if they are to receive any state income at all (Burghes, 1992).

Two terms are coined here to describe the effects of inconsistency and lack of congruence in policy: policy 'holes' and knots'. 'Holes' occur where a void is left in the provision of needed care, support or financial maintenance because state assistance is withheld on the assumption of family obligations which cannot be enforced, and the result is an *absence* of care/support/maintenance. 'Knots' occur where policies convey contradictory messages and conflicting rewards/penalties, resulting perhaps in a 'no-win' situation where any option may be penalised.

In fact, however, while 'knots' may do this, and may cause a sense of injustice, they may also convey an advantage. For example, you do not entirely 'lose' by *either* marriage or cohabitation when both attract some rewards *and* penalties; or by single parenthood or dual parenthood when the general advantages of the two parent form are offset by some specific benefits for single parents. It is also the case that inaccurate assumptions may produce a gain as well as a loss (a 'surfeit' as well as a hole) as noted when discussing this model for the family–state relationship in Chapter 5: that is, where it is assumed that something is *not* being provided which in fact *is*, state provision is added on to other provision.

The existence of policy phenomena like these can give rise to the demand for a *more coherent* 'family policy', in which inconsistencies, anomalies and contradictions are as far as possible smoothed out. In support of this it may be argued first that lack of coherence, confusion, overlap, inconsistency and so on in policies and services cause practical problems for consumers and suppliers of services alike, and may cause a sense of injustice, and be bad for families in some ways. They may produce general hostility to state bureaucracies and a lack of take-up of certain benefits. People may feel that they are 'trapped' by the system, or that they 'can't win'. The interaction of tax and benefit policies to produce the 'poverty trap' and the 'poverty plateau' might be one example (see, for example, Burghes, 1993).

Second, it may be argued that lack of coherence undermines any strong sense of agreed social norms about the family. Those who take a strong normative position on the family might wish for a coherent policy, but of course different norms point to different types of coherent policy. Those who hold diverging family ideologies might agree that there ought to be a coherent policy, but disagree violently as to what it should contain. Most obviously, a 'pro-family' or moral lobby would diverge from feminist perspectives as to what a coherent family policy should look like.

A third type of argument is that greater coherence and co-ordination might mean more effective policies; approaching problems from an integrated and rational viewpoint, for example, rather than from a narrow departmental stance, might result in more effective solutions. However, this type of argument does raise the question as to what are the preferred goals against which a policy might be judged to be effective/ineffective. Fourth, it is argued that greater coherence would make the family more of a central focus of public attention and debate, by ensuring that family policy was discussed, and by making policy more explicit; fifth, that greater coherence in policy would enable a better response to rapid family change (this still begs the question of what *sort* of response to change would be desired); and finally, that stresses on family relationships arising from policies could be identified and possibly alleviated. A coherent family policy would enable some highlighting of destructive policies and a base for challenging them; again, however, value judgements would be involved about what effects were in fact undesirable.

There is also a set of arguments which may be put *against* a unified family policy, some of which are already implied by what has been said. The chief danger is that a more coherent policy might utilise a narrow and inflexible definition of family, or a moralistic view of what is good for the family. As Kamerman and Kahn (1978, p. 8) say: 'Family policy has the potential of conservative or regressive application and use to support what some people define as the traditonal family exclusively and to acknowledge only traditional family roles.' If family policy is to have a clear direction, this assumes some consensus of values about family life which is not in fact present. Kamerman and Kahn acknowledge this when they say (p. 482): 'Brief consideration will disclose that any deliberately unified family policy has a strong normative foundation. Some normative choices preclude others.' The attempt to establish a unified policy is likely to give rise to conflict, therefore. A related point is that the values of a majority, or of a particularly vocal and well-organised minority, might be imposed on the rest; or that the values and norms of professionals, bureaucrats and a variety of 'experts' might be imposed on others. And an over-rigid family policy based on values of whatever hue might be extremely harsh on those whose lifestyles did in fact differ from what the norms assumed. An obvious example would be the fate of single parents and their children under a coherent family policy of a neo-traditionalist bent. Indeed, an 'inconsistent' policy might yield some advantages in terms of effective tolerance of a variety of groups and norms; inconsistency may make sense in a pluralistic society. A coherent policy would tend to be authoritarian. Finally, a coherent *family* policy might overlook the separate interests of *individuals* within families, who may be disadvantaged by a strong emphasis on families as units and keeping families together (most obviously those individuals whose power position is weak owing to factors of age and gender).

Can 'family policy' be value-free?

The above line of argument points to the central question of whether 'family policy' can ever be value-free. It has been suggested that an integrated family policy assumes some sort of consensus about family norms and values, although this consensus does not in fact exist. Where policy is to some degree authoritarian, then clearly something is being imposed, regardless of consensus. But even an ostensibly *laissez-faire* policy may contain implicit values, assumptions and understandings about what families are and should be like. Furthermore, between these two extremes, the contested boundaries of state and family responsibility reflect a debate which is by no means value-free, but linked to wider political and moral arguments and ideologies.

This issue also returns us to the problem of unintended side effects. Certain types of family pattern may be 'rewarded' or 'punished' by policy effects even if this was not consciously intended; therefore it would appear that the policy is not in practice value-free, and is open to criticism accordingly.

While actual policy, then, may almost invariably reflect values about preferred family forms, or appear to do so, perhaps all that can be achieved in terms of value neutrality is the *study* of such policy (or perhaps not even that?).

Conclusion

This chapter has considered a number of aspects of the notion of 'family policy': definitions of family policy, rhetoric and actual policy, family policy as smokescreen for other objectives, the question of policy side-effects, the incoherence of policies, and briefly whether policy can be value-free. The topic of 'family policy' is unsatisfactory because of the lack of clear boundaries, the inter-meshing of family and non-family policies, and the absence of any clear family policy in Britain which would provide a defined subject for analysis. Nevertheless the interrelationship of family and state demands study in a rapidly changing scene, and the notions of family policy, family policy as perspective, family impact analysis and so on, may provide a useful means of approach.

Conclusion

This conclusion will be brief, as much has been said by way of summary already (the reader is referred to the beginnings and ends of the various chapters). On family change, the author's conclusion is that change has been considerable yet patchy and inconsistent, and far from uniform (neither need it be unidirectional, of course). Change *is* significant and does have implications for the state. Opinions divide, however, on how much change there is, how significant it is, and what its effects are.

On the state, the conclusion is that the state and its policy have ambiguous effects on family life. The state does not just coerce or control. Its relationship with families is more subtle than that, and in some ways the state supports a variety of family forms and helps to extend choice. The family–state boundary is contested, however, and one's view of this boundary connects with wider ideologies and perspectives on where responsibilities for care and maintenance for a variety of groups should lie, and how extensive such responsibilities should be. The state and family may be seen as 'uneasy bedfellows', with many issues requiring constant renegotiation. There is a power relationship, and increased control from the state is always a possibility. One problem with clear ideas about where families *should* go, in terms of their roles and functioning, is that these ideas tend to involve more state control. Yet democratic, liberal culture militates against carrying this too far, even when family forms are demonstrated to have some socially adverse effects. However, the issue of family and state does matter. Abdication of state responsibility in this area, as in the complete *laissez-faire* model, would not, it is suggested, be widely supported.

The author, finally, argues for an approach to families which is more 'objective' and empirically based, and less ideological. Of course this is not entirely possible, partly because of the nearness of the field of inquiry to our own experiences and emotions; but values should at least be made explicit and analysed, and an accurate picture of social reality attempted. It is possible to distort the picture of the degree and nature of family change/continuity and of the family–state relationship in the service of wider ideologies. Academics and other commentators, pressure groups and policy-makers have, however, *different* responsibilities in this debate. To be 'value-free' is not the calling of the politician, perhaps; but politicians do need to heed what empirical evidence and cogent argument we have about families in all their rich variety and their two-way relationship with the state in the pragmatic (and probably short-term) decisions which they take.

Bibliography

Abbott, P. and Wallace, C. (1992), *The Family and the New Right* (London: Pluto Press).

Abrams, P. and McCulloch, A. (1976), *Communes, Sociology and Society* (Cambridge: Cambridge University Press).

Aldridge, J. and Becker, S. (1993) *Children who Care* (Loughborough: Loughborough University).

Allan, G. (1985), *Family Life, Domestic Roles and Social Organisation* (Oxford: Basil Blackwell).

Anderson, D. and Dawson, G. (1986), *Family Portraits* (London: Social Affairs Unit).

Anderson, M. (1979), 'The relevance of family history', in M. Anderson (1980), *The Sociology of the Family* (Harmondsworth: Penguin).

Anderson, M. (1983), 'Some salient features of the modern family', in British Society for Population Studies, *The Family* Occasional Paper 31 (London: OPCS), pp. 8–15.

Archbishop of Canterbury (1964), *Putting Asunder: A Divorce Law for Contemporary Society* (London: Society for Promoting Christian Knowledge).

Aries, P. (1962), Centuries of Childhood (New York: Random House).

Armstrong, P. and Armstrong, H. (1988), 'Women, Family and Economy', in N. Mandell and A. Duffy (eds), *Reconstructing the Canadian Family: Feminist Perspectives* (Toronto and Vancouver: Butterworths).

Askham, J. (1984), *Identity and Stability in Marriage* (Cambridge: Cambridge University Press).

Askham, J. *et al.* (1992), *Life After 60 – A Profile of Britain's Older Population* (London: Age Concern).

Audit Commission (1986), *Making a Reality of Community Care* (London: HMSO).

Baker, L. and McGarry, J. (1992), 'The price of maintaining owner occupation', *Poverty*, 83 (Winter), pp. 11–13.

Bakewell, J. (1993), 'Search for the secular soul', *Guardian*, 26 November 1993.

Balchin, P. N. (1985), *Housing Policy: An Introduction* (London: Routledge).

Baldwin, S. and Falkingham, J. (eds) (1994), *Social Security and Social Change: New Challenges to the Beveridge Model* (New York, London: Harvester Wheatsheaf).

Baldwin, S. and Parker, G. (1989), 'The Griffiths Report on Community Care', in M. Brenton and C. Ungerson (eds), *Social Policy Review 1988–89* (Harlow: Longman).

Bayley, M. (1973), *Mental Handicap and Community Care: A Study of Mentally Handicapped People in Sheffield* (London: Routledge & Kegan Paul).

Bebbington, A. (1991), 'The expectation of life without disability in England and Wales: 1976–88', *Population Trends*, 66 (Winter), pp. 26–9.

Bebbington, A. and Miles, J. (1989), 'The background of children who enter local authority care', *British Journal of Social Work*, 19, pp. 349–68.

Belson, P. (1993), 'The care of children in hospital', in G. Pugh (ed.), *Thirty Years of Change for Children* (London: National Children's Bureau).

Berger, P. and Berger, B. (1983), *The War over the Family* London: Hutchinson.

Bernard, J. (1972), *The Future of Marriage* (New Haven, CT: Yale University Press).

Besharov, D. J. (1989), 'Targeting long-term welfare recipients', in Cottingham and Ellwood (1989).

Beveridge, W. (1942), *Social Insurance and Allied Services*, Cmd 6404 (London: HMSO).

Bird, R. (1992), *Child Maintenance – The New Law* (Bristol: Family Law, Jordan & Sons).

Bittman, M. and Bryson, L. (1989) 'Persistence and change in the family and gender in Australian society', in Close (1989).

Bly, R. (1991), *Iron John – A Book about Men* (Shaftesbury: Elmet).

Bornat, A. *et al.* (1993) *Community Case: A Reader* (London: Macmillan/ Open University).

Bowlby, J. (1953), *Child Care and the Growth of Love* (Harmondsworth: Penguin).

Bowlby, J. (1969, 1973), *Attachment and Loss* (London: Hogarth), 2 volumes.

Boyd, M. (1988), 'Changing Canadian Family Forms: Issues for Women', in N. Mandell and A. Duffy (eds), *Reconstructing the Canadian Family: Feminist Perspectives* (Toronto and Vancouver: Butterworths).

Bradshaw, J. (1989), *Lone Parents: Policy in the Doldrums* (London: Family Policy Studies Centre), Occasional Paper No. 9.

Bradshaw, J. (1990), *Child Poverty and Deprivation in the UK* (London: National Children's Bureau).

Bradshaw, J. and Millar, J. (1991), *Lone Parent Families in the United Kingdom*, Department of Social Security Research Report No. 6 (London: HMSO).

Brannen, J. and Collard, J. (1982), *Marriages in Trouble: The Process of Seeking Help* (London: Tavistock).

Brannen, J. and Wilson, G. (1987), *Give and Take in Families: Studies in Resource Distribution* (London: Allen & Unwin).

British Society for Population Studies (1983), *The Family*, Occasional Paper 31 (London: OPCS).

British Social Attitudes Survey (1993), reported in *Guardian*, 1 December 1993.

Brochlain, N. M. (1986), 'Women's paid work and the timing of births: longitudinal evidence', *European Journal of Population*, 2, pp. 43–47.

Brown, A. (1986), 'Family circumstances of young children', Population Trends, 43, pp. 18–23.

Brown, A. and Kiernan, K. (1981), 'Cohabitation in Great Britain', *Population Trends*, 25, pp. 4–10.

Brown, C. (1981), 'Mothers, fathers and children: from private to public patriarchy', in L. Sargent (ed.), *Women and Revolution: The Unhappy Marriage of Marxism and Feminism* (London: Pluto Press).

Brown, J. (1984), *Children in Social Security* (London: Policy Studies Institute).

Brown, J. (1987), *The Future of Family Income Support* (London: Policy Studies Institute).

Brown, J. (1988), *Child Benefit Investing in the Future* (London: Policy Studies Institute).

Bryson, L. (1992), *Welfare and the State – Who Benefits?* (London: Macmillan).

Bulmer, M. (1987), *The Social Basis of Community Care* (London: Unwin Hyman).

Bunk, B. P. and van Driel, B. (1989), *Variant Lifestyles and Relationships* (London: Sage).

Bureau of Labor Statistics (1988) 'Labor Force Participation Unchanged Among Mothers with Young Children', USDL 88–431 (Washington, DC: US Government Printing Office).

Burghes, L. (1992), *Working for Benefits: Lessons from America* (London: Low Pay Unit), pamphlet No. 57.

Burghes, L. (1993), *One-Parent Families: Policy Options for the 1990s* (York: Family Policy Studies Centre, Joseph Rowntree Foundation).

Burgoyne, J. (1987), 'Rethinking the family life cycle: sexual division, work and domestic life in the post-war period', in A. Bryman *et al.* (eds), Rethinking the Life Cycle (London: Macmillan).

Burgoyne, J. & Clark, D. (1984), *Making a Go of It: A Study of Stepfamilies in Sheffield* (London: Routledge & Kegan Paul).

Campbell, B. (1988), *Unofficial Secrets Child Sexual Abuse – The Cleveland Case* (London: Virago).

Cannan, C. (1992), *Changing Families Changing Welfare Family Centres and the Welfare State* (Hemel Hempstead: Harvester Wheatsheaf).

Caplan, I. (1987), 'Hitler's Women's Movement', *Guardian*, 15 May 1987.

Cashmore, E. (1985), *Having to: The World of One Parent Families* (London: Allen & Unwin).

Charlesworth, A. *et al.* (1984), *Carers and Services: A Comparison of Men and Women Caring for Dependent Elderly People* (London: Equal Opportunities Commission).

Chester, R. (1983), 'A social agenda: policy issues relating to the family', in British Society for Population Studies, *The Family*, Occasional Paper 31 (London: OPCS), pp. 96–105.

Chester, R. (1985), 'The rise of the neo-conventional family', *New Society*, 9 (May), pp. 185–8.

Chester, R. and Peel, J. (eds) (1977), *Equalities and Inequalities in Family Life* (London: Academic Press).

Child Poverty Action Group (1990a), *Poverty*, 76, p. 18, quoting *Daily Telegraph*, 11–13 June 1990.

Child Poverty Action Group (1990b), *The Poverty of Maintenance* (London: Child Poverty Action Group).

Child Poverty Action Group (1992a), *A Better Budget: The Chancellor's Choice* (London: Child Poverty Action Group).

Child Poverty Action Group (1992b), Press release: *Home Owners' Guide Published as Mortgage Arrears Problems Soar* (London: Child Poverty Action Group).

Child Poverty Action Group (1993a), Press release: *Benefits Guide Published with Call for Urgent Action* (London: Child Poverty Action Group).

Child Poverty Action Group (1993b), Press release: *Debt Advice Handbook published as Debt Problems Reach 'Catastrophic Proportions'* (London: Child Poverty Action Group).

Chiplin, B. and Sloane, P. (1974), 'Sex discrimination in the labour market', *British Journal of Industrial Relations*, 12 (3), pp. 371–402.

Clark, D. (ed.) (1991), *Marriage, Domestic Life and Social Change: Writings for Jacqueline Burgoyne 1944–88* (London: Routledge).

Clark, K. *et al.* (1993), 'An act of conflict', *Community Care* 11 November, pp. 14–15.

Clifford, D. (1990), *The Social Costs and Rewards of Caring* (Aldershot: Avebury).

Close, P. (1985), 'Family form and economic production', in P. Close and R. Collins (eds), *Family and Economy in Modern Society* (London: Macmillan).

Close, P. (ed.) (1989), *Family Divisions and Inequalities in Modern Society* (London: Macmillan).

Cohen, B. (1990), *Caring for Children: The 1990 Report* (London: Family Policy Studies Centre).

Cohen, B. (1993), 'Childcare policy in the European Community: finding a place for children', in R. Simpson and R. Walker (eds), *Europe for Richer or Poorer?* (London: Child Poverty Action Group).

Cohen, B. and Fraser, N. (1991), *Child Care in a Modern Welfare System – Towards a New National Policy* (London: Institute for Public Policy Research).

Collins, R. (1989), 'Illegitimacy, inequality and the law in England and Wales', in Close (1989).

Community Care (May–August 1993), Articles on elder abuse.

Cooper, J. (1991), 'Births outside marriage: recent trends and associated demographic and social changes', *Population Trends*, 63 (Spring), pp. 8–18.

Cottingham, P. H. and Ellwood, D. (eds) (1989), *Welfare Policy for the 1990s* (Cambridge, Mass: Harvard University Press).

Craven, E. *et al.* (1982), *Family Issues and Public Policy* (London: Study Commission on the Family).

Crimmins, E. M. *et al.* (1989), 'Changes in life expectancy and disability-free life expectancy in the United States', *Population and Development Review* 15, pp. 235–67.

Crow, G. and Hardey, M. (1991), 'The housing strategies of lone parents' in Hardey and Crow (1991).

CSO (various years) *Social Trends* (London: HMSO).

Dale, J. and Foster, P. (1986), *Feminists and State Welfare* (London: Routledge & Kegan Paul).

David, M. (1993), *Parents, Gender and Education Reform* (Cambridge: Polity Press).

Davies, J. (1993), *The Family: Is it just another Lifestyle Choice?* (London: Institute of Economic Affairs Health & Welfare Unit).

Deakin, N. and Wicks, M. (1988), *Families and the State* (London: Family Policy Studies Centre).

Delphy, C. and Leonard, D. (1992), *Familiar Exploitation: A New Analysis of Marriage in Contemporary Western Societies* (Cambridge: Polity Press).

Dennis, N. and Erdos, G. (1992), *Families without Fatherhood* (London: IEA Health & Welfare Unit).

Department of Health (1989), *Caring for People: Community Care in the Next Decade and Beyond*, Cm 849 (London: HMSO).

Department of Health (1992), *Adoption Law Review* (London: HMSO).

Department of Health (1993), *Adoption: The Future* (London: HMSO).

Department of Health and Social Security (1974), *Report of the Committee on One Parent Families* (Finer Report), Cmnd 5629 (London: HMSO).

Department of Health and Social Security (1981) *Growing Older*, Cmnd 8173 (London: HMSO).

Department of Health and Social Security/Law Commission (1985), *Review of Child Care Law: Report for Ministers of an Inter-Departmental Working Party* (London: HMSO).

Department of Health and Social Security (1987), *The Law on Child Care and Family Services*, Cm 62 (London: HMSO).

Derricourt, N. (1983), 'Strategies for community care', in ed. M. Loney *et al.* (eds), *Social Policy and Social Welfare* (Milton Keynes: Open University Press).

Dewar, J. (1992), *Law and the Family* (London: Butterworths).

Dingwall, R. *et al.* (1983), *The Protection of Children: State Intervention and Family Life* (Oxford: Basil Blackwell).

Donzelot, J. (1980), *The Policing of Families: Welfare versus the State* (London: Hutchinson).

Douglas, G. (1991), *Law, Fertility and Reproduction* (London: Sweet & Maxwell).

Duffy, A. *et al.* (1989), *Few Choices: Women, Work and Family* (Toronto: Garamond Press).

Durham, M. (1991), *Sex and Politics: The Family and Morality in the Thatcher Years* (London: Macmillan).

Ehrenreich, B. (1983), *The Hearts of Men: American Dreams and the Flight from Commitment* (London: Pluto Press).

Elliott, B. J. (1991), 'Demographic trends in domestic life 1945–87', in D. Clark (1991).

Elliott, B. J. *et al.* (1990), 'Divorce and children: a British challenge to the Wallerstein view', *Family Law*, 20, pp. 309–10.

Elliott, F. R. (1986), *The Family: Change or Continuity?* (London: Macmillan).

Elliott, F. R. (1989), 'The family: private arena or adjunct of the state', *Journal of Law and Society*, 16, pp. 443–63.

Ellwood, D. (1988), *Poor Support Poverty in the American Family* (New York: Basic Books).

Equal Opportunities Commission (1991), *Women and Men in Britain* (London: HMSO).

Ermisch, J. (1983), *The Political Economy of Demographic Change: Causes and Implications of Population Trends in Great Britain* (London: Heinemann).

Ermisch, J. (1989), 'Divorce: economic antecedents and aftermath', in Joshi (1989).

Ermisch, J. (1990), *Fewer Babies, Longer Lives* (London: Family Policy Studies Centre/Rowntree Foundation).

Ermisch, J. (1991?), 'Policy implications of demographic change', unpublished conference paper.

Fagin, L. and Little, M. (1984), *The Forsaken Families: The Effects of Unemployment on Family Life* (Harmondsworth: Penguin).

Faludi, S. (1991), *Backlash: The Undeclared War Against American Women* (New York: Doubleday).

Family Policy Studies Centre (1990), *Bulletin*, 8 (Spring) (London).

Family Policy Studies Centre (1991), *Fact Sheet: The Family Today; One Parent Families*, No. 3 (London).

Family Policy Studies Centre (1992), *Bulletin*, June (London).

Family Research Council (1991), *In Focus*, INF6* 2/91 (Washington, DC).

Farber, B. (1973), *Family and Kinship in Modern Society* (Brighton: Scott Foresman).

Farrell, W. (1988), *Why Men Are the Way They Are* (Berkley Pub.).

Farrell, W. (1994), *The Myth of Male Power* (London: Fourth Estate).

Field, F. (1978), *Priority for Children: A Labour Success* (London: Child Poverty Action Group), Poverty Pamphlet 36.

Field, F. (1982), *Poverty and Politics: The Inside Story of the Child Poverty Action Group Campaigns of the 1970s* (London: Heinemann).

Finch, J. (1989), *Family Obligations and Social Change* (Cambridge: Polity Press).

Finch, J. and Groves D. (1980), 'Community care and the family: a case for equal opportunities', *Journal of Social Policy*, 9 (4), pp. 487–511.

Finch, J. and Groves, D. (1983), *A Labour of Love: Women, Work and Caring* (London: Routledge and Kegan Paul).

Finch, J. and Mason, J. (1993), *Negotiating Family Responsibilities* (London: Tavistock/Routledge).

Finch, J. and Morgan, D. (1991), 'Marriage in the 1980s: a new sense of realism? in D. Clark (1991).

Fletcher, R. (1988a), *The Abolitionists: Family and Marriage under Attack* (London and New York: Routledge).

Fletcher, R. (1988b), *The Shaking of the Foundations* (London and New York: Routledge).

Fowler, N. (1990), speeches in *Parliamentary Debates*, Commons, vol. 169, (12–23 March, 1989–90).

Fox Harding, L. (1991a), 'The Children Act 1989 in context: four perspectives in child care law and policy', (I) and (II), *Journal of Social Welfare and Family Law*, 3 and 4 pp. 179–93; 285–302.

Fox Harding, L. (1991b), *Perspectives in Child Care Policy* (Harlow: Longman).

Fox Harding, L. (1993), '"Alarm" versus "liberation"? Responses to the increase in lone parents', 1 and 2 *Journal of Social Welfare and Family Law*, 2 and 3, pp. 101–12; 174–84.

Fox Harding, L. (1994), '"Parental responsibility": a dominant theme in English child and family policy for the 1990s', *International Journal of Sociology and Social Policy*, 14 (1/2), pp. 84–108.

Freeman, M. D. A. (1983), 'Freedom and the welfare state: child-rearing, parental autonomy and state intervention', *Journal of Social Welfare Law*, March, pp. 70–91.

Friedan, B. (1963), *The Feminine Mystique* (Harmondsworth: Penguin).

Frost, N. (1990), 'Official intervention and child protection: the relationship between state and family in contemporary Britain', in Violence Against Children Study Group (ed.), *Taking Child Abuse Seriously* (London: Unwin Hyman).

Frost, N. and Stein, M. (1989), *The Politics of Child Welfare* (Hemel Hempstead: Harvester Wheatsheaf).

Fyfe, A. (1989), *Child Labour* (Cambridge: Polity Press).

Garfinkel, I. and McLanahan, S. (1986), *Single Mothers and their Children: A New American Dilemma* (Washington, DC: Urban Institute).

Garnham, A. and Knights, E. (1993), *Child Support Handbook* (London: Child Poverty Action Group).

Garnham, A. and Knights, E. (1994), *Putting the Treasury First The Truth about Child Support* (London: Child Poverty Action Group).

Gavron, H. (1966), *The Captive Wife: Conflicts of Housebound Mothers* (London: Routledge & Kegan Paul).

George, M. (1992), 'Sacrificing children on the altar of care', *Community Care*, 11 (June) 1992 p. 19.

George, V. and Wilding, P. (1984), *The Impact of Social Policy* (London: Routledge).

Gershuny, J. *et al.* (1986), 'Time budgets: preliminary analysis of a national survey', *Quarterly Journal of Social Affairs*, 2 (1) pp. 13–39.

Gershuny J. and Robinson J. P. (1988) 'Historical Changes in the Household Division of Labor' *Demography*, 25(4) (Nov. 1988) pp. 537–54.

Gil, D. (1971), 'Violence against children', *Journal of Marriage and the Family*, 33, pp. 637–57.

Gilding, M. (1991), *The Making and Breaking of the Australian Family* (Sydney: Allen & Unwin).

Gittins, D. (1985), *The Family in Question: Changing Households and Familiar Ideologies*, 2nd ed 1993 (London: Macmillan).

Glennester, H. (1991), 'Social policy since the Second World War', in J. Hills *et al.* (eds), *The State of Welfare* (Oxford: Clarendon Press).

Glennester, H. and Evans, M. (1992), *Beveridge and his Assumptive Worlds: The Incompatibilities of a Flawed Design – Fifty Years After Beveridge*, Vol. 1 (London: Benefits Agency/Stationery Service).

Glick P. C. (1979) 'Children of Divorced Parents in Demographic Perspective', *Journal of Social Issues*, 35.

Goldscheider, F. K. and Waite, L. (1991), *New Families, No families? The Transformation of the American Home* (Berkeley and Los Angeles: University of California Press.

Goldstein, J., Freud, A. and Solnit, A. (1973), *Beyond the Best Interests of the Child* (New York: Free Press).

Goldstein, J. Freud, A. and Solnit, A. (1980) *Before the Best Interests of the Child* (London: Burnett Books).

Goldthorpe, J. (1987), *Family Life in Western Societies* (Cambridge: Cambridge University Press).

Goode, R. (1993), *Pension Law Reform: The Report of the Pension Law Review Committee*, Vol. I (London: HMSO).

Goode, W. (ed.) (1964), *Readings on the Family and Society* (Englewood Cliffs, NJ: Prentice-Hall).

Graham, H. (1984), *Women, Health and the Family* (Brighton: Wheatsheaf).

Green, L. H. (1988), *General Household Survey – Informal Carers* (London: HMSO).

Greenwood, V. A. and Young, J. (1976), *Abortion on Demand* (London: Pluto Press).

Griffiths, Sir R. (1988), *Community Care: Agenda for Action* (London: HMSO).

Grundy, E. and Harrop, A. (1992) 'Co-residence between adult children and their elderly parents in England and Wales', *Journal of Social Policy*, 21 (3), pp. 325–48.

Hakim, C. (1979), 'Occupational segregation: a comparative study of the degree and pattern of the differentiation between men and women's work in Britain, the US and other countries', *Department of Employment Research Paper* (London: Department of Employment).

Hakim, C. (1980), 'Census reports as documentary evidence: the census commentaries 1801–1951', *Sociological Review*, 28(3), pp. 551–80.

Hakim, C. (1981), 'Job segregation trends in the 1970s', *Employment Gazette* December, pp. 521–9.

Halsey, A. H. (1993), 'Changes in the family', in G. Pugh (ed.) *Thirty Years of Change for Children* (London: National Children's Bureau).

Hantrais, L. (1993), 'Towards a Europeanisation of family policy?', in R. Simpson and R. Walker (eds), *Europe For Richer or Poorer?* (London: Child Poverty Action Group).

Hardey, M. and Crow, G. (eds) (1991), *Lone Parenthood: Coping with Constraints and Making Opportunities* (Hemel Hempstead: Harvester Wheatsheaf).

Harding, L. (1987), 'The debate on surrogate motherhood: the current situation, some arguments and issues; questions facing law and policy', *Journal of Social Welfare Law*, January, pp. 37–63.

Harding, L. (1993), 'The Children Act in practice: underlying themes revisited', *Justice of the Peace*, 157(38) (18 September), pp. 600–2; 157(39) (25 September) pp. 616–18.

Hardyment, C. (1983), *Dream Babies: Child Care from Locke to Spock* (London: Cape).

Harris, J. (1987), *William Beveridge A Biography* (Oxford: Clarendon Press).

Harrison, P. (1983), *Inside the Inner City: Life under the Cutting Edge* (Harmondsworth: Penguin).

Hartmann, H. (1987), 'Changes in women's economic and family roles in post-World War II United States', in L. Beneira and C. R. Simpson (eds), *Women, Households and the Economy* (New Brunswick, NJ: Rutgers University Press).

Haskey, J. (1984), 'Social class and socio-economic differentials in divorce in England and Wales', *Population Studies*, 38, pp. 419–38.

Haskey, J. (1987), 'Social class differentials in remarriage after divorce: results from a forward linkage study', *Population Trends*, 47, pp. 34–42.

Haskey, J. (1989), 'Current prospects for the proportion of marriages ending in divorce', *Population Trends*, 55, pp. 34–7.

Haskey, J. (1990), 'The children of families broken by divorce', *Population Trends*, 61, pp. 34–42.

Haskey, J. (1991b), 'Lone parenthood and demographic change', in Hardey and Crow (1991).

Haskey, J. (1991a), 'Estimated numbers and demographic characteristics of one-parent families in Great Britain', *Population Trends*, 65, pp. 35–47.

Haskey, J. (1992), 'An examination of trends since 1950 in first marriages, divorces, and cohabitation in the different countries of Europe', *Population Trends*, 69, pp. 27–36.

Haskey, J. and Kelly, S. (1991), 'Population estimates by cohabitation and legal marital status – a trial set of new estimates' *Population Trends*, 66, pp. 30–44.

Haskey, J. and Kiernan, K. (1989), 'Cohabitation in Great Britain – characteristics and estimated numbers of cohabiting partners', *Population Trends*, 58, pp. 23–32.

Hayes, P. *et al.* (1989), *Social Work in Crisis* (London: National and Local Government Officers' Association).

Henderson, J. and Karn. V. (1987), *Race, Class and State: Housing Inequality and the Allocation of Public Housing in Britain* (Aldershot: Gower).

Hendrick, H. (1990), 'Constructions and reconstructions of British childhood: an interpretive survey, 1800 to the present', in A. James and A. Prout (eds), *Constructing and Reconstructing Childhood* (London: Falmer).

Hendrick, H. (1993), *Child Welfare in England 1872–1989* (London: Routledge).

Hendry, J. (1989), 'The continuing case of Japan', in Close (1989).

Henwood, M. *et al.* (1987), *Inside the Family* (London: Family Policy Studies Centre).

Hobart, C. W. (1983), 'Marriage or cohabitation', in K. Ishwaran (ed.), *Marriage and Divorce in Canada* (Agincourt, ON: Methuen).

Hoggett, B. (1980), 'Ends and means: the utility of marriage as a legal institution', in J. Eekelaar and S. Katz (eds), *Marriage and Cohabitation in Contemporary Societies* (Toronto: Butterworths).

Hoggett, B. (1987), *Parents and Children: The Law of Parental Responsibility* (London: Sweet & Maxwell).

Holman, R. (1980), *Inequality in Child Care* (London: Child Poverty Action Group), Poverty Pamphlet 26.

Holman, B. (1988), *Putting Families First: Prevention and Child Care* (London: Macmillan).

Holme, A. (1985), *Housing and Young Families in East London* (London: Routledge and Kegan Paul).

Holt, J. (1975), *Escape from Childhood* (Harmondsworth: Penguin).

House of Commons (1984), *Second Report from the Social Services Committee* (session 1983–4) *Children in Care* (The Short Report) (London: HMSO).

Howe, D. *et al.* (1992), *Half a Million Women: Mothers Who Lose Their Children by Adoption* (Harmondsworth: Penguin).

Humphries, S. (1981), *Hooligans or Rebels: An Oral History of Working Class Childhood and Youth 1889–1939* (Oxford: Basil Blackwell).

Hunter, D. and Wistow, G. (1987), *Community Care in Britain: Variations on a Theme* (London: King Edward's Hospital Fund for London).

Jackson, P. R. and Walsh, S. (1987), 'Unemployment and the family', in D. Fryer and P. Ullah (eds), *Unemployed People: Social and Psychological Perspectives* (Milton Keynes: Open University Press).

Jackson, S. (1993), 'Under fives: thirty years of no progress?', in G. Pugh (ed.), *Thirty Years of Change for Children* (London: National Children's Bureau).

Jamieson, A. (1991), 'Community care for older people policies in

Britain, West Germany and Denmark', in G. Room (ed.), *Towards a European Welfare State?* (Bristol: School for Advanced Urban Studies).

Jefferys, M. and Thane, P. (1989), 'Introduction: an ageing society and ageing people', in M. Jefferys (ed.), *Growing Old in the Twentieth Century* (London: Routledge).

Jeffreys, S. (1985), *The Spinster and her Enemies: Feminism and Sexuality 1880–1930* (London: Pandora).

Jensen, A-M. (1989), 'Reproduction in Norway: an area of non-responsibility?', in Close (1989).

Johnson, A. M. (1994), 'Data sheet on ageing', *Epworth Review*, 21(2) (May), pp. 78–84.

Jones, C. (1992), 'Fertility of the over thirties', *Population Trends*, 67, quoted by Family Policy Studies Centre, *Bulletin*, June.

Jones, K. (1989), 'Community care: old problems and new answers', in P. Carter *et al.* (eds), *Social Work and Social Welfare Yearbook*, Vol. I (Milton Keynes: Open University Press).

Joseph Rowntree Foundation (1994), *Findings: Children Living in Re-ordered Families (York).*

Joshi, H. (ed.) (1989), *The Changing Population of Britain* (Oxford: Basil Blackwell).

Kamerman, S. B. and Kahn, A. J. (eds) (1978) (International Working Party on Family Policy), *Family Policy: Government and Families in Fourteen Countries* (New York: Columbia University Press).

Karn, V. and Henderson, J. (1983), 'Housing atypical households: Understanding the practices of local government housing', in A. W. Franklin (ed.), *Family Matters: Perspectives on the Family and Social Policy* (Oxford: Pergamon Press).

Keegan, V. (1994), 'Girls on top in jobs market', *Guardian*, 9 April 1994.

Kett J. F. (1977) *Rites of Passage: Adolescence in America, 1790 to the Present* (New York: Basic Books).

Kiernan, K. (1989), 'The Family: Formation and Fission', in Joshi (1989).

Kiernan, K. (1990), 'The rise of cohabitation', Family Policy Studies Centre, *Bulletin*, 8 (Spring) London.

Kiernan, K. (1992), 'The impact of family disruption in childhood on transitions made in young adult life', *Population Studies*, 46, pp. 213–14.

Kiernan, K. and Wicks, M. (1990), *Family Change and Future Policy* (Rowntree/Family Policy Studies Centre).

Koonz, C. (1987), *Mothers in the Fatherland – Women, The Family and Nazi Politics* (London: Cape).

Laczko, F. and Phillipson, C. (1991), *Changing Work and Retirement* (Milton Keynes: Open University Press).

Lampard, R. (1990), cited in *Guardian*, 1 June 1990.

Lampard, R. (1994), 'An examination of the relationship between marital dissolution and unemployment', in D. Gallie and C. Vogler (eds), *Social Change and the Experience of Unemployment* (Oxford: Oxford University Press).

Land, H. and Parker, R. (1978), 'United Kingdom', in Kamerman and Kahn (1978).

Langan, M. (1990), 'Community care in the 1990s: the community care White Paper "Caring for People"', *Critical Social Policy*, 10(2) (Autumn), pp. 58–70.

Lasch, C. (1977), *Haven in a Heartless World: The Family Beseiged* (New York Basic Books).

Laslett, P. (1971), *The World We Have Lost* (London: Methuen).

Laslett, P. (1980), 'Characteristics of the Western European family', *London Review of Books* 16 Oct.–5 Nov. pp. 7–8.

Laslett, P. and Wall, R. (eds) (1972), *Household and Family in Past Times* (Cambridge: Cambridge University Press).

Law Commission (1981), *The Financial Consequences of Divorce*, No. 112 (London: HMSO).

Law Commission (1988a), *Facing the Future: A Discussion Paper on the Grounds for Divorce*, No. 170 (London: HMSO).

Law Commission (1988b), *Family Law Review of Child Law, Guardianship and Custody*, No. 172 (London: HMSO).

Law Commission (1990), *The Grounds for Divorce*, No. 192 (London: HMSO).

Lawson, A. (1983), *Adultery: An Analysis of Love and Betrayal* (Oxford: Basil Blackwell).

Leete, R. and Anthony, S. (1979), 'Divorce and re-marriage: a record linkage study', *Population Trends*, 16, pp. 5–11.

Leonard, D. and Hood-Williams, J. (1988), *Families* (London: Macmillan).

Leridon, H. (1990), 'Cohabitation, marriage, separation: an analysis of life histories of French cohorts from 1968 to 1985', *Population Studies*, 44, pp. 127–44.

Lerman, R. I. (1989), 'Child support policies', in Cottingham and Ellwood (1989).

Lewis, J. (1984), *Women in England 1870–1950* (Hemel Hempstead: Harvester Wheatsheaf).

Lewis, J. (1989), 'Comment: lone parent families: politics and economics', *Journal of Social Policy*, 18 (4), pp. 595–600.

Lewis, J. (1992), *Women in Britain since 1945* (Oxford: Basil Blackwell).

Lewis, J. and Meredith, B. (1988), *Daughters Who Care* (London: Routledge).

Lister, R. (1972?), *As Man and Wife? A Study of the Cohabitation Rule*, Poverty Research Series 2 (London: Child Poverty Action Group).

Lister, R. (1994), 'Back to the family: family policies and politics under the Major Government', unpublished conference paper, Social Policy Association.

Lonsdale, S. (1987), 'Patterns of paid work', in C. Glendinning and J. Millar (eds), *Women and Poverty in Britain* (Hemel Hempstead Harvester Wheatsheaf).

Lord Chancellor *et al.* (1990), *Children Come First: The Government's Proposals on Child Maintenance*, Cm1264 (London: HMSO).

Lord Chancellor (1993), *Looking to the Future: Mediation and the Ground for Divorce* (London: Lord Chancellor's Department).

Lund, M. (1984), 'Research on divorce and children' *Family Law*, 14 pp. 198–201.

Lyndon, N. (1992), *No More Sex War – The Failures of Feminism* (London: Sinclair-Stevenson).

Macklin, E. D. and Rubin, R. H. (1983), *Contemporary Families and Alternative Lifestyles: Handbook on Research and Theory* (Beverly Hills and London: Sage).

Malpass, P. and Murie, A. (1987), *Housing Policy and Practice* (London: Macmillan).

Mandell, N. and Duffy, A. (eds) (1988), *Reconstructing the Canadian Family: Feminist Perspectives* (Toronto and Vancouver: Butterworths).

Mann, K. (1992), *The Making of an English 'Underclass'? The Social Divisions of Welfare and Labour* (Milton Keynes: Open University Press).

Mansfield, P. and Collard, J. (1988), *The Beginning of the Rest of Your Life? A Portrait of Newly-Wed Marriage* (London: Macmillan).

Marchant, C. (1993), 'Single minded', *Community Care*, 5 August, pp. 14–15.

Martin, T. C. and Bumpass, L. L. (1989) 'Recent Trends in Marital Disruption', *Demography*, 26.1 (Feb. 1989) pp. 37–51.

Martin, J. and Roberts, C. (1984), *Women and Employment: A Lifetime Perspective* (London: HMSO).

Mattox, W. R. Jr (1991), 'The parent trap: so many bills, so little time', *Policy Review*, Winter, pp. 6–13.

McFarlane, A. (1978), *The Origins of English Individualism: The Family, Property and Social Transition* (Oxford: Basil Blackwell).

McGlone, F. (1992), *Disability and Dependence in Old Age* (London: Family Policy Studies Centre).

McGurk, H. *et al.* (1993), 'Controversy, theory and social context in contemporary day care research', *Journal of Child Psychology and Psychiatry*, 34(1), pp. 3–23.

McIntyre, S. (1977), *Single and Pregnant* (London: Croom Helm).

McQueen, J. (1993), 'Old seeking a future with a caring face', *Guardian*, 13 January 1993.

Mearns, A. (1883), *The Bitter Cry of Outcast London: An Inquiry into the Condition of the Abject Poor* reprinted 1970 (London: Cass).

Meissner, M., Humphreys, E. W., Meis S. M. and Scheu W. J. (1975) 'No Exit for Wives: Sexual Division of Labour', *Canadian Review of Sociology and Anthropology*, 12 (Nov. Part 1), pp. 424–39.

Millar, J. (1987), 'Lone mothers', in C. Glendinning and J. Millar (eds), *Women and Poverty in Britain* (Hemel Hempstead: Harvester Wheatsheaf).

Millar, J. (1989), *Poverty and the Lone Parent Family: The Challenge to Social Policy* (Aldershot: Gower).

Mitchell, A. (1988), 'Children's experience of divorce', *Family Law*, 18, pp. 460–3.

Moore, M. (1989), 'How long alone? The duration of female lone parenthood in Canada' *Transition*, March, pp. 4–5.

Morgan, D. (1975), *Social Theory of the Family* (London: Routledge and Kegan Paul).

Morgan, D. (1985), *The Family, Politics and Social Theory* (London: Routledge and Kegan Paul).

Moroney, R. M. (1976), *The Family and the State: Considerations for Social Policy* (London: Longman).

Morris, L. (1984), 'Redundancy and patterns of household finances', *Sociological Review*, 32 (2), pp. 492–523.

Morris, L. (1985a), 'Local social networks and domestic organisation', *Sociological Review*, 33 (1), pp. 327–42.

Morris, L. (1985b), 'Renegotiation of the domestic division of labour in the context of male redundance', in B. Roberts, R. Finnegan and D. Gallie (eds), *New Approaches to Economic Life* (Manchester: Manchester University Press).

Morris, L. (1990), *The Workings of the Household: A US UK Comparison* (Cambridge Polity Press).

Moss, P. and Lau, C. (1985), 'Mothers without marriages', *New Society*, 9 August.

Moss, P. and Sharpe, D. (1979), 'Family policy in Britain', in M. Brown and S. Baldwin (eds), *The Yearbook of Social Policy in Britain 1979* (London: Routledge and Kegan Paul).

Mount, F. (1982), *The Subversive Family* (London: Allen and Unwin).

Mumtaz, K. and Shaeed, F. (1987), *Women of Pakistan – Two Steps Forward One Step Back* (London: Zed Books).

Murray, C. (1984), *Losing Ground American Social Policy 1950–80* (New York: Basic Books).

Murray, C. (1990), *The Emerging British Underclass* (London: Institute of Economic Affairs Health & Welfare Unit).

National Audit Office (1990) (DSS/HoC 328), *Department of Social Security: Support for Lone Parent Families* (London: HMSO).

National Children's Bureau (1990), *Divorce and Children Highlight*, No. 93 (London).

National Children's Bureau (1991), *Homeless Families Highlight*, No. 99 (London).

National Children's Bureau (1992), *Family-based Day Care Highlight*, No. 110 (London).

National Children's Bureau (1993), *Day Care for Children Under Three Highlight*, No. 116 (London).

Nave-Herz, R. (1989) 'The significance of the family and marriage in the Federal Republic of Germany', in Close (1989).

New Society, series on 'The Family in Crisis', 6 March–10 April 1987.

New Society, 'Crisis in Community Care', Special supplement, 18 September 1987.

New, C. & David, M. (1985) *For the Children's Sake* (Harmondsworth: Penguin).

Norman, A. (1987a), *Severe Dementia: The Provision of Long-Stay Care* (London: Centre for Policy on Ageing).

Norman, A. (1987b), *Aspects of Ageism: A Discussion Paper* (London: Centre for Policy on Ageing).

Oakley, A. (1974), *The Sociology of Housework* (Oxford: Martin Robertson).

OECD (1993), *Breadwinners or Child Rearers: The Dilemma for Lone Mothers* (Paris: OECD).

Oldfield, N. (1993), 'The cost of a child', in J. Bradshaw (ed.), *Household Budgets and Living Standards* (York: Joseph Rowntree Foundation).

Oldfield, N. and Yu, A. C. S. (1993), *The Cost of a Child* (London: Child Poverty Action Group).

OPCS, *General Household Survey*, 1977, 1979, 1987, 1989, 1990, 1991, 1992, 1994 (London: HMSO).

OPCS (1990a), *Population Trends*, 60.

OPCS (1990b), *Population Trends*, 61, reported in *Guardian*, 20 September.

OPCS (1991a), *Marriage and Divorce Statistics England and Wales*, Series FM, No. 19 (London: HMSO).

OPCS (1991b), 'A Review of 1990', *Population Trends*, 66, pp. 1–13.

OPCS (1993), *1991 Census: Persons aged 60 and over – Great Britain* (London: HMSO).

Oppenheim, C. (1990), *Poverty: The Facts* (London: Child Poverty Action Group).

Owens, D. J. (1988), 'Marriage and the family in contemporary Britain: some implications for social work policy', *Adoption and Fostering*, 12 (4), pp. 44–8.

Pahl, J. (1985), *Private Violence and Public Policy: The Needs of Battered Women and the Response of the Public Services* (London: Routledge).

Pahl, J. (1989), *Money and Marriage* (London: Macmillan).

Pahl, J. (1990), 'Household spending, personal spending and the control of money in marriage', *Sociology*, 24 (1), pp. 119–38.

Parker, S. (1990), *Informal Marriage, Cohabitation and the Law, 1750–1989* (London: Macmillan).

Pascall, G. (1986), *Social Policy: A Feminist Analysis* (London Tavistock).

Pensions Management Institute (1991), *Pensions and Divorce* (London).

Phillipson, C. and Walker, A. (eds) (1986), *Ageing and Social Policy: A Critical Assessment* (Aldershot: Gower).

Piachaud, D. (1984), *Round About Fifty Hours a Week* (London: Child Poverty Action Group).

Piachaud, D. (1986), 'A family problem', *New Society*, 13 June, pp. 15–16.

Pillinger, J. (1992), *Feminising the Market: Women's Pay and Employment in the European Community* (London: Macmillan).

Pinchbeck, I. and Hewitt, M. (1969), *Children in English Society II* (London: Routlege & Kegan Paul).

Pitkeathley, J. (1989), *It's my Duty isn't it? The Plight of Carers in our Society* (Lava: Souvenir Press).

Pizzey, E. (1973), *Scream Quietly or the Neighbours Will Hear* (Harmondsworth: Penguin).

Platt, S. (1984), 'Unemployment and suicidal behaviour: a review of the literature' *Social Science and Medicine*, 19, pp. 93–115.

Platt, S. and Kreitmann N. (1985), 'Parasuicide and unemployment among men in Edinburgh 1968–1982', *Psychological Medicine*, 15, pp. 113–23.

Pollitt, N. with Booth, A. and Kay, H. (1989), *Hard Times: Young and Homeless* (London: Shelter).

Pollock, L. (1983), *Forgotten Children Parent–Child Relations from 1500–1900* (Cambridge: Cambridge University Press).

Popay, J. *et al.* (1983), *One Parent Families: Parents, Children and Public Policy* (London: Study Commission on the Family), Paper No. 12.

Pritchard, J. (1992), *The Abuse of Elderly People A Handbook for Professionals* (London: Jessica Kingsley).

Quah, S. (1994), 'Social policy in family life: the case of child-care in Singapore', *International Journal of Sociology and Social Policy*, 14 ($\frac{1}{2}$), pp. 126–48.

Qureshi, H. and Walker, A. (1989), *The Caring Relationship: Elderly People and their Families* (London: Macmillan).

Rapoport, R. (1981), *Unemployment and The Family* (London: Family Welfare Association).

Rapoport, R. and Rapoport, R. N. (1976), *Dual Career Families Re-examined* (Oxford: Martin Robertson).

Rapoport, R. and Rapoport, R. N. (eds) (1982), *Families in Britain* (London: Routledge and Kegan Paul).

Raymond, J. (1987), *Bringing up Children Alone*, Issues Paper No. 3, Social Security Review (Canberra: Department of Social Security).

Redding, D. (1991), 'Exploding the Myth', *Community Care*, 12 December pp. 18–20.

Reid, I. (1986), *The Sociology of School and Education* (London: Fontana).

Reid, I. and Stratta, E. (eds) (1989), *Sex Differences in Britain* (Aldershot: Gower).

Renvoize, J. (1985), *Going Solo: Single Mothers by Choice* (London: Routledge and Kegan Paul).

Rickford, F. (1992), 'Baby boom', *Social Work Today*, 5 November, p. 10.

Rigby, A. (1974), *Alternative Realities* (London: Routledge and Kegan Paul).

Roberts, E. (1984), *A Woman's Place: An Oral History of Working Class Women 1800–1940* (Oxford: Basil Blackwell).

Roberts, E. (1988), *Women's Work 1840–1940* (London: Macmillan).

Robinson, A. (1989), 'Taxation and the family', in D. Collard, (ed.) *Fiscal Policy: Essays in Honour of Cedric Sandford* (Aldershot: Avebury).

Roll, J. (1992), *Lone Parent Families in the European Community* (London: European Family and Social Policy Unit).

Rose, H. (1981), 'Re-reading Titmuss: the sexual division of welfare', *Journal of Social Policy*, 10 (4), pp. 477–502.

Rose, H. (1985), 'Women's refuges: creating new forms of welfare?', in C. Ungerson (ed.), *Women and Social Policy: A Reader* (London: Macmillan).

Rutter, M. (1972), *Maternal Deprivation Re-assessed* (Harmondsworth: Penguin).

Schultheis, F. (1990), 'Familles d'Europe sans frontières: un enjeu social par dessus le marché', Conference Proceedings, *Familles d'Europe sans frontières*, 4–5 December 1989, Paris.

Secretary of State for Social Services (1974), *Report of the Committee of Inquiry into the Care and Supervision Provided in Relation to Maria Colwell* (London: HMSO).

Secretary of State for Social Services (1988), *Report of the Inquiry into Child Abuse in Cleveland*, Cm 412 (London: HMSO).

Segal, L. (1987), *Is the Future Female? Troubled Thoughts on Contemporary Feminism* (London: Virago).

Segal, L. (1990), *Slow Motion: Changing Masculinities Changing Men* (London: Virago).

Sexty, C. (1990), *Women Losing Out: Access to Housing in Britain Today* (London: Shelter).

Shorter, E. (1975), *The Making of the Modern Family* (New York: Basic Books).

Simmons, M. (1993), 'Why women lose out in the housing stakes', *Guardian*, 6 August.

Skeens, M. (1994), 'School's out forever', *Guardian*, 19 January 1994.

Smart, C. (1984), *The Ties that Bind: Law, Marriage and the Reproduction of Patriarchal Relations* (London: Routledge).

Smart, C. (1989), *Feminism and the Power of the Law* (London: Routledge).

Smart, C. (1992), 'The woman of legal discourse', *Social and Legal Studies*, 1, pp. 29–44.

Smart, C. (1994), 'Good wives and moral lives: marriage and divorce after the War', in C. Gledhill and G. Swanson (eds), *Nationalising Femininity* (Manchester: Manchester University Press).

Smith, C. R. (1984), *Adoption and Fostering: Why and How?* (London: British Association of Social Welfare, Macmillan).

Smith, S. J. (1989), *Housing and Health: A Review and a Research Agenda* (London: Economic and Social Reserved Council).

South, S. J. (1985), 'Economic conditions and the divorce rate: a time-series analysis of the post-war United States', *Journal of Marriage and the Family*, 47, pp. 31–41.

Stanworth, M. (ed.) (1987), *Reproductive Technologies: Gender, Motherhood and Medicine* (Cambridge: Polity Press).

Statistics Canada (1981) *Marriage, Divorce and Mortality: A Life Table Analysis for Canada* (by O. B. Adams and D. N. Nagnun) Catalogue 84–536 (Ottawa: Minister of Supply and Services Canada).

Stepfamily (1993), *Stepfamilies in England and Wales, Fact File 1*, March.

Stone, L. (1977), *The Family, Sex and Marriage in England 1500–1800* (Harmondsworth: Penguin).

Stone, L. (1990), *The Road to Divorce* (Oxford: Oxford University Press).

Strathdee, R. (1989), *Nobody Wants to Know* (London: Gingerbread).

Study Commission on the Family (1982), *Values and the Changing Family* (London: Study Commission on the Family).

Study Commission on the Family (1983), *Families in the Future* (London: Study Commission on the Family).

Sutton, D. (1993), 'Attacking single parents', *Community Care*, 15 July, p. 8.

Taylor, J. (1986), *Mental Handicap Partnership in the Community* (London: Office of Health Economics).

Thane, P. (1989), 'Old age: burden or benefit?', in Joshi (1989).

Thomas, D. (1993), *Not Guilty: In Defence of Modern Man* (London: Weidenfeld and Nicolson).

Thornes, B. and Collard, J. (1979), *Who Divorces?* (London: Routledge and Kegan Paul).

Tilly, L. and J. Scott (1978), *Women, Work and Family* (New York: Holt, Reinhart & Winston).

Titmuss, R. M. (1963), 'The position of women', in R. M. Titmuss, *Essays on 'The Welfare State'*, 2nd ed. (London: Unwin).

Townsend, P. (1979), *Poverty in the United Kingdom* (London Allen Lane).

Townsend, P. (1986), 'Ageism and Social Policy', in Phillipson and Walker (1986).

Townsend, P. and Davidson, N. (1988), *Inequalities in Health: The Black Report* and *The Health Divide* (Harmondsworth: Penguin).

Trent, K. and South, S. J. (1989), 'Structural determinants of the divorce rate: a cross-societal analysis', *Journal of Marriage and the Family*, 51, pp. 391–404.

Ungerson, C. (ed.) (1990), *Gender and Caring: Work and Welfare in Britain and Scandinavia* (Hemel Hempstead: Harvester Wheatsheaf).

US Bureau of the Census (1981) *Vital Statistics of the United States: Natality, 1981 ed* (Washington, DC: US Government Printing Office).

US Bureau of the Census (1985) 'Living Arrangements of Children' by Characteristics of the Parent, by Marital Status of the Parent: March 1985'. unpublished data.

Veevers, J. E. (ed.) (1991), *Continuity and Change in Marriage and Family* (Toronto: Holt, Reinhart & Winston).

Wainwright, H. (1978), 'Women and the division of labour', in P. Abrams (ed.), *Work, Urbanism and Inequality* (London: Weidenfeld & Nicolson).

Walby, S. (1986), *Patriarchy at Work* (Cambridge: Polity Press).

Walby, S. (1990), *Theorising Patriarchy* (Oxford: Basil Blackwell).

Walker, A. (1989) 'Community care', in M. McCarthy (ed.), *The New Politics of Welfare* (London: Macmillan).

Walker A. (1993), 'Community care policy: from consensus to conflict', in Bornat *et al.* (1993).

Walker, A. *et al.* (1986), *The Debate About Community*, Policy Studies Institute Discussion Paper 13 (London: Policy Studies Institute).

Wallerstein, J. and Kelly, J. (1980), *Surviving the Break-up: How Children and Parents Cope with Divorce* (London: Grant McIntyre).

Wallerstein, J. and Blakeslee, S. (1989), *Second Chances* (London: Bantam Press).

Walvin, J. (1982) *A Child's World: A Social History of English Childhood 1800–1914* (Harmondsworth: Penguin).

Wargon, S. (1987), *Canada's Lone-Parent Families*, Catalogue 99–993 (Ottawa: Department of Supply and Services Statistics).

Warnock, M. (1984), Department of Health and Social Security *Report of the Committee of Inquiry into Human Fertilisation and Embryology*, Cmnd. 9314 (London: HMSO).

Warr, P. (1987), *Work, Unemployment and Mental Health* (Oxford: Clarendon Press).

Watson, S. (1987), 'Ideas of the family in the development of housing form', in M. Loney *et al.* (eds), *The State or the Market* (London: Sage).

Watson, S. (1988), *Accommodating Inequality: Gender and Housing* (Sydney: Allen and Unwin).

Watson, S. and Austerberry, H. (1986), *Housing and Homelessness: A Feminist Perspective* (London: Routledge and Kegan Paul).

Webb, M. (1989), 'Sex and gender in the labour market', in Reid and Stratta (1989).

Weeks, J. (1981), *Sex, Politics and Society: The Regulation of Sexuality since 1880* (Harlow: Longman).

Weeks, J. (1985), *Sexuality and its Discontents: Meanings, Myths and Modern Sexualities* (London: Routledge and Kegan Paul).

Weeks, J. (1991), *Against Nature: Essays on History, Sexuality and Identity* (London: Rivers Oram Press).

Wenger, C. (1986), *The Supportive Network: Coping with Old Age* (London: Allen & Unwin).

Whitehead, B. D. (1993), 'Dan Quayle was right', *The Atlantic Monthly*, April 1993, pp. 47–84.

Whitehead, M. (1987), 'The health divide' in Townsend and Davidson (1988).

Whitfield, R. (ed.) (1987), *Families Matter: Towards a Programme of Action* (Basingstoke: Marshall Pickering).

Wicks, M. (1987) 'Family policy: rights and responsibilities', Family Policy Studies Centre, *Bulletin*, No. 3 (Summer) London.

Williams, F. (1989), *Social Policy: A Critical Introduction* (Cambridge: Polity Press).

Willmott, P. (1986), *Social Networks, Informal Care and Public Policy*, Policy Studies Institute Research Report 655 (London: Policy Studies Institute).

Willmott, P. and Young, M. (1973), *The Symmetrical Family* (London: Routledge & Kegan Paul).

Wilson, E. (1977), *Women and the Welfare State* (London: Tavistock).

Wilson, G. (1987), *Money in the Family: Financial Organisation and Women's Responsibility* (Aldershot: Avebury).

Woodroofe, C. *et al.* (1993), *Children, Teenagers and Health: The Key Data* (Buckingham: Open University Press).

Wright, F. D. (1986), *Left to Care Alone* (Aldershot: Gower).

Wynn, M. (1971), *Family Policy* (London: Michael Joseph).

Zimmerman, S. (1979), 'Policy, social policy and family policy: concepts, concerns and analytical tools', *Journal of Marriage and the Family*, 41 (August) pp. 487–95.

Zimmerman, S. (1988), *Understanding Family Policy: Theoretical Approaches* (Newbury Park: Sage).

Zimmerman, S. (1992), *Family Policies and Family Well-being* (Newbury Park: Sage).

Index

Matrimonial and Family
Proceedings Act (1984)
56, 115–16
Matrimonial Property and
Proceedings Act (1970)	115
men
and changing ideas of gender
22–5
involvement in housework
15–17
and labour market	22–3
see also male–female
relationships
Millar, J.	64, 84–5
see also Bradshaw, J. and
Millar, J.
Ministry for the Family	220
models of family–state
relationships	177–203
authoritarian	178, 179–82
enforcement of certain family
responsibilities	187–8
laissez-faire	178, 183–6, 226,
228
manipulation of incentives
188–91
responding to needs and
demands	198–201
substituting for or supporting
families	195–8
working within constraining
assumptions	191–5
'moral lobby'	98–101, 125–6
Morgan, D.	*see* Finch, J. and
Morgan, D.
Morris, L.	16
Moss, P. and Sharpe, D.	207–9
mothers
as head of single-parent
households	62, 64, 65–7, 68
surrogate	122, 125
unmarried	65–7, 82, 83–4,
85–6, 117–18
working	5, 6–8, 33–5
Mount, F.	90, 92, 184

National Assistance	132–4,
199–200

National Campaign for the
Family	99
National Council for One
Parent Families	69
National Family Trust	99
National Insurance benefits
132–3, 135
for women	136–7, 192
needs, model of state response
to	198–201
neo-traditionalist approach to
family life	98–101, 105,
125–6, 217
Netherlands	7–8, 65
New Zealand	68
Norway	16, 30, 45, 205
nuclear families	89–90, 91–2,
94–5, 99, 169–70
in housing policy	143–4,
145–6, 152, 153–4, 160–1

Oakley, A.	14
occupational segregation of
working women	10–11
One Parent Benefit	131
one parent families	*see*
single-parent families
Orkney sex abuse cases	166
Owens, D. J.	71, 79
owner-occupied houses	116,
142, 147–50

Pahl, J.	8, 12
parental leave	170
parental responsibilities	117–18,
126–7, 187–8, 221–2
in cohabitation	117, 221–2
as Conservative theme	213
in extra-marital births	120
of unmarried mothers	117–18
parenthood
legal concept	117, 118
poor state support for	170–1
and reproductive
technology	125
parent–child relationships	31–3,
34–6, 162–5, 167–8, 171
changing	91–2, 93, 102–3